LAUREATES AN ERETICS

LAUREATES AND HERETICS

SIX

CAREERS

IN

AMERICAN

POETRY

Yvor Winters

Robert Pinsky

James McMichael

Robert Hass

John Matthias

John Peck

ROBERT ARCHAMBEAU

University of Notre Dame Press
Notre Dame, Indiana

Manufactured in the United States of America

From "Meditation at Lagunitas" and "Picking Blackberries with a Friend Who Has Been Reading Jacques Lacan" in *Praise* by Robert Hass, Copyright © 1979 by Robert Hass, by permission of HarperCollins Publishers.

From "Spring Drawing" in *Human Wishes* by Robert Hass, Copyright © 1989 by Robert Hass, by permission of HarperCollins Publishers.

Ohio University Press/Swallow Press, for poetry of John Matthias and Yvor Winters.

Excerpts from the poems by James McMichael in *The World at Large*, Copyright © 1996 by The University of Chicago. All rights reserved.

Excerpts from John Peck, *Collected Shorter Poems* (Evanston, Ill.: TriQuarterly, 2004), by permission of Northwestern University Press.

From "The Figured Wheel" in *The Figured Wheel: New and Collected Poems, 1966–1996* by Robert Pinsky, Copyright © 1996 by Robert Pinsky, by permission of Farrar, Straus and Giroux, LLC.

From "The Geysers" in *Collected Poems* by Thom Gunn, Copyright © 1994 by Thom Gunn, by permission of Farrar, Straus and Giroux, LLC.

Library of Congress Cataloging-in-Publication Data
Archambeau, Robert Thomas, 1968–
    Laureates and heretics : six careers in American poetry / Robert Archambeau.
        p.   cm.
    Includes bibliographical references and index.
    ISBN-13: 978-0-268-02036-1 (pbk. : alk. paper)
    ISBN-10: 0-268-02036-1 (pbk. : alk. paper)
1. American poetry—20th century—History and criticism.   2. Winters, Yvor, 1900–1968—Influence.   I. Title.
    PS323.5.A73   2010
    811'.5—dc22   2009053249

 This book is printed on recycled paper.

Contents

Acknowledgments

First, my thanks go to the poets themselves: to James McMichael, for all his work; to Robert Pinsky, for meeting with me in Lake Forest and in South Bend; to Robert Hass, for talking with me in Chicago and for his comments on the manuscript; to John Peck, for his correspondence and his patience; to John Matthias, for his generosity and for his feedback along the way; and to the late Yvor Winters, for leaving his mark on all of his students.

Also to Michael Anania of the University of Illinois–Chicago, who read much of the manuscript and made many important suggestions; to Alan Golding of the University of Louisville, for his attention to the papers I gave at the Twentieth Century Literature Conferences over the years; to David Kellogg of Northeastern University, for providing a paradigm and a sympathetic ear; to Charles Altieri, for finding my early work on Pinsky irritating and telling me why; to Piotr Gwiazda of the University of Maryland, for disagreeing with Altieri; and to Keith Tuma of Miami University of Ohio, the last honest man in literary criticism. I would also like to thank the contributors to *Word Play Place: Essays on the Poetry of John Matthias*, especially Romana Huk of the University of Notre Dame and Vincent Sherry of Washington University, without whom at least one chapter of this book would not have been possible.

I would be remiss in not thanking the formidable Joe Francis Doerr, Michel Delville, and Christine Pagnoulle of the University of Liège, Belgium; Lars-Håkan Svensson of the University of Lund, Sweden; David Sanders of Ohio University Press; Burt Kimmelman of New Jersey Institute of Technology, the editors of *Mantis*, the *Chicago Review*, and the *Notre Dame Review*, and Don Bogen at *Cincinnati Review*; the staff of the Modernist Studies Association; the English Department at the University of Copenhagen; the Institute for Advanced Studies at the University of London; and all the editors and conference organizers who provided support for this project as it developed. I would be remiss, too, in not citing Philip Clover of Malmö University and Stefan Hollander of Finnmark University College for keeping me sane, if not always sober, during a year in Scandinavia. Let me also thank Ron Ellingson of Chicago's much-missed Aspidistra Bookshop, a graduate school in its own right.

Closer to home, I would like to thank Lake Forest College for supporting me in this project in a number of ways, not the least being a sabbatical and a year's leave. At Lake Forest, let me particularly thank Dan LeMahieu for providing a model of intellectual integrity. Thanks also to Caleb Gordon, Doug Light, and Ben Goluboff for knowing how to take my mind off the book, and to Derek Lambert for understanding the meaning of *gemeinschaft*. Also Dave Park, sort of. Still closer to home, let me thank Valerie, for everything, always. This book is for her, and for Lila.

Introduction

Laureates and Heretics of the American Poetic Field

Gertrude Stein, in her essay "Composition as Explanation," has said almost everything that I want to say in this book:

> No one is ahead of his time, it is only that the particular variety of creating his time is the one that his contemporaries who also are creating their own time refuse to accept.
>
> The things refused are only important if unexpectedly somebody happens to need them. (521)

In just two sentences, Stein lays out a whole theory of literary composition (creating the time), and a theory of canonization and marginalization, with a sidebar on the recovery of neglected works. In one sense, this book is a series of footnotes to Stein's observations about literature and literary reputations, an application in practical criticism of her condensed theory of poetry and its reception.

Other recent critics share similar concerns, and one of these, David Kellogg, has been of particular use to me in the writing of this book. When I first read Kellogg's essay "The Self in the Poetic Field," I knew I had found a paradigm for understanding poetry that would make the project I had in mind possible. Kellogg's work, based on the cultural sociology of Pierre Bourdieu, provided both a set of compass points by which one could begin to understand the vastness and the variety of American poetry, and a way of reading that could account for the conditions of composition and reception. His model proposed a reading of American poetry in terms of the social and aesthetic claims made for it by its readers, and he offered a way of constructing models of the poetic field as it shifted over time. Kellogg gave Bourdieu's general observations about the dynamics of culture a specific application to contemporary poetry.

Kellogg's article defines the field of American poetry in terms of two axes of value: one aesthetic, ranging from the traditional to the experimental; the other sociological, ranging from the individual to the communal. Readers, critics, reviewers, prize committees, anthologists, and publishers define the relative prestige of these different values as well as the relation of individual poets to the various values. They do this not only through the selection of works for publication or prizes but also in subtler ways, such as by claiming that a certain poet represents an identity group, or by placing a poet's work in the context of a tradition or a school of innovative writing. To simplify greatly, you could say that the poet who is claimed from the most positions (or is claimed most strongly for a certain position) wins—if by "winning," we mean gaining a large readership or a prestigious reputation. If the critics, anthologists, and prize-givers from a number of different communities happen to need what you have to offer, you could be claimed from several sides at once.

The career of John Ashbery is a shining example of a poet benefitting from multiple claims. For some, Ashbery carries into our own time the great tradition that runs from Keats through Wallace Stevens (people like this write articles with titles such as "John Ashbery's Revision of the Post-Romantic Quest"). For others, he is the great linguistic innovator who inaugurated a new era in poetry with *The Tennis Court Oath* (people like this write articles with titles such as "Nimbus of Sensations: Eros and Reverie in the Poetry of John Ashbery and Ann Lauterbach"). For still others, Ashbery is the most personal and private of poets (people like this write articles with titles such as "John Ashbery: The Self against Its Images"). And for some, he is a representative of the gay male community (people like this write articles with titles such as "Reports of Looting and Insane Buggery behind Altars: John Ashbery's Queer Politics").[1] If not exactly all things to all people, Ashbery is, at any rate, many things to many people. His way of creating his time happens to be useful to representatives of all quadrants of the American poetic field. It is surely no coincidence that Ashbery is one of the most canonical American poets of our time.

Looking at the works of poets in Kellogg's terms allows us to understand them and their reputations in a somewhat systematic way. The symmetry of his system of analysis is the perfect tool with which to investigate asymmetrical reputations, differing in both degree (of sales) and kind (of prestige). The model helps explain not only the popular appeal but also high-culture veneration. While Kellogg does not, in the limited space of his article, go on to apply his theory or test it in practical criticism, he offers a way to examine poetry both sociologically and aesthetically.

Kellogg's work comes out of a long debate about the nature of canonization, with a rich literature of its own. One thinks immediately of Jed Rasula's *The American Poetry Wax Museum*, for example, and of Alan Golding's *From Outlaw to Classic: Canons in American Poetry*. In fact, a few words are in order by way of explaining my title which, with its "heretics," invokes the "outlaws" in Golding's. (I should also own up to going back to Stein's "Composition as Explanation" after seeing an excerpt as the epigraph to Golding's book.) One way of considering the six poets here—Yvor Winters and his last generation of graduate students, Robert Hass, Robert Pinsky, James McMichael, John Matthias, and John Peck—is to divide them into a group of "laureates" and a group of "heretics." In this view, those who were literally laureates, Hass and Pinsky, both of whom served multiple terms as U.S. Poet Laureate, are the laureates of popular fame and institutional canonization, while Matthias, McMichael, Peck (and, to a degree, Winters) are heretics in the sense of writing largely outside of the laws of canonization. Whatever its very real merits, their work has not resulted in strong canonization or wide readership. Their different kinds of reception cannot be explained by anything so simple as the "mainstream"

1. These articles are by Frank Lepkowski, James McCorkle, David Bromwich, and John Vincent, respectively.

nature of the popular work versus the "experimental" nature of the less popular. While Peck is surely an innovative writer, and Matthias is at times a profoundly experimental one, McMichael is perhaps the most formally traditional poet in the group. Moreover, Yvor Winters' chances at achieving full canonical status faded just at the point when he left a promising career as a modernist and proto-objectivist and took up a less experimental poetic.

We can only understand the different aesthetic choices made by these poets, and their appeals to various reading publics, when we examine the social forces that played into making them write as they did, and the forces that made their publics value certain kinds of poetry more than others. Such forces include the postwar growth of universities, the coincident movement of poetry into universities, the radicalism of the 1960s, the post-1960s radical exhaustion, and the birth of identity politics and identity poetics. Some poets emerged from this maelstrom clutching the laurels of fame, and others did not.

There is no judgment inherent in this last observation. Poets are not lesser artists because they are less than popular. Nor should one fall into that somewhat adolescent elitism, the reflex that tells us that something popular cannot be good, not if all of *those* people like it. Then again, I have operated on the assumption that the importance and value of the popular are, ipso facto, clear to many and do not need an advocate. The importance of the less-well-known poets not being common knowledge, I have made gestures of advocacy in certain cases. These are not, though, to be taken as exclusive gestures made at the expense of other poets: I value all of those dealt with here.

Any study of a group of poets has to make its exclusions as well as to make some case for those exclusions. The five men under consideration here do not represent anything like a full roster of the poets who had been Winters' students at Stanford. Such a roster, when drawn up, is impressive indeed, including Thom Gunn, J. V. Cunningham, N. Scott Momaday, Edgar Bowers, and Donald Hall. Instead, this is a study of Winters and his last generation of students, those who arrived in Palo Alto around 1962. Even as such it is incomplete, since so many of Winters' students went on to write poetry. (Ken Fields, for example, was a member of this final generation.) It does, though, represent what I take to be the poets of that generation who contributed most significantly to American poetry, for reasons ranging from mass popularity (and therefore sociological interest) to what I find myself calling philosophical depth.

Heresy and Orthodoxy at Stanford

Winters, late in life, was known for the extremity, exclusivity, and orthodoxy of his literary views. A rigorous formalist, an idiosyncratic traditionalist with his own narrow version of the canon, a moralist who felt that the wrong poetics could lead to disastrous errors in life, he was a commanding presence. F. R. Leavis comes to mind as a corresponding figure—he did, anyway, to Gunn, who had studied under both men and had observed the same tendency of both men's students to split into zealous champions of the great man's orthodoxy, on the one hand, and into rebels against the tyrant's authority, on the other. The champions of Wintersian orthodoxy among the final generation of Winters' students—those who come closest to his opinions—are McMichael and, to a degree, Pinsky. The Wintersian rebels or heretics include Matthias and Peck. Hass, interestingly, treads right along the border of Winters' kingdom. It often seems that he holds both Wintersian and anti-Wintersian ideas simultaneously, and for this reason I call him an agnostic Wintersian.

It is perhaps surprising that there is some correlation between a moderate Wintersian poetic and poetic canonization. While Mc-Michael's Wintersianism has been too austere for most audiences, the more ecumenical Pinsky and the agnostic Hass have gone on to great fame and have received the highest honors available to American poets. While Winters found himself excluded by the poetic establishment of his time—he once told Hall that the Ivy League "thought he was lower than the carpet" (Hall, "Rocks and Whirlpools" 247)—some of his more faithful students now find themselves honored by that same establishment. The phenomenon can be explained with reference to the modifications Hass and Pinsky made to Winters' poetics, and, more important, to the changes in the values of many readers of American poetry from the 1950s through the 1980s. In Pinsky's case, Winters' Augustan poetics and Enlightenment ideas of the self have appealed to those threatened by the growth of identity politics in the 1970s and early 1980s. In Hass's case, negative capability with regard to Winters' ideas led him to write a poetry that has appealed to both sides of the "theory wars" of the 1980s and 1990s. A poem such as "Picking Black-berries with a Friend Who Has Been Reading Jacques Lacan," for in-stance, ends up being praised by deconstructionists and antitheorists alike. Hass's reputation grew in large measure due to a kind of bidding war over his work between radical and conservative forces.

The uncanonical status of the Wintersian heretics, Peck and Matthias, can be explained with reference to similar changes in the poetic field, as can the reputation of one other Wintersian outlaw who has languished in obscurity. This is Winters himself, or at any rate the young Yvor Winters, whose experimental work the mature poet all but disowned. I treat this poet not only because the work of the ma-ture Winters can only be explained in the context of the work of the young Winters, but also because I firmly believe that his achievement was larger than his more orthodox critics maintain. Just as his legacy includes poets as diverse in style and substance as Pinsky and Peck, his own career includes substantial work in a wide breadth of styles. If there is one element of this book that I think will enrage some of the more orthodox Wintersian true believers, it is the assertion, implicit on many pages, that all of Winters' work is legitimate, as is the whole of his legacy.

Chapter One

Yvor Winters

A Journey into the Dark

Two Men at Midlife

Poet-Critic A and Poet-Critic B are both fifty-nine years old. But what else do they have in common? Not much, it seems, when you look at where their careers have led them.

Earlier this year, Poet-Critic A began an unprecedented third term as Poet Laureate of the United States of America. His books are issued by the most prestigious literary publishers in New York and are well reviewed in the literary and popular press. He has been one of the most frequently appearing living poets in the big-league anthologies during the fifteen years since he made the cut for the *Norton Anthology of American Literature*. He has credibility with academics, too: punch his name into the subject-search line of the Modern Language Association (MLA) database and you will find dozens of references. He has, too, what most of us in academe would consider an enviable job at an eminent university in a major East Coast metropolis. His position has, inevitably, made him a power broker in the poetry world, with a great deal of influence over publications and prizes. He ought to know about prizes: he has managed to collect nearly all of them.

Poet-Critic B, whose poetics have much in common with those of Poet-Critic A, began his fifty-ninth year in much humbler circumstances. While he is tenured at a reputable institution, he has not been the star of the department. In fact, some of his colleagues wish they could let him go. The department kept him teaching Freshman Composition as long as it could, and the chairman once told him his publications were a disgrace. No university press will put out his criticism, so his just-completed work on Yeats will appear next year in pamphlet form. His poetry has not done well lately, either: he had to publish his collected poems on his own letterpress. He has taken a drubbing from the critics, and the growing view of him is that he is outmoded, outdated, and more than a bit outlandish in his views.

Poet-Critic A is, of course, Robert Pinsky. The year is 1999. And his much-less-popular companion in the art is Yvor Winters forty years earlier.

The story I want to introduce here is how the poetics of Yvor Winters put him out of step with the cultural movements and institutions of his time, and how Robert Pinsky later rose to fame by using those same poetics. The poetics did not much change; they were handed down from Winters to his Stanford graduate student, Pinsky. What changed was the field of poetic production, and the more general field of cultural production, in response to shifts in American culture from the 1960s to the 1990s. Winters' way of "creating his time," in Gertrude Stein's phrase, was rejected by his contemporaries. Later in the century a powerful set of culture brokers, prize givers, reviewers, and fellowship committee members happened to "need" that same way of creating the times. By then, though, Winters was gone, and the exemplar of that way of creating was his student, Robert Pinsky.

The New Augustans

The banner to unfurl when discussing the poetics shared by Winters and Pinsky is that of neo-Augustanism. Winters and Pinsky hold a number of significant ideas in common with the Augustan poets of the eighteenth century. Broadly speaking, these ideas can be described as elaborations of four main principles: the idea that art is largely, even primarily, an ethical enterprise; the idea that emotional impulse is not to be trusted; the idea that there is a general nature (a common human nature shared transhistorically and transculturally); and the idea that clear discursive statement is a literary virtue.

"We are perpetually moralists, but we are geometricians only by chance," wrote Samuel Johnson in *Lives of the Poets* (95). Paul Fussell, in *The Rhetorical World of Augustan Humanism*, glosses Johnson's statement by saying that, for the Augustans, "our nature in itself does not oblige us to function as geometricians—or patriots, or Tories, or consumers, or other kinds of exclusive specialists—but it does oblige us to function as moral adjudicators." The Augustan humanist, says Fussell, "sees man not primarily as a maker or even as a knower, but rather as a moral actor" (7). This carries over into the Augustan view of the arts, where the old Horatian definition of the function of poetry (to delight and instruct) is taken up with special emphasis on the ethical element of the latter quality. As it was for the eighteenth-century Augustans, so it is for Winters and Pinsky. The moralistic vein runs so deep for Winters that he is able to begin a sentence in *Primitivism and Decadence* with the words, "Poetry, as a moral discipline . . ." (*Primitivism*, in *In Defense of Reason* 28). "The act of judgment prior to the vision of any poem is a social judgment," writes Pinsky, sounding the same neo-Augustan note in "Responsibilities of the Poet" (*Poetry and the World* 97). Doctor Johnson certainly would have approved.

We can turn to Johnson again as an exemplar of the second Augustan principle, the distrust of emotional impulse. Boswell captures Johnson delivering a concentrated dose of this sort of distrust when he relates how Johnson reacted to Boswell's breezy observation that, on a fine day, he felt the sudden urge to be benevolent to all mankind, without exception. Johnson, says Boswell, stared him down and "took occasion to give me wise and salutary caution. 'Do not, Sir, accustom yourself to trust to *impressions*. . . . By trusting impressions, a man may gradually come to yield to them, so as not to be a free agent. . . . There can be no confidence in him, no more than in a tyger'" (*Life of Johnson* 694).

In his deep distrust of emotional impulse and spontaneity of feeling, Johnson is fighting what is already becoming a rearguard action. Shaftesbury's cult of sensibility, which emphasized the validity of spontaneous individual impressions, was set to sweep the field, preparing the way for Romanticism and the American transcendentalists. When, a century and a half after Johnson, Winters condemns Emerson for his belief in the moral efficacy of "immediate inspiration," he is picking up the fallen standard under which Johnson fought. And when Winters tells us his reasons for condemning Emerson—that "immediate inspiration amounts to the same thing as unrevised reactions to stimuli; unrevised reactions are mechanical, man in a state of [what Emerson would call] perfection is an automaton"—the resemblance to Johnson's views is striking. In fighting against impulse as a moral guide, Johnson wants to preserve the "free agen[cy]" of man; Winters wants to keep us free of automatism (*In Defense of Reason* 54–55).[1]

While Pinsky is never so overtly anti-Romantic as Winters, we still see a distrust of spontaneous, unexamined impulse running through his work. We find this frequently in criticism, as in his cautionary words about Keats[2] and those who follow him in *The Situation of Poetry*: "for all of these poets . . . . something which they feel drawn to be with leads them to realms perilous and forlorn" (71). We find the same distrust in his poetry, most notably in "Essay on Psychiatrists," where his meditations on *The Bacchae* are distinctly anti-Bacchus, and where madness is defined as "a desperate sweet yielding to some broad,/Mechanical simplification."

The third principle of Augustan and neo-Augustan poetics, the belief in a universal human nature, common in its composition across the chasms of space and time, is also well articulated by Johnson, perhaps most famously in his *Preface to Shakespeare*. "Nothing can please many, and please long, but just representations of general nature" (23). Augustans did not deny that there were differences between the

1. If Winters' more immediate target for antiautomatism was, at times, the Surrealist automatic writing of André Breton and his associates, this is nevertheless an anti-Romantic, neo-Augustan position, especially when we remember that Winters saw the twentieth-century avant-garde as a development and continuation of Romanticism.

2. The reflections on Keats in *The Situation of Poetry* (47–61) are some of the most Wintersian moments in Pinsky's prose. The conflict he perceives between "conscious and unconscious forces within the mind" (47) and his sense of the poet's obligation to side with the former are so similar to the arguments Winters makes in "The Significance of *The Bridge*" that one almost feels certain passages could be transposed into Winters' book, if only the word "Keats" were replaced by "Crane."

ancient Roman and the contemporary Englishman or Scot, but they appealed to the part of the reader that represented a common humanity, rather than to the peculiarities of manners of any particular social or historical subgroup. It is on the same foundation that Winters rests what he famously, or infamously, called his moral absolutism (*In Defense of Reason* 11), that bald rejection of moral relativism of any sort, including historical and cultural varieties.[3] While Pinsky never thunders forth with an overtly Wintersian moral absolutism, there is, nevertheless, a strong emphasis in his poetry on broadly shared subjectivity and common values. We find this most strongly in his discursive or essayistic poems, such as "Sadness and Happiness" and *An Explanation of America*, where Pinsky addresses an audience imagined as possessing a common, Johnsonian general nature.

The fourth principle, the insistence that poetry speak clearly and paraphrasably, rather than cryptically—that it should mean, as well as be—accords both with Johnson's practice and with the general ideals of Augustan classicism. Classicism, as Roland Barthes maintains, insists on a certain degree of prosy discursiveness in poetry, or, rather, on the fundamental similarity of good poetry and good prose. "Poetry is always different from prose," says Barthes in *Writing Degree Zero*, but in the classical period "this difference is not one of essence, it is one of quantity. It does not, therefore, jeopardize the unity of language, which is an article of classical dogma" (41). In other words, the classical or Augustan writer does not grant to poetry one of the rights that we moderns and postmoderns grant it: the right to follow rules significantly different from those governing discursive prose.

The Augustan dogma of clarity and the unity of language manifests itself in the works of both Winters and Pinsky. Winters' very definition of poetry—"a poem is a statement in language about a human experience" ("Introduction" to *Forms of Discovery* xvii)—is predicated

---

3. Winters' ideas of general nature have been noted by some of his most careful readers. When Robert Von Hallberg writes of Winters' poem "The Grave" in 1981, for example, he tells us that the poem "rests upon the conviction that poetry engages the grand, perennial, urgent human issues" ("Yvor Winters" 795). The phrase "perennial . . . human issues" implies a transhistorical, transcultural human subjectivity—that is, it implies Augustan general nature. There is some question as to whether Winters' more sympathetic readers simply note these ideas or, in fact, perpetuate them.

upon the idea of clear discursive paraphrasability. The idea of the poem as a special sort of utterance is anathema to Winters because it violates the nature of language itself: "since language is conceptual in its nature, this statement [the poem] will be more or less rational or at least apprehensible in rational terms, or else the medium will be violated and the poem weakened" (xvi). This is exactly the sort of thinking that made Winters a literary heretic in the era of Cleanth Brooks's "The Heresy of Paraphrase." One imagines the grinding of Brooks's teeth when he came across Winters' quip that "many poems cannot be paraphrased and are therefore defective" (see Von Hallberg 804).

The argument for clarity and the unity of prosaic and poetic language is even more overt in Pinsky's *The Situation of Poetry*. In a chapter entitled "The Discursive Aspect of Poetry," Pinsky takes up Ezra Pound's familiar contention that poetry atrophies when it gets too far from music and answers it with a question: "What happens to poetry when it gets too far from prose, and the prose virtues?" (162). Straying from these virtues, says Pinsky, can be deadly to poetry. "The 'surrealist' diction" of work that eschews the prose virtues fails to give us an image of a shared or objective world, substituting a "hermetically primitive" world without paraphrasable meaning or a shared sense of objective reality (162–63).

It is easy to understand how Pinsky came to these ideas. They were, after all, the beliefs of his professor at graduate school. But Winters' path to Augustan poetics was undertaken without a mentor. Indeed, it was a journey made against the general current of the period in which he came of age as a poet, and against the modernist principles of his own early work. The turn to Augustanism came late, but it came with force, because Winters came to see it as the only way to cage his personal demons.

An Unlikely Prospect

If Samuel Johnson were recruiting new talent for his team, as it played in the eternal overtime championship match between Classics and Romantics, he would not think much of the undergraduate prospect from the University of Chicago, young Yvor Winters. An associate of *Poetry*

(Chicago)'s Harriet Monroe, Winters was fascinated with the experimental poetry that her magazine was publishing, and he seemed intent on becoming a stay-at-home cousin of the American expatriates working in the Imagist mode. The first published prose of the precocious Winters, which appeared in the *Little Review* in 1919 when he was nineteen years old, would surely have been disowned by the neo-Augustan poet he later became. The article, "Concerning Jessie Dismorr," was a review of a now largely-forgotten poet and is of little interest, except for how it shows the young Winters following directly in the footsteps of Pound. Winters condemns Dismorr for attempting to introduce ideas into poetry as direct statements. In fact, the pattern of Winters' praising-and-blaming throughout the early 1920s, when he frequently reviewed for *Poetry*, came straight out of the Poundian-Imagist playbook, with prosiness and abstraction condemned and the juxtaposition of sharp physical details held up as exemplary.

In his first published poems, too, we see Winters aspiring to modernism rather than Augustanism. His fragile health having forced him to leave the University of Chicago before graduating, Winters followed the work of the great modernists at a distance, trying to emulate Imagism from the confines of a tuberculosis sanatorium in New Mexico. In 1919 and 1920, Winters broke into print as a poet, peppering the more adventurous little magazines with poems such as "Hawk's Eyes," "The Immobile Wind," and "Two Songs of Advent," most of them very much in an Imagist mode inflected by the landscapes of the American Southwest. Consider, for example, the last of these, which, like many of Winters' early poems, is short enough to quote in its entirety:

I.
On the desert, between pale mountains, our cries—
Far whispers creeping through an ancient shell.

II.
Coyote, on delicate mocking feet,
Hovers down the canyon, among the mountains,
His voice running wild in the wind's valleys.

Listen! Listen! for I enter now your thought.

The Imagist credentials of the poem are beyond reproach. Seven years earlier, Pound had announced that the Imagist poem should follow the rhythms of the musical phrase, not the metronome (Pound, *Literary Essays* 3), and Winters has certainly absorbed the lesson of a carefully calibrated *vers libre*. And the poem follows another Poundian injunction in that it walks in fear of abstractions: the valleys here are hard and tangible, not the "dim lands of peace" that Pound had condemned for combining the abstract with the concrete (5). In its handling of time, too, the poem follows the Imagist model. Its curious suspension of motion, in which even the coyote's movements are rather passive and indeterminate in duration, gives it the frozen-moment quality of the Poundian "intellectual and emotional complex in an instant of time" (4). Moreover, the first section of the poem is a textbook illustration of the Imagist technique that T. E. Hulme described as a "visual chord" (*Selected Writings* 64): the juxtaposition of two images in adjacent lines to create a whole greater than the sum of the parts. Had Pound failed to boil "In a Station of the Metro" down to its final, two-line form, Winters' poem could serve in a thousand poetry seminars to illustrate this central precept of Imagist poetics.

More important than these Imagist bona fides, though, is the way the poem follows the Poundian dictate to present rather than describe. Pound makes the distinction between presentation and description on a number of occasions, most famously in "A Retrospect," where he admonishes poets not to be "viewy" or philosophical in their writing (*Literary Essays* 6). While he is never too clear on the exact nature of the distinction, the idea that presentation is somehow less chatty and overtly discursive than description seems to be at the heart of the matter. Certainly this appears to be what Pound was getting at when he wrote "the artist seeks out the luminous detail and presents it. He does not comment" (*Selected Prose* 23). "Two Songs of Advent" is, in this sense, a poem of presentation rather than of abstract statement or chatty commentary. In its resistance to easy paraphrase, it is at a far pole from the neo-Augustan poetics of the late Winters, who would define a poem as "first of all a statement in words" (*In Defense of Reason* 363). Between the young Imagist poet and the Augustan lies a chasm. How—or rather, why—did the one poet become the other?

From the available evidence, it seems entirely likely that the Yvor Winters who wrote "Two Songs of Advent" would become someone altogether different from the author of *The Anatomy of Nonsense* and of such neo-Augustan volumes as *Before Disaster* and *The Giant Weapon.* It certainly appeared that way to Winters himself when, in 1949, he looked back on his career and wrote that, had he not mended his ways, "it is quite possible that I should still be a minor disciple of W.C. Williams, doing little impressionistic notes on landscapes" (*Uncollected Essays* 308).

So the young Winters was much more "Y.W., *Imagiste*" than potential star player for the Classics team. But by 1929, just around the time a Bay Area poet with his background should have been talking about new poetic developments with Kenneth Rexroth, we find Winters gathering his fellow-travelers around him at Stanford to launch a decidedly nonexperimental project, the little magazine *Gyroscope.* Winters wrote and published *Gyroscope*'s manifesto in the form of a brief "Statement of Purpose" that upheld "a classical state of mind," condemned cultural movements that "minimize[d] the moral and intellectual responsibilities of man as man," and opposed "all doctrines which advocate that the poet 'express' his country (Whitmanian Rousseauism) or his time (Dadaism and allied heresies)" (*Uncollected Essays* 216–17). These claims are declarations of the neo-Augustan faith.

The *Gyroscope* manifesto is thoroughly neo-Augustan in that it upholds art as subordinate to morality. *Gyroscope* is also opposed to the expression of inadequately motivated emotion—a very neo-Augustan distrust of emotional overflow, with classical origins in the work of the Greek critic Longinus. These concerns and convictions, combined with *Gyroscope*'s preference for formal poetry of clear statement, show us a Winters far more eligible for the Classics team than one would ever have expected, had one known him only as the precocious modernist he had been in the early and mid-1920s.

"Not in Paris, Nor Even at Harvard"

Winters stuck with Imagism longer, and thought about it harder, than any other American poet. He was writing Imagist poems prior to the publication of *The Immobile Wind* in 1921, and one could argue that he was still occasionally working the same vein up to 1930 when *The Proof* rolled off the presses. This is quite extraordinary: Hugh Kenner plausibly dates the Imagist movement as lasting from mid-1912 to mid-1913 (*Pound Era* 173), while Mary Ann Caws somewhat generously gives the years from 1914 to 1918 as the span of the movement (*Manifesto* xxxiii). There is simply no individual case comparable to that of Winters' decade-long engagement with Imagism. Ever the magpie, Pound flew off to new isms long before the hedgehog Winters had even begun to burrow his way into Imagist poetics. And there is no statement of Imagist poetics to compare with Winters' 1924 *Secession* essay "The Testament of a Stone" (*Uncollected Essays*). In terms of simple bulk (some 15,000 words, versus about one tenth of that for Pound's "A Few Don'ts by an Imagiste") as well as philosophical depth, it is the weightiest existing document of Imagist poetics. Clearly, Imagism meant more to Winters than it would if he had turned to it merely as the latest thing from London. Indeed, it was far from the latest thing when he first picked up on it: as Michael Schmidt puts it, Winters "is an Imagist arriving late at the feast" (753).

In Winters' hands, Imagism became a more fully developed theory and practice than it did for any other poet of his generation, or the previous one. But his particular, rather idiosyncratic version, combined with his early experiences of isolation and illness and his years of convalescence in the Southwest, made the abandonment of Imagism urgent for the young Winters. Neo-Augustan poetics came to seem like the cure for his particular anxieties, and one imagines him reaching, around 1930, for the works of Doctor Johnson, much as one would reach for the right bottle from the medicine chest. Neo-Augustanism appeared to offer the remedy for the limitations he saw in the version of Imagism that he had developed for himself.

When Winters wrote, in his later years, about his turn from Imagist modernism to neo-Augustan poetics, he tended toward circumspection. In fact, he described the radical shift from one set of poetics to another in negative terms. He claimed, for example, in the introduction to a 1966 edition of his early poems, that the turn was "not due to the influence of Stanford nor to any sudden intellectual or religious conversion," nor was it "a shift from formlessness to form; it was a shift from certain kinds of forms to others" (*Uncollected Essays* 314, 315). This is fair enough, but also not particularly informative about what exactly did lead to the change. If we look at Winters' statements about Imagist poetics from the 1920s, though, what we see makes up for his later reticence. We see a young poet whose idea of Imagism implied that an extreme state of mind, involving the almost mystical loss of self, was necessary for poetic creation.

"The Testament of a Stone: Being Notes on the Mechanics of the Poetic Image," offers us a great deal of insight into young Winters' idea of the mystical selflessness of the poet. The foreword to the essay is devoted to what we might somewhat ponderously call the phenomenology of poetic perception—that is, Winters writes here of the relation of the poet-as-subject to the object of his poetic perception. The relation is one in which the poet's very identity is under threat of dissolving. Poetic perception, in Winters' view at the time, involved the "fusion of the poet with his material"; and "[t]he cause of a perfectly fused poem is the fusion of the poet's consciousness with an object or group of objects of whatever nature" (*Uncollected Essays* 195). More surprisingly for anyone who comes to Winters through his later work, the poem is presented as nothing less than "a permanent gateway to waking oblivion" (195). Ordinary categories of experience collapse in the act of poetic perception, and the division of subject and object disappears. The self as a conscious mind separate from the object of perception simply vanishes.

This sort of mystic irrationalism is carried to further extremes, as in this passage, where Winters contrasts the poet with the philosopher:

> The poet moving in a world that is largely thought, so long as he regards it curiously and as a world, perceives certain specific things, as a walker in a field perceives a grassblade. These specific things are the material of the image, of art. When he loses his sense of the infinite nature of his world and organizes it into a knowable and applicable principle, he loses sight of the particulars themselves and sees their relationships to each other and his newly-created whole, and so becomes a philosopher; for it is only in the finite that the particular can be

detected as a complete and uncoordinated whole; for he may still have occasional perceptions, and at times revert to the poet. (197)

The rational ordering of the world is antithetical to poetic perception, which is of the infinite, beyond reason, irrational.

The collapse of distance between the poet and the object of poetic perception leads toward an absolute selflessness. This selflessness extends to matters of style, because, as Winters has it, "the poet who is preoccupied with his object"—that is, the true poet—"desires a speech without idiom" (198). The poem, as the product of a loss of self, is shorn of stylistic signs of the self. Grosvenor Powell glosses this element of Winters' poetics by telling us that "the two poles" of "self and nonself . . . fuse inextricably—the intensity of the experience determining the degree of the fusion. In the most intense moments of vision, the polarity disappears" (126–27).

The idea of poetic perception involving a mystical union of subject and object, self and nonself, ego and universe, is not a new one with Winters, although his Imagism is the only version of that particular aesthetic to incorporate the idea systematically. And poets have not always seen such ideas of mystical poetic perception as problematic or threatening: indeed, such ideas are celebrated in the visionary traditions of Romanticism and Surrealism. But the idea never sat comfortably with Winters, even during the decade in which he worked with it constantly. Even in his early Imagist poems, one detects reservations about the poetic process and the selflessness that Winters felt it entailed. Consider "Alone," from Winters' first volume of poems:

> I, one who never speaks
> Listened days in summer trees,
> Each day a rustling leaf.

> Then, in time, my unbelief
> Grew like my running —
> My own eyes did not exist,
> When I struck I never missed.

Noon, felt and far away —
My brain is a thousand bees.

The poem begins with a passive subject, "one who never speaks," whose activities are limited to listening. In the second stanza this passivity passes over into a loss of self, and a disappearance, to use Powell's terms, of the polarity of self and nonself. The last two lines of the second stanza drive home the point: "My own eyes did not exist"—if eyes continue to exist, they are no longer the possession of an owning subject. "When I struck I never missed"—there can be no misses, because the distance between striking self and the object of the strike has collapsed. At the end of the poem we are left in what Robert Von Hallberg calls "the terrifying present," where "the speaker's mind is left a scramble" (787). The unified self is gone, the mind hums with the agitation of "a thousand bees." This buzzing carries with it the connotations of individuality lost in the collective identity of the hive. It also carries the connotation of buzzing anger, of primitive alarm. The poem goes one step beyond the poetics articulated in "The Testament of a Stone" by hinting at a discomfort not yet present in the criticism.

It is important, when reading an early poem such as "Alone," to remember the circumstances under which such poems were composed. With very few exceptions, Winters' first two collections were written during those forced years of convalescence after he was diagnosed with tuberculosis in the winter of 1918. "It is impossible to understand Winters without taking account of the bitter isolation tuberculosis conferred upon him," writes Donald Hall (237), while Helen Pinkerton Trimpi tells us that after his diagnosis and "for the next five years his career was shaped by the need to recuperate from his illness" (xvii). Winters found both the symptoms of his disease and the enforced inactivity difficult, and a constant threat to his alertness and consciousness. Later he would look back on his tubercular years and write that "the disease filled the body with a fatigue so heavy that it was an acute pain, pervasive and poisonous" (see Trimpi xviii).

The dry, barren extremes of the New Mexican landscape, experienced under these conditions of illness, also seemed to undermine Winters' sense of self-control and rational consciousness. Writing of a New Mexico landscape painted by Marsden Hartley (whom Winters knew at the Sunmount sanatorium in Santa Fe), Winters said that it embodied the "ominous physical mysticism" that was "the principal characteristic of this country" (Trimpi xvii). When we put "Alone" in this context, the ominous quality of the ending (Von Hallberg's "terrifying present") becomes palpable. The loss of self in a delirium was not merely hypothetical for the Winters who wrote those poems but also a very real, and very constant, possibility.

If we return with this context in mind to "Two Songs of Advent," we see an even more powerful expression of ambivalence about the poetic state of mind that Winters was to articulate in "The Testament of a Stone." Here, again, is the first song:

> On the desert, between pale mountains, our cries —
> Far whispers creeping through an ancient shell

The landscape is recognizably the vast quiet of the Southwest, where human voices are reduced to "far whispers" and even lose their human quality, becoming the inarticulate noise of a shell pressed to one's ear. Alien, bare, and inhuman, the landscape reduces the humanity of the speaker and his unnamed companions. This is the emotional staging ground for the second, more ominous song:

> Coyote, on delicate mocking feet,
> Hovers down the canyon, among the mountains,
> His voice running wild in the wind's valleys.
>
> Listen! Listen! For I enter now your thought.

As Trimpi has pointed out in her excellent reading of the poem, the coyote-object who merges with the speaker-subject is "regarded as hostile, for he proposes to take over the consciousness" in breaking into the speaker's thought. Here, as in "Winter Echo," "The Aspen's Song," and other poems, Winters gives an ominous quality to the collapsing of distance between subject and object in the act of poetic perception. Trimpi again: "In this and other early poems Winters uses the Native American poetic form of speaking in the persona of an animal or some other less-than-human condition, as a technique to explore . . . a dissolution of consciousness" (xxviii). The haunted Winters came to distrust his own poetics.

Like his unease about the loss of self in Imagist perception, Winters' sense that Imagism was flawed by its inability to investigate the causes of emotions appears in his poetry before it becomes the subject of his prose. It is present, for example, in "The Rows of Cold Trees," which first appeared in 1924. Toward the conclusion, we find the following lines:

> It was the dumb decision of the
> madness of my youth that left me with
> this cold eye for the fact; that keeps me
> quiet, walking toward a
> stinging end . . .

Terry Comito, one of Winters' most sensitive and sophisticated critics, reads the madness of his youth here as the "ecstatic communion" of self and world that we have seen in "The Testament of a Stone" (67). But surely the muteness of the speaker ("quiet" and "dumb") and his inability to rise above "fact" to the level of judgment support a slightly different reading. It is the incomplete nature of the early poetics, their limited ability to analyze emotion and motive through discursive statement, that leads the speaker toward his "stinging end."

Winters' early experiences of fear without apparent motivation made this incompleteness inherent in Imagist poetics a matter of very real urgency. His single work of fiction, the 1932 story "The Brink of Darkness," makes clear the extent to which these experiences of isolation in the extreme landscapes of the Southwest were experiences of fear without directly apparent motivation. The story is based on Winters' time in Moscow, Idaho, where he taught from 1925 to 1927. The unnamed protagonist is clearly autobiographical, so much so that Hall has claimed that it is not only "clearly consonant with known facts of [Winters'] life" but also a deliberate "clue to the function throughout his life of what he called reason" (238). Indeed, Comito has suggested that "it is in some ways misleading to think of ["The Brink of Darkness"] as fiction" (4). Like Winters, the protagonist is a teacher, the owner of two Airedales, who boards with a local family. But the external resemblances are merely circumstantial: what is essential are the psychological parallels between Winters and his protagonist.

The protagonist finds himself living in isolation in a largely abandoned house, of which he cedes more and more to the encompassing cold and the ever-present mice as the story progresses. Human territory becomes less and less differentiated from the elemental world in a process that is the exact inverse of what Winters had described in 1929 as the task of the human spirit, "to differentiate itself a little more distinctly from the remainder of the universe . . . which is continually endeavoring to absorb and destroy it" (*Uncollected Essays* 245). It is in these conditions that the protagonist becomes possessed by irrational fears, without direct motive or known cause. Alone one night in the house, and aware of the vast cold emptiness outside, he tells us: "I felt that I saw farther and farther into the events about me, that I perceived a new region of significance, extending a short distance behind that of which I had always been aware, suggesting the existence of far more than was even now perceptible" (219).

The terror of the "demonic" silence stays with him until spring draws near. At that point he is able to reflect on his irrational perception of a world of demonic force:

> I thought back over the past months, of the manner in which I had been disturbed, uncentered, and finally obsessed by an insidious power. I remembered that I had read somewhere of a kind of Eastern demon who gains power over one only in proportion as one recognizes and fears him. I felt that I had been the victim of a deliberate and malevolent invasion, an invasion utilizing and augmenting to appalling and shadowy proportions all the most elusive accidents of my life. (223)

Like the coyote of "Two Songs of Advent," the demon of isolation forces its way into the mind. But even now, in the spring and in human society, the protagonist is unable to rest assured that his fears have left him. The emotion remains, as does his inability to attribute it to any rational cause: "It was as if there were a darkness evenly underlying the brightness of the air, underlying everything, as if I might slip suddenly into it at any instant, and as if I held myself where I was by an act of the will from moment to moment" (224). If the story is as autobiographical as Comito claims it is, we would not be going too far in calling Winters' experience of isolation in the West traumatic, as much so as his life-threatening experience of tuberculosis. It can hardly be seen as surprising that a man so shaken would grow to distrust a poetics that he felt incapable of tracing the relation between emotions and their motivations. A poetics that presented the experience of fear in a landscape without understanding the real cause of that fear could even be described, in the terms of "The Brink of Darkness," as demonic.

Certainly one does not want to say that Winters was only the product of his environment. Had he not thought long and hard about poetics, and taken his Imagism more seriously than any other poet who wrote under that banner, it would have mattered little where he had lived, and in what degree of health. But it would be wrong to deny the important role that his particular experiences played in his poetic development. "In the twenties," wrote Winters, "I was not in Paris, nor even at Harvard" (*Uncollected Essays* 314). Had he been at either place, or in the London where Pound, Richard Aldington, and Hilda Doolittle launched the good ship *Imagiste*, he would never have followed his particular Imagist journey to its dark conclusions. The history of his poetic development, and the development of his students, would be altered beyond recognition.

The Augustan Solution

One of the passages from Robert Pinsky's poem "Essay on Pyschiatrists" most remembered among Winters' former students reads as follows:

> it is all bosh, the false
> Link between genius and sickness,
>
> Except perhaps as they were linked
> By the Old Man, addressing his class
> On the first day: "*I know why you are here.*

You are here to laugh. You have heard of a crazy
Old man who believes that Robert Bridges
Was a good poet; who believes that Fulke

Greville was a great poet, greater than Philip
Sidney; who believes that Shakespeare's Sonnets
Are not all they are cracked up to be. . . . Well,

I will tell you something: I will tell you
What this course is about. Sometime in the middle
Of the Eighteenth Century, along with the rise

Of capitalism and scientific method, the logical
Foundations of Western thought decayed and fell apart.
When they fell apart, poets were left

With emotions and experiences, and with no way
To examine them. At this time, poets and men
Of genius began to go mad. Gray went mad. Collins

Went mad. Kit Smart was mad. William Blake surely
Was a madman. Coleridge was a drug addict, with severe
Depression. My friend Hart Crane died mad. My friend

Ezra Pound is mad. But you will not go mad; you will grow up
To become happy, sentimental old college professors,
Because they were men of genius, and you

Are not; and the ideas that were vital
To them are mere amusements to you. I will not
Go mad, because I have understood those ideas"

The Old Man, of course, is Yvor Winters, or a very close approxima-
tion of him, as Pinsky himself admits,[4] and the ideas about madness

4. In a 1996 interview with Jere Odell, Pinsky responds to Odell's question
about the identity of the Old Man by saying that the character "[i]s a fictionalized

are recognizably those expressed in *Forms of Discovery*.[5] For the Old Man Winters of Pinsky's poem, the last great age for poetry was the Augustan early eighteenth century. We have seen Winters' reasons for moving away from Imagist poetics around 1930, but in turning aside from Imagism, why did he move in the direction of the Augustan poets? For Winters, Imagism was a poetry of particulars and presentation, but Augustanism was a matter of commentary, abstraction, and moral statement. Augustan poetics filled perfectly the perceived lacunae of Imagism.

There is more at work here than this, though. One corollary of Winters' turn toward Augustan statement as an antidote to Imagist presentation is his embrace of Augustan sociability in place of what he saw as the isolation of the poetic consciousness in Imagist poetics. The collapse of distance between subject and object detailed in "The Testament of a Stone" left little room for a social poetry in which the self acknowledges and speaks to other selves. Winters came to see this as a problem, claiming in 1940 that his early poems "vacillate between an attitude—it was hardly more than that—of solipsism and mystical pantheism" (note to *Selected Poems* 58). The turn toward Augustan statement allows for that most social of poetic modes, the occasional poem, a form Winters came to exploit extensively in his later work. In fact, the change that strikes one most in the evolution of Winters' poetry is the growing sociability of the poems. "To William Dinsmore Briggs Conducting His Seminar," "To a Young Writer," and "On the Death of Senator Thomas J. Walsh" all emerge from and speak to particular social contexts in an Augustan manner antithetical to Winters' early work. The solipsism of the early work is cured by the social nature of Augustan poetics.

---

version of Winters. I knew him well, but the passage is based largely on a version of Winters talking to the opening of a class I didn't take. My friend Bob Hass did a little monologue on Winters, and I used some of that. . . . Winters said much of what was in the poem, but I don't think he'd refer to Ezra Pound as his friend. They corresponded. Little touches like that are different." (79).

5. See, for example, pages 157–59, where Winters discusses how, "from the eighteenth century onward, and not . . . before, we have a high incidence of madness among poets of more or less recognized talent: Collins, Gray, Chatterton, Smart, Blake, and others later." (158).

In addition, Augustanism offered a solution to the problem of the vagueness of motives that Winters found in modernist poetry. When, in 1930, Winters criticizes Hart Crane for his tendencies to extasis without clear motive, it is the original Augustan model of ancient Rome that Winters holds up as an alternative. "[D]estiny, for Aeneas, is not a vague surge toward an infinite future," he writes, thinking of Crane's and Walt Whitman's moments of epic ecstasy, "it is a deliberate effort to achieve a definite aim, and the effort is composed of specific moral duties; it is the serious attitude toward those duties that made him *pius* to the Augustan Roman" (*Uncollected Essays* 75). The Augustan is deliberate, contextual, and self-possessed, while Crane's poetics were, in Winters' view, dangerously unhinged in their unchecked impulsiveness and lack of self-understanding. Augustan restraint seemed like the best cure, and Winters was to hold to it, with little exception, until the end.

The Heretic of Paraphrase

It is by no means obvious why Winters' move away from a solipsistic, hermetic poetic and toward a sociable, plainspoken one should lead to his marginalization. In fact, it seems somewhat counterintuitive, until we look at the context in which Winters' marginalization occurred. That context, of course, is the postwar America in which radically expanded universities became the arbiters of poetic reputation, and in which a triumphant New Criticism ruled the English departments. The rise of the New Criticism led to many things, good and bad, but one consequence of its rise was particularly significant for the reception of Yvor Winters' poetry: the predominance of a theory of the autonomous art-object.

"The literary or artistic field is at all times the site of struggle between the two principles of hierarchization," writes Pierre Bourdieu, "the heteronomous principle . . . (e.g., 'bourgeois art') and the autonomous principle (e.g., 'art for art's sake')" (40). If art is judged on the basis of formal concerns without reference to other criteria, the autonomous principle of art prevails. If, however, the formal concerns of art are subordinated to other concerns, the heteronomous principle prevails. The formalism into which the New Criticism had evolved by the 1950s was, in Bourdieu's terms, an autonomous theory of literature. In contrast, the subordination of poetry's formal elements to its morality made Winters' poetry and poetics of this period a kind of heteronomous art, at odds with the New Criticism and the academic institutions it dominated.

In 1951, Cleanth Brooks codified the New Critical method in a number of "articles of faith" published in the *Kenyon Review* under the title "The Formalist Critic." These articles included the following:

> That the primary concern of criticism is with the problem of unity—the kind of whole which the literary work forms or fails to form, and the relation of the various parts to each other in building up this whole. . . .
> That in successful work, form and content cannot be separated.
> That form is meaning. . . .
> That literature is not a surrogate for religion.
> . . . that the purpose of literature is not to point to a moral. (72)

Brooks establishes the autonomy of the literary field from history and ethics. His methods are perfect to the explication of a certain kind of modernist poem, but absolutely inimical to a plainspoken, overtly moralistic poetry such as Winters was then writing. We could say that, in renouncing modernism in the years before the New Critics began to make it respectable for a generation of educated readers, Winters sold his shares just before a bull market.

It is unsurprising, then, that the New Critics could be merciless in their evaluation of Winters. In the same year that Brooks published his articles of faith, for example, Randall Jarrell wrote:

> *Is* Clarity the handmaiden of Popularity, as everybody automatically assumes? How much does it help to be immediately plain? In England today few poets are as popular as Dylan Thomas—his magical poems have corrupted a whole generation of English poets, yet he is surely one of the most obscure poets who ever lived. Or take an opposite

example: the poems of the students of Yvor Winters are quite as easy to understand as those which Longfellow used to read during the Children's Hour; yet they are about as popular as those other poems (of their own composition) which *grave Alice, and laughing Allegra, And Edith with golden hair* used to read to Longfellow during the Poet's Hour. If Dylan Thomas is obscurely famous, such poets as these are clearly unknown. ("The Obscurity of the Poet" 307–8)

These comments are flippant but telling, in that they encapsulate much of the New Critical critique of Wintersian poetry and poetics. While Winters, in one of his less tolerant moods, could write that "many poems cannot be paraphrased and are therefore defective" (see Von Hallberg 804), it would only be stretching things a little to say that the standard New Critical assessment of Winters was that his later poems were defective because they could be too readily paraphrased.

This was the basic substance of John Crowe Ransom's quarrel with Winters, and the substance of the critique that his student, Cleanth Brooks, would level at Winters. Both Ransom and Brooks objected to the statement-oriented, paraphrasable side of Winters' neo-Augustan poetics, and for the same two reasons: Winters' work violated the autonomous principle of poetry, and it upheld a neoclassical unity of language that was anathema to the New Critical notions of the nature of poetry. Two other New Critics, W. K. Wimsatt and Monroe C. Beardsley, would also object to his work on the same grounds. The repeated rejections were strong enough to sting even the thick-skinned Winters.

Ransom explicitly objects to Winters' heteronomous principles of poetry in the 1941 volume that became the namesake of a movement, *The New Criticism.* Here he maintains that "Winters believes that ethical interest is the only poetic interest" (214). This is a problem, Ransom argues, because it looks to poetry for reasons other than "poetical interest" itself:

Now I suppose [that Winters] would not disparage the integrity of a science like mathematics, or physics, by saying that it offers discourse whose intention is some sort of moral perfectionism. It is motivated by an interest in mathematics, or in physics. But if mathematics is for mathematical interest, why is not poetry for poetical interest? A true-blue critic like Eliot would certainly say that it is, though he would be unwilling to explain what he meant. I think I know why all critics do not answer as Eliot would: because criticism, a dilettante and ambiguous study, has not produced the terms in which poetic interest can be stated. Consequently Winters is obliged to think that mathematics is for mathematical interest—or so I suppose he thinks—but that poetry, in order that there may be an interest, must be for ethical interest. And why ethical? Looking around among the stereotyped sorts of interest, he discovers, very likely, that ethical interest is as frequent in poetry as any other one. (214)

The passage reverberates with the energies that were to bring the New Criticism to power in the universities: the science-based emphasis on a division of knowledge into discrete, autonomous fields; the condemnation of "dilettante" critics; the call for an articulation of "terms in which poetic interest can be stated" (terms, one imagines, such as *irony, balance,* and *unity,* which stress complex structure over moral statement). Ransom takes a position that will advance the New Criticism to the center of academic and literary authority. Winters, in this process, serves as a foil: the poet-critic who fails to grasp the autonomous principle, he is the representative of an outmoded, heteronomous aesthetic.

Ransom is also opposed to the neo-Augustan unity of language (or essential continuity of prose and poetry) so valuable to Winters, and this plays into his disdain for a poetry of paraphrasable statement. As early as 1934, Ransom denigrated statement as an element of poetry. He makes the point in "Poetry: A Note in Ontology," where the title itself stresses that a poem should "be" ontologically rather than "mean" hermeneutically. Ransom uses the image/statement distinction to help separate poetic language from the everyday language of statement: "a discourse which employed only abstract ideas," he tells us, "would be a scientific document and not a poem at all" because the poem is not primarily about any "idea to be propagated" (868). A poetry that uses the language of plain or abstract statement, he reiterates, is "a bogus poetry" and "not really a poetry" at all (870).

Cleanth Brooks's major contribution to the anti-Wintersian argument comes in the middle section of his famous essay of 1947, "The Heresy of Paraphrase," where Inquisitor Brooks fingers Winters as the leading heretic. Like Ransom, Brooks objects to Winters' emphasis on statement on the grounds that it violates the autonomous nature of literature. "Mr. Winters' position will furnish perhaps the most respectable example of the paraphrastic heresy," intones the Inquisitor, naming Winters as a heretic because "he assigns primacy to the 'rational meaning' of the poem" (963). This is a violation of the autonomous principle of poetry because "to refer the structure of the poem to what is finally a paraphrase of the poem is to refer it to something outside of the poem" (964). For true believers free from heteronomous heresies, poems are to be judged in terms of structure and "internal order" (964) only. In addition, Winters is condemned for conceiving of the language of poetry as continuous with the language of "science or philosophy or theology" (964). Brooks, like Ransom, holds to the New Critical dogma that poetry is a special kind of language, and so he is unsympathetic to Winters' idea that poetry does not differ in essence from prose. While no dunking stools were in use for heretics in the New Critical academy, the most powerful weapon available was deployed against the heretic Winters: he was derided and, worse, ignored.

Bourdieu waxes about as eloquent as is possible for a French sociologist on this matter of combating heresy through ignorance. "One of the difficulties of orthodox defense against heretical transformation of the field by a redefinition of the tacit or explicit terms of entry is the fact that polemics imply a form of recognition," he writes. "The 'nouveaux philosophes' came into existence as active elements in the philosophical field," for example, "as soon as consecrated philosophers felt called upon to take issue with them" (42). The New Critics increasingly took the position of ignoring Winters rather than refuting him. Robert Von Hallberg even seems to indicate that this kind of hostility played a part in Winters' increasing interest in criticism over poetry from the mid-1940s onward, "probably because he had come to a coherent understanding of the canons of contemporary taste that interfered with the appreciation of his own poems. . . . Winters seems to have decided at that time to devote most of his energy to criticism and teaching" (812). It may seem counterintuitive to class as resilient and stoic a man as Winters with the delicate version of Keats we find in Shelley's "Adonais" (his "soft Form" rent by the "barbed tongues" of critics), but Von Hallberg has a very real point: Winters' turn from poetry to criticism is coincident with the spreading hostility to his work, and more than likely the link between the two is causal.

One of the last major attacks on Winters—or perhaps we should say, one of the last moments when his work is taken seriously enough by a New Critic to merit sustained attack—comes in Wimsatt and Beardsley's 1954 study, *The Verbal Icon*. In addition to making light of Winters' concerns about improperly motivated emotion, they repeat the standard New Critical case against Wintersian poetics when they say they will not embrace "the extreme doctrine of Winters, that if a poem cannot be paraphrased it is a poor poem" (35). Winters, for them, is largely passé.

For the New Critics from Jarrell to Ransom to Brooks to Wimsatt and Beardsley, the poems most favored were "obscurely famous," centered on formal concerns and consecrated because of those concerns. Had the Robert Lowell of *Lord Weary's Castle* not been born, the New Critics would have had to invent him in a secret laboratory beneath Kenyon College's biology building. But the poems of Yvor Winters, like those of his unnamed students in Jarrell's "The Obscurity of the Poet," were "clearly unknown." It was their clarity, in fact, that kept them that way.

On Not Breaking Through in the 1960s

While the New Criticism was to remain a powerfully entrenched force in English departments for many years, other factors came into play in the continued marginalization of Winters' neo-Augustan poetics in the 1960s. One of these factors concerned a large-scale cultural movement: the growth of a counterculture with ideals that were remarkably unclassical and therefore un-Wintersian. If, as Susan Sontag maintained in 1966 in the closing chapter of *Against Interpretation*, the "new sensibility" must reject a literature of "moral judgement" (21), then it must perforce reject Wintersian poetics. Or if, as Irving Howe put it in his 1968 essay "The New York Intellectuals," the prevailing ethos of the 1960s was one of emotional impulse and "a psychology of unobstructed need," then that ethos would be anathema to neo-Augustan restraint (*Decline of the New* 111).

In the poetic field this new ethos manifested itself in what James Longenbach has called the "break-through narrative" of poetic development. This was the story of the poet's breakthrough from restrictive formalism to personal expression: a pattern of development that seemed to run counter to Winters' movement from his early free verse to his later Augustan formalism. The invention of the term "confessional poetry" by M. L. Rosenthal in 1967 to describe poets such as Robert Lowell, Anne Sexton, Sylvia Plath, and John Berryman (*The New Poets* 83) helped to popularize this idea. In the breakthrough narrative, the strongest poets struggle against thorny formal constraints, to achieve victory at last by discarding them for the lucidity of sincere personal expression. Lowell, scion of the New Criticism, became the most notable hero of this story. Indeed, Rosenthal says that "Lowell's poetry has been a long struggle to remove the mask, to make the speaker unequivocally himself" ("Robert Lowell and the Poetry of Confession," *The New Poets* 45).

Lowell himself helped to create this myth of the poet's development, describing his own in detail and generalizing that development as the story of a generation. Looking back in 1970 at his poetic evolution, Lowell painted a picture of himself in the 1940s as a kind of *uber*-New Critical poet, too formalist even for the formalists. As a recent graduate of Kenyon, Lowell tells us that he was reading William Empson's *Seven Types of Ambiguity* while teaching at the college, and writing poems more and more full of ironies and ambiguities. Even Ransom, Lowell says, found the poems intimidatingly complex: "Ransom, editing the *Kenyon Review*, was impressed, but didn't want to publish them. He felt they were forbidding and clotted." While this type of poetry formed the basis of his early success, in hindsight Lowell saw it as a dead end, and formalism as an obstacle to be overcome: "I seemed to have reached a great impasse. The kind of poem I thought was interesting and would work on became so cluttered and overdone that it wasn't really poetry" ("An Interview with Robert Lowell" 265).

The breakthrough came, famously, with the poems of *Life Studies*, which appeared in 1959. *Après Lowell, le déluge*, one might say, as poet after poet seemed to follow in Lowell's footsteps. As Longenbach points out, this story, despite its limitations, was to become the most common one for describing the lives of poets in the 1960s. Readers in the 1960s looked at Lowell's development as a paradigm for poets in general and "found a similar aesthetic 'breakthrough' (often accompanied by a psychological 'breakdown') in the careers of many of Lowell's contemporaries" (*Modern Poetry* 5). Poets, too, came to see their careers in this way: even as conservative a poet as John Hollander would, at the end of the 1960s, look back on his development from the writing of rather impersonal sonnets and sestinas to a somewhat more autobiographical, looser formality: "opening up at all is harder than meeting a measure" ("Helicon," *Selected Poetry* 286). The heroism of the poet comes in breaking through to simplicity and personal expressivity.

The prevalence of the breakthrough narrative did not bode well for Winters, whose neo-Augustan poetics emphasized those traditional verse forms that were being jettisoned by those young poets who were following in Lowell's considerable wake. Perhaps the best illustration of Winters' sad fate in this period comes in a short essay of 1968, "Looking for an Opening," by Winters' one-time student, Philip Levine. Here, Levine describes his own poetic development from 1952 to 1965. The story he tells is quite clearly the "breakthrough narrative," and Winters represents the crusty old forces that needed to be overthrown. Levine begins with an image of himself in 1952, already longing to break through to simple expression: "As early as my 24th year, that is to say long before I became tolerably proficient at traditional meters, I had an idea for a poem in free verse and conversational English, a poem which would be harsh, natural, and somehow powerful without employing a heightened vocabulary or a single word suggesting the presence of an idea" (388).

The noble savage was soon corrupted by the vices of tradition, though. Levine goes on to tell how the "dreary fifties" and the formalism he picked up while studying at the University of Iowa with the still–New Critical Lowell suppressed his natural expressivity. Despite his education, Levine says, he was able to continue as a poet: "occasionally I was even able to get some of the experiences of my life into the poetry without raising it to the level of the emotions of princes." Enter, at this point, the villain: "at the same time I so mastered the poetry of princes that Yvor Winters awarded me a fellowship in the creative writing [*sic*] at Stanford" (388). How the young Levine suffered under Yvor's baleful gaze! "I would show him one of my new poems," writes Levine, "and he would read me something by [Tristan] Corbière that turned my tongue to stone. He neither understood nor valued what I did, and he said so" (389).

But the breakthrough was to come for Levine while under Winters' tutelage. It was, in fact, through Winters' syllabus that the young Levine broke.

> On Winters' suggestion I was reading the dull, ladylike poetry of Elizabeth Daryush; it was very easy to see the technique in her syllabic poetry because there was almost nothing else there, and so after two hours in the rare book room at Stanford, where Daryush was housed, I was ready to write. . . . I wrote about the one time I went out hunting alone and scared myself half to death and never went hunting again. Whatever intensification I gave to the experience did not come from a falsely elevated diction, for with the exception of one slip in the first stanza I had written in the language I used when I spoke. Rhythmically I had used Mrs. Daryush as a base, put her line and stanza down as a norm, and then had broken through it as quickly as I could. (389)

Levine, as hero of his own narrative, bursts through the barrier of mere form and into natural expression. Winters, we are told, was unappreciative of the poem and "couldn't see that it was about anything except details" (390).

It is deeply ironic that the same Augustan Winters who was not formalist enough (in the art-for-art's-sake sense) for the New Critics was too much of a formalist (in the sense of regularity in meter and rhyme) for the poets of the "breakthrough" generation. Marjorie Perloff has called Winters "the great counter-critic" of the 1950s (*The Dance of the Intellect* 2), but it is perhaps more accurate to say that he was the great counter poet of two decades—too plainspoken for the 1950s, too formal for the 1960s. Small wonder, then, that our Poet-Critic B wears so few of the medals and ribbons of the kind that adorn our much-lauded Poet-Critic A.

Chapter Two

Robert Pinsky

American Laureate

Wintersians, Orthodox and Otherwise

In 1963, Robert Pinsky arrived at Stanford to pursue his doctorate in literature. He had been writing poems for years, and he had enough confidence to publish some in *The Anthologist*, the literary magazine at Rutgers University, where he had studied as an undergraduate. Knowing little about Winters except that he was the senior poet on campus, Pinsky took a selection of his early efforts with him to an early meeting with Winters. This initial meeting was not auspicious, with Winters displaying his usual preference for honest disdain over tact when discussing student writing. The relationship soon improved, though, with Winters directing much of Pinsky's reading and providing guidance for the dissertation on Walter Savage Landor that would become Pinsky's first published book five years later. The Wintersian inheritance would play a crucial role in Pinsky's rise to prominence in American poetry. But while much of his considerable early achievement was the direct result of his engagement with Winters, two circumstances have conspired to limit the public recognition of this link. It has been obscured by a general reticence in our literary culture when it comes to acknowledging influence and, more important, by the need felt by Pinsky to disassociate himself from the most dogmatic followers of Winters.

Inside the thorny, overgrown, Freudian-Longinian garden of Harold Bloom's *Anxiety of Influence* lies at least one kernel of truth: it is often difficult for poets to give credit to their most vital influences. In a literary culture far from free of Romantic notions of the virtue of originality, poets can be a bit reticent about the role played by others in their development. And if originality is a virtue, professional courtesy dictates that poets should be very careful even when describing the influence of a mentor on other poets. This, I think, is the cultural matrix behind a comment by Thom Gunn, in which he dances very carefully around the issue of Winters' influence on the poets who studied at Stanford: "Many others of his students, before and after . . . were to keep their poetic identities intact—Donald Hall, Edgar Bowers, Philip Levine, Robert Pinsky, Alan Stephens, Scott Momaday, Kenneth Fields and so on—some even coming to reject him. But all of us learned from him, even the most reluctant" (690). With the one hand, Gunn giveth the Wintersian influence, with the other he taketh away.

While Gunn's circumspection is certainly the product of our Romantic inheritance, it also has to do with more local concerns. It would not be so important to stress the relative independence of poets such as Pinsky were there not another contingent of Stanford students who clung much more fiercely to Wintersian ideas. When Gunn describes the attitudes and motives of those students in the 1950s, they come off sounding like nothing so much as a cult:

> For some of [Winters'] students his formulations provided a refuge, a harmonious world where everything had already been decided in accordance with certain rules. It became a temporary or lifelong asylum for those who might otherwise have fallen into the hands of a church or political party. The attraction lay in the logical *completeness* with which he had worked out his ideas, and such students became disciples in a literal sense, limiting themselves to another man's world. . . . I had seen the whole thing happen before, among the students of F. R. Leavis at Cambridge. (690)

Donald Hall, like Gunn a student of Winters in the 1950s, reports on the phenomenon in strikingly similar terms:

> Certain strong teachers and writers develop not students but disciples. Everyone compares Leavis at Cambridge to Winters at Stanford, teachers and students largely incomparable except in their relationships to students. Charles Olson was another. Intelligent leaders with power of character attract men and women who have a vocation for following, whose ecstasy is obedience or replication, whose bliss is to lose their identities in a leader or parent. (234)

It was the meeting of two types of personalities—the naturally submissive follower and the magnetically charismatic master—that created the cult of Winters.

The tendency of some of his students to take up Winters' ideas with something like the gleam of fanaticism in their eyes continued long after the 1950s, even carrying on after his death in 1968. Alan Shapiro reports on the prevalence of the phenomenon in the 1970s and makes an explicit comparison with religious extremism. He recalls one episode from his graduate school years in particular, when he was being berated by an old friend who had converted to Hasidism. "I listened with superior, somewhat contemptuous amusement," he writes, "for I too (though I didn't recognize it then) was a true believer, and the faith I clung to . . . had its sacred doctrine, replete with clear and definitive prescriptions." While Shapiro's friend had turned to Menachem Mendel Schneerson, leader of the Lubavitcher movement, as his spiritual leader, "mine," says Shapiro, "was Yvor Winters" (*Last Happy Occasion* 131–32).

Pinsky was certainly never one of these orthodox Wintersians, and given the association of the Wintersian label with such extremists, it is quite understandable that he resists it, as he does in a 1996 interview with Jere Odell, when he says, "I never was one of what were called the Wintersians" (80). "I can remember being sneered at in his seminar by my pal John Peck and others because I was soft on Yeats," Pinsky continues, adding, "I wouldn't admit that Yeats wasn't as good a poet as Sturge Moore." But if Pinsky was not a card-carrying member of the Wintersian party, he was certainly a fellow-traveler. Of his years with Winters at Stanford, Pinsky has said that "I knew I was learning as much from him as I ever have from anybody in my life" (81).

It would not, I think, be going too far to say that Winters played an essential role in making the young Pinsky who walked into his office in 1963 into the author of such considerable Augustan works as *The Situation of Poetry* and *An Explanation of America*. Pinsky acknowledges Winters' importance to his development when, in an autobiographical sketch, he recounts his first meeting with him:

> He asked me to sit down, and he thumbed through the manuscript while I was there. It took him four minutes, stopping once or twice at certain ones. Then he looked up at me, and said, "You simply don't know how to write."
>
> He added that there was some gift there, but because I was igno-rant of what to do with it, he could not estimate how much of a gift it was. If it was blind luck or happy fate or smiling Fortune that must be thanked for leading me to Stanford, let me congratulate myself for having the sense not to leave the room when he said that. (*Contempo-rary Authors Autobiography Series* 245)

While few of us would look at the Winters depicted in this passage as the model of an ideal literary pedagogue, Pinsky certainly found the man's influence salutary, the gift of a smiling Fortune.

Fortune saved Pinsky from a too-narrow sense of literary tradi-tion. He had arrived in Winters' seminar room as a potential disciple of William Carlos Williams or of Allen Ginsberg. In 1963, Pinsky had, by his own account, a very limited sense of English literature, having focused on modern American poets. He had, he says, "read everything I could get my hands on by Allen Ginsberg. I'd read most of Williams that was available. I'd read *Paterson*." Winters, says Pinsky, "gave me a heightened understanding of what poetry was, partly— maybe largely—by introducing me to the English 16th and 17th cen-turies" (Interview 79). In that seminar room, as in few other places in American academe, those centuries were considered important for producing the plain-style poets. Before coming to Winters' seminars,

Pinsky "hadn't even heard of Gascoigne or Greville," plain-style poets who came to serve as his "models of . . . urgent moral energy" (81). Small wonder then, that Pinsky's major critical work, *The Situation of Poetry*, is dedicated to the memory of "A.Y.W."—Arthur Yvor Winters.

Pinsky's Augustan Moralism and Emotional Restraint

Critics have been quick to note the moralism of Pinsky's early work, but they have seldom been as ready to note the role of Winters in shaping that moralism, perhaps because of the stigma of extremism connected with the word "Wintersian." Willard Spiegelman, for example, finds "ethical ambition" to be the thread that binds Pinsky's poetry and prose into a unified whole, but he asserts that "the tradition of Jewish ethical seriousness" is the source of that ambition (99). One hesitates to claim that Pinsky had no sense of art as a moral or ethical act before he came to Stanford: his early interest in the ever-moralizing Ginsberg argues otherwise. But the form and degree of Pinsky's moralism surely bear the mark of Winters' Augustanism. Spiegelman actually comes quite close to seeing the Wintersian roots of Pinsky's first two books of poetry, *Sadness and Happiness* and *An Explanation of America*, when he says that they "reveal the ethical nature of Pinsky's meditations" as "his inheritance of a Horatian sanity" (99).

The classical Augustan basis of Pinsky's moralism is most apparent in part two of *An Explanation of America*, where the ethical meditations take place within a frame of reference that is explicitly Horatian. After working over material from Horace's *Epistulae*, Pinsky comes to the following conclusion:

> we should aspire,
> For ourselves, to struggle actively to save
> The Republic—or to be, if not like Brutus,
> Like Quinctius: a citizen of affairs . . .

Not only is this a passage of classical civic sentiment: the path of civic virtue is marked by evocations of figures from Rome at the time of the coming of Augustus.

The moralism of poems such as *An Explanation of America* is, in fact, a close cousin of Pinsky's Wintersian wariness of emotional impulse. Like Pinsky's moralism, this can also come clothed in a classical imagery indicative of its Augustan lineage. "Ceremony for Any Beginning," from *Sadness and Happiness*, is a case in point. Here is the first stanza:

> Against weather, and the random
> Harpies—mood, circumstance, the
> Laws of biography, chance, physics—
>
> The unseasonable soul holds forth,
> Eager for form as a renowned
> Pedant, the emperor's man of worth,
> Hereditary arbiter of manners.

The poem sets the overtly classical form exemplified by the "emperor's man of worth" against the forces of emotional impulse, represented by the harpies of mood and circumstance. The forces cataloged along with mood and circumstance—"laws of biography, chance, physics"— are all forces that would reduce us to automatons, deprived of free will. Like Winters and Samuel Johnson, Pinsky associates emotional impulse with an automatism against which we must hold out.

It is not the case, though, that Pinsky is immune to the lure of emotional impulse. Like Winters, he acknowledges the pull of raw emotion even as he argues the need to distance oneself from it. We have a rather vivid dramatization of this process in the title poem of *Sadness and Happiness*. Here, Pinsky allows himself, for a moment, to follow his impulses and wallow in a self-indulgent and self-pitying image of himself as an unacknowledged and mistreated genius. Thinking of his frequent "hard-ons of self concern," he confesses to his

> melodramas and speeches
> of myself, crazy in love with
> my status as a sad young man: dreams
> of myself old, a vomit-stained

ex-Jazz-Immortal, collapsed
in a phlegmy Bowery doorway
on Old Mr. Boston lemon-flavored
gin or on cheap wine—that romantic

fantasy of my future bumhood
excused of all manner of lies, fumbles,
destructions

He then goes on to imagine himself as the kind of poet who follows his
momentary impulse to howl out his visionary curses:

even this minute, "*Mea
culpa!*" I want to scream, stealing
the podium to address the band,
the kids, the old ladies awaiting
buses, the glazed winos . . .

. . . "Oh you city of
undone deathcrotches! Terrible
the film of green brainpus! Fog
of corruption at the great shitfry! No

grease-trickling sink
of disorder in your depressed
avenues is more terrible
than these, and not your whole

aggregate of pollution
is more heavy than the measure
of unplumbed muttering
remorse, shame, inchoate pride

and nostalgia in any one
sulphur-choked, grit-breathing
citizen of the place."

The moral outrage, the scatology, the hurling of neologisms such as "deathcrotches," "brainpus," and "shitfry" out into the street—all indicate that this is Pinsky's vision of himself as Ginsberg, or as the Ginsbergian poet he was well on his way to becoming before he went to Winters' Stanford. But the poem turns, after these lines, heading off in an important new direction. The howling stops, and the measured voice returns to comment on what has come before:

> Sad,
> the way one in part enjoys
>
> air pollution, relishes
> millennial doom . . .

Having acknowledged the pull of self-pity and self-indulgent rage, Pinsky turns away from them, gives himself a little distance, and makes a judgment about them: such emotions are real, but sad, and ultimately must be kept from dominating us. The howling Ginsbergian version of the self is set aside.

Perhaps the best frame of reference for these passages from "Sadness and Happiness" is Pinsky's book of criticism, *The Situation of Poetry*. John Matthias summarizes the argument of that book quite well: "a 'sane' work of art . . . is one which accomplishes its meaning consciously," and "sanity in writing is the tonal adjustment that changes confession into character making. Authentic clarity is the style's proof that the fiction is true: not a patient's tortured, oblique version of a dream, but the authoritative dream itself" (*Reading Old Friends* 174). This might well be taken as a commentary on the lines from "Sadness and Happiness" quoted above. The poem that Pinsky offers is not the spontaneous rant itself, not the "first-thought best-thought" rush of ecstatic inspiration and improvisation behind many of Ginsberg's poems. Instead, it is a matter of "character making," in which the ranting self is a creation of a deliberate self.

It may well be the case that the ultimate impulse behind Pinsky's moralism is, as Spiegelman maintains, "the Jewish tradition of ethical seriousness"(99); and it may well be, as James Longenbach says, that Pinsky "knew intuitively that the reading and writing of poetry was a moral act" (*Modern Poetry after Modernism* 143). But the importance of Winters in shaping any ethical impetus that Pinsky may have brought to Stanford cannot be understated. After all, Ginsberg is another poet in whom Spiegelman sees manifested the tradition of ethical seriousness, and Pinsky, in "Sadness and Happiness," clearly distances himself from the Ginsbergian mode of ethical poetry as righteous harangue.

In the Wintersian Matrix: Realism and Nominalism

Not least among Winters' legacies to Pinsky was the realist theory of language. "Realism" and its opposite, "nominalism," are, unfortunately, two of the most overdetermined terms in philosophy, and the word "realism" also carries a great deal of freight in the history of post-Romantic literature and literary criticism. The realism that Pinsky inherits from Yvor Winters, though, is quite specific, and it has its source in scholastic philosophy and theology. According to Winters, Aristotle and Thomas Aquinas represented the realist tradition, in which "philosophical knowledge was possible" (*In Defense of Reason* 374), and language was considered adequate for conveying this knowledge. In this view, ideas or essences are real, existing independently of our perceptions. Words can embody these ideas, so language can contain real truths and apprehend the real essences of things.

The nominalist tradition, according to Winters, begins "by attacking the reality of universals, by endeavoring to show the illusory nature of all ideas whatsoever" (*In Defense of Reason* 374–75). William of Ockham, to Winters' mind "the most profound of medieval nominalists," masterminded the assault on the fortress of realism. In Ockham's view, the things of the world do not have essences, and all language is, in a sense, arbitrary. It cannot communicate what reality is actually like: instead, it is a fallible human invention, a matter of mere names. Abstractions have no real existence, so the category "sadness," say, would not refer to an essential state, but would simply be an invented name aimed in the general direction of a disparate collection of individual experiences.

For Winters, this view was not only wrong but dangerous: it left us with an unintelligible world. In effect, it left us with the world of

Winters' early Imagist poetry, in which the things of the world were presented but not explained, and in which the conscious mind had no real ability to make sense of experience. Of his early period, Winters was to say in 1964, "I was a nominalist, although I did not know the word" ("By Way of Clarification" 131). Being a nominalist was not just a matter of holding a particular philosophical viewpoint, either: it mattered tremendously. As Terry Comito puts it, nominalism for Winters was "a limitless terror, the vision of a universe receding into the silence of particulars" (242).

Poetry, rightly understood, would save us from this terror, or so thought Winters in his later years. It would do this because the true poet recognized that each word of our language "has a conceptual content, however slight," that bears a real relation to the world (*In Defense of Reason* 363). Winters came to see his own career as a progression from the nominalist error of his youth to the redemptive realism of his maturity. And he came, also, to see the whole of literary history as a war between the realist and nominalist traditions, with nominalism dangerously ascendant from Romanticism onward.

Pinsky inherits this sense of an ongoing cold war between realist and nominalist poetics. We see this most clearly in the leadup to his reading of Keats' "Ode to a Nightingale" in *The Situation of Poetry*. Pinsky begins with a sense of the continuous struggle between the nominalist "flow of absolutely particular moments" and the realist "arrangement of perfectly abstract categories":

> Certain ideas and emotional conflicts suggest a continuity between contemporary and modernist poetry—and, beyond that, a continuity with the Romantic poetry of the nineteenth century. Monumental and familiar, the conflicts are between conscious and unconscious forces within the mind: between the idea of experience as unreflective, a flow of absolutely particular moments, and the reality of language as reflective, an arrangement of perfectly abstract categories. (47)

The Manichean conflicts of Winters' literary history are evident, as is the preference for the realist theory of language, which appears here as "the reality of language."

The reading of Keats that follows is eminently Wintersian, describing Keats as a poet who "loves and wishes to approach unconscious being" (50). Fed through Pinsky's Wintersian thought-matrix, the longing for unconscious being becomes a longing for an experience of the absolutely particular moment, irreducible to abstraction. It becomes, in effect, the longing of a nominalist:

> Alone, exiled from the rest of the physical world by his consciousness which organizes, reflects and articulates sensory particulars, the Romantic poet [Keats] regards the natural world nostalgically, across a gulf which apparently can be crossed only by dying, either actually or through induced oblivion. That gulf is closely related to the gulf between words and things. Various philosophical descriptions might apply to the situation. The broadest of these (if any such description is necessary) stems from the terms "nominalism" and "realism." Nominalism can be loosely defined as the doctrine that words and concepts are mere names, convenient counters of no inherent reality, though they may be useful means of dealing with the atomistic flux of reality. I understand philosophical realism as the opposite doctrine that universals—and, therefore, concepts and words—embody reality. The Romantic poet tends to look for values to emerge from particular experiences—associated sense perceptions and states of mind at particular moments—and insofar as that is true, he is a nominalist. (56–57)

For Winters, this sort of nominalism represented a misunderstanding of the nature of language. Pinsky, then, is following Wintersian doctrine when he goes on to say of Keats that "insofar as he is a poet he must to some extent be a realist, for those reasons which may bear repeating: words are abstractions, sentences are forms disposing their parts in time, and rhythm is based upon the recurrence of pattern" (57). That is, a true nominalist would not write at all. He would not attempt meaning, through the use of language, but satisfy himself through mere being, or through seeking union with the natural world he longs for "by dying, either actually or through induced oblivion." This sense of the ominous consequences of nominalism comes directly from Winters, who blamed an American Romantic nominalism

for the self-destructive behavior and eventual suicide of his friend
Hart Crane:

> I saw Crane during the Christmas week of 1927, when he was approx-
> imately 29 years old: his hair was graying, his skin had the dull red
> color with reticulated grayish traceries which so often goes with ad-
> vanced alcoholism, and his ears and knuckles were beginning to look
> like those of a pugilist. About a year later he was deported from France
> as a result of his starting an exceptionally violent commotion in a bar-
> room and perhaps as a result of other activities. In 1932 he committed
> suicide by leaping from a steamer into the Caribbean sea.
>
> The doctrine of Emerson and Whitman, if really put into prac-
> tice, should naturally lead to suicide. (*In Defense of Reason* 589–90)

There is nothing of Winters' urgency or anguish in Pinsky's realism,
but otherwise the doctrines are virtually identical.

A Test of Language: "Sadness and Happiness"

The poem "Sadness and Happiness" is Pinsky's most thorough exploration of the nominalist/realist debate. Playing nominalist and realist
themes against one another in an ode-like structure of strophe and antistrophe, he acknowledges the power of the nominalist argument but
finally takes his stand on the realist side, where Winters stood before
him. The taking of this realist stand affirms Pinsky's belief in the power
of language to speak about human experiences. The poem begins with
a quandary: Is emotion fathomable? Are words adequate to the task of
comprehending human feeling? The first lines of the opening section
offer us a sense of the complexity of sadness and happiness and acknowledge the difficulty of describing them with words:

> That they [sadness and happiness] have no earthly measure
> is well known—the surprise is
> how often it becomes impossible
> to tell one from the other in memory:

the sadness of past failures, the strangely
happy—doubtless corrupt—
fondling of them. Crude, empty
though the terms are, they do

organize life . . .

Difficult though the task may be, and crude as our words are, the poem
does seem to take a realist stance here: words are not empty, the world
is not without discernible meaning. Words do organize life.

In the next section, though, Pinsky undoes this too-easily attained
conclusion. A contemplation of *postcoitum tristesse* leads him to a contemplation of his own romantic failures and missed erotic chances. A
curious pleasure in self-pity accompanies the sorrow of lost opportunity, and words such as "sadness" and "happiness" seem incapable of
describing the muddled state of emotion. While he begins the section
confident in the terms—"pain" and "bliss"—that Elizabethan sonne-
teers used for erotic frustration and fulfillment, by its end such language
has failed. "'Bale' and 'bliss' merge/in a Petrarchist grin"—Petrarch's
grin, presumably, being one of simultaneous erotic fulfillment and
frustration. If the initial section was a rationalist strophe, then this
section comprises a nominalist antistrophe.

The third section of the poem begins by deepening this nominalism, and then it seems, for a moment, to deliver us from it. Imagin-
ing himself as a "holy idiot" who, in his befuddlement, misses out on
"the best prizes of life," Pinsky goes on to compare himself to "Korsh,
Old Russia's bedlam-sage." For Korsh, language is a mere babble of
vague but ultimately meaningless prophecy. Aristocrats visit him, and
"into his muttered babble they read tips//on the market, court, marriage," but the babble remains just that, a mere fluttering of airy words.
Pinsky envisions himself as a similar spouter of babble—"I too/mutter:
Fool, fool! or *Death!/* or *Joy!*" Language, it seems, is as empty as a lu-
natic's park-bench ramblings: a tool unfit for describing the muddle of
human emotion with any precision. But the poem is not ready to give
up on language, or let "sadness" and "happiness" mean nothing. "Well,"
Pinsky continues,

somewhere in the mind's mess
feelings are genuine, someone's
mad voice undistracted, clarity
maybe of motive and precise need
like an enameled sky, cool
blue of Indian Summer, happiness

It looks like happiness, anyway; and an undistracted mind could name it accurately with a simple word. The section ends on such a note, but the sentence does not: it runs over into the next section, in which things become more complicated. The "happiness" at the end of the third section is, we learn in the fourth, "like the sex-drowsy saxophones/rolling flatted thirds of the blues/over and over" and "rocking the dulcet rhythms of regret." Happiness, like "Black music . . . / tumbles loss over in the mouth/like a moist bone full of marrow." The happiness that seemed clear and genuine in the last section turns out to contain its opposite, just as the joy of blues music contains an immensity of suffering. The word "happiness" ceases to be adequate to an emotion that deconstructs itself before our eyes.

Bereft of a language adequate to experience, Pinsky proposes to "feel/the senses." He begins a catalog of the word, moving from what looks like a rather nice lunch to what appear to be a couple of semester-break vacations: "cheese, bread, tart/apples and wine, broiling acres/ of sunflowers in Spain,/mansards in Vermont, painted shay and pard." This catalog continues in sections five and six, in which we accompany Pinsky as he drives from Vermont to Cambridge, Massachusetts. Watching the scenery go by through the car window, Pinsky finds that everything is all "fraught//full of emotion, and yet empty —/how can I say it?—all empty/of sadness and happiness." Bereft of a meaningful language, the speaker finds himself in a situation that is, in a mild, professorial way, like that of the Romantic poets described by the old man (based on Winters) in Pinsky's "Essay on Psychiatrists." He, like those poets, is *"left// With emotions and experiences, and with no way/ To examine them."* The situation may not represent the "limitless terror" of a "universe receding into the silence of particulars" that Winters had felt during his nominalist period (Comito 242). It is a problem, though: the world becomes "a profound emptiness," and the jumble of sensations appears "crazy . . . crazy" in its irreducible, language-resistant particularity.

Section seven finds our speaker still mired in the world of mere sensation. This is a world confined to the eternal present, in which the poet wonders what it would be like to exist without a past of failures and a future without ambitions:

> how happy I would be, or else
> decently sad, with no past: you
> only and no foolish ghosts
> urging me on to become some redeeming

> Jewish-American Shakespeare

Happy or "decently sad": it hardly matters which words one uses, at this point, with language emptied of meaning and unable to fix itself firmly to its referents in the world.

The consequences of lacking any workable language for describing and analyzing emotions become clear in sections eight through ten. In sections eight and nine, Pinsky imagines himself as a poet without such a language. He pictures himself filled with rage, hurling invective at the injustices of the world. In his fiery wrath, this poet never realizes that his anger is really a kind of happiness in self-righteousness, a complacency or smugness that mistakes itself for the zeal for justice. The ranting Pinsky figure, lost in sensation and with a language that is little more than sound and fury, cannot understand that it is "sad,/ the way one in part enjoys//air pollution, relishes//millennial doom." He has emotions and experiences, but no meaningful way to examine them.

Section ten, perhaps the most overtly Wintersian part of the poem, proposes that it is "terrible, to think that mere pretty/scenery . . . can bring joy/or fail to." In a nominalist world of sensation we lack an emotional gyroscope. The terrible ease with which the natural world can dictate emotion here is familiar from Winters' early poetry: it is the terror of the coyote's "mocking feet" in "Two Songs of Advent." It is also exactly what Winters described as a Romantic vice in *Primitivism and Decadence*, where he tells us:

> Shelley's "Ode to the West Wind," and in a measure Keats' "Ode to a Nightingale," are examples . . . of expressing a feeling, not as among the traditional poets in terms of its motive, but in terms of something irrelevant or largely so, commonly landscape. No landscape, in itself, is an adequate motive for the feelings expressed in poems such as these. . . . as an act of moral contemplation the poem [that follows this procedure] is incomplete and may even be misleading and dangerous. (*In Defense of Reason* 50–51)

In an attempt to overcome his susceptibility to sensations such as the sight of pretty scenery, Pinsky wonders if he should aim for a stoic self-sufficiency and "vow/to seek only within myself/my only hire." Not for him, though, the Wintersian white-knuckle grip on the emotions. He cannot help but be buffeted by experience: "all my senses/. . . counsel gratitude//for the two bright-faced girls/crossing the Square" with their "long legs flashing bravely above//the grime." What looks at first like a simple happiness leaps forth from such sense moments— but again, the emotion proves elusive and self-deconstuctive, quickly leading Pinsky to an obscure sadness where bale and bliss merge.

After this long journey into nominalism, the poem turns again in sections eleven and twelve. The connection between word and referent is reaffirmed at last: there can, we are told, be moments that may be described as "pure joy." And language, raised to an art, can be worked to encompass the most poignant of moments. In section twelve, Pinsky summons the figure of Miguel de Cervantes as his representative virtuoso of "the bizarre art of words." Cervantes offers the "confirmation/ of a good word" as sufficient to experience. *El polvo*, or dust, becomes the *mot juste* for joy in Cervantes' "poem of the girl dancing" with "*el polvo*/rising in pale puffs to glaze lightly/the brown ankles and brown bare feet." Through his verbal virtuosity, Cervantes can form language to fit and express experience. And through a comparable virtuosity, Pinsky works the same word to express a different experience. "All dust now," writes Pinsky of Cervantes, "poet, girl." It is "intolerable," he continues, "to think of my daughters, too, dust/*el polvo*." It is not that language is arbitrary, applying to anything at which it is aimed. Rather, it is the careful fitting of word to verbal and literal contexts that allows language to be sufficient to the world and to carry definite meanings. We have returned to the realist position, where Pinsky's ode will, in its final section, take its stand.

The final section begins with Pinsky's daughters playing a game invented by his wife—a game called "Sadness and Happiness," in which the daughters are asked to name "one sad/thing that happened today" and whether they can "think/of one happy thing to tell me that/happened to you today?" They are, as Pinsky says, "organizing life" through language: these are the first steps on the road to using language with the precision and virtuosity necessary for it to bear meaning. The game initiates the daughters into the realist's sense of language.

The realist view of language that we see the daughters learning will give them an interpretable world, where meaningful statements are possible. This is certainly a kind of logocentrism, but it is far from a naïve one, acknowledging as it does the lure of the nominalist position. It is also a position that makes possible Pinsky's essay-poems, such as "Essay on Psychiatrists," in which he will, with a realist's confidence, offer a "Peroration, Defining Happiness." His poetics of statement will be built on the foundations of Wintersian realism.

Making a Statement

Pinsky won the literary equivalent of a biathlon gold medal with the appearance of *Sadness and Happiness* in 1975 and *The Situation of Poetry* soon thereafter: one of the best-received books of poetry of its year was immediately followed by a highly acclaimed book of criticism. Clearly, both books offered things that readers and reviewers were ready to receive, even to celebrate. One of these things was a poetics of discursive statement, shown by example in *Sadness and Happiness*, and through theoretical exposition and practical criticism in *The Situation of Poetry*. It is a small irony of literary history that, while Winters' statement-poetics condemned him to obscurity during the rise of the New Criticism, those same poetics would, thirty years later, help launch Pinsky on his voyage to fame. What was once the heresy of the paraphrasable was now experienced as a liberation from a stale paradigm.

The principal poems of discursive statement in *Sadness and Happiness* include the title poem, the long "Tennis," and, most famously, the "Essay on Psychiatrists." The two share a great deal: they are fearless in their use of abstraction; they use straightforward, propositional language; they take up a single topic and divide it into constituent parts for examination and explanation. In these respects they resemble nothing so much as the essay-poems of that great Augustan, Alexander Pope. The Augustan past in which these poems were so firmly rooted had become largely invisible, though, slipping off the radar of reviewers, so that it was possible for someone as astute as David Bromwich to write that "the title poem of *Sadness and Happiness* . . . gives one a jolt." "To call 'Sadness and Happiness' the best of its kind would be fatuous," Bromwich continues, "since there is nothing else like it" ("Robert Pinsky" 416).

Pinsky, no doubt, was prepared for such startled responses. The "situation" indicated in the title of *The Situation of Poetry* is, in fact, one where poets and critics have lost much of their historical sense and have come to take a particular version of modernist poetics as the norm. At the outset of the book, Pinsky seeks to create the taste by which he would like to be judged:

> Modern poetry was created by writers born about a hundred years ago. The premises of their work included a mistrust of abstraction and statement, a desire to escape the blatantly conventional aspects of form, and an ambition to grasp the fluid, absolutely particular form of the physical world by using the static, general medium of language. Those premises are paradoxical, or at least peculiar, in themselves. Moreover, the brilliant stylistic inventions associated with the premises—notably the techniques of "imagism," which convey the powerful illusion that a poet presents, rather than tells about, a sensory experience—are also peculiar as techniques.
>
> Or they once seemed peculiar. These special, perhaps even tormented premises and ways of writing have become a tradition: a climate of implicit expectation and tacit knowledge. (3)

The approach is gentle, but the polemical aim is clear, and with the exception of the gentleness with which the argument is introduced, everything about the passage is Wintersian. The placing of Imagism at the center of modernism, for example, is familiar from Winters, as is the distrust of a poetry that seeks to present rather than comment upon experience.

The theories of language and tradition on display in the opening of *The Situation of Poetry* also show the influence of Winters. When Pinsky claims, for example, that it is paradoxical both to eschew abstraction and to try to grasp the physical world by using language, an inherently general or abstract medium, his words could come straight from the "Preliminary Problems" of Winters' *The Anatomy of Nonsense*. And later, when he speaks of a peculiar system of poetics becoming a "climate of expectation," he is echoing Winters, who could very easily have made Pinsky's claim that "in general, the more any style is taken for granted, the more abusive the practice of it can become" (165).

If Pinsky's major work of discursive poetics is so thoroughly Wintersian, why then, did Pinsky became something of a wunderkind, while Winters became a pariah? Part of the answer may have to do with the nondogmatic nature of Pinsky's discursive poetics. When Winters' hectoring tone and moral absolutism did not win disciples, they alienated readers and created enemies. Pinsky, in contrast, is less the absolutist or fanatic, and more the ecumenical.

Another important factor in Pinsky's success relative to Winters, though, is the changed nature of the literary field in which his books appeared. While Winters came to his discursive position at a time when the New Critics were coming to power, Pinsky's books of the mid-1970s appeared when New Critical norms had been challenged, and when many poets and critics who had internalized those norms were ready to cast them off. In such a climate, poets and critics could receive Pinsky's discursive poetry and poetics as a welcome liberation. This is certainly the case when Louis Martz, writing for the *Yale Review* in 1976, claims that *Sadness and Happiness* has led American poetry into "a new era of confidence," and that Pinsky, with his poetry of "abstract utterance" and his lack of reticence about having "something to say," was "point[ing] the way toward the future of poetry" (126–27). That poems could make statements—that they could *mean* as well as *be*—excited the reader of Pinsky's debut book of poetry.

One finds a similar feeling of liberation in the wake of Pinsky's next major essay-poem, *An Explanation of America*. Michael Hamburger, for example, writing for *The Nation,* claims with some exhilaration that the poem "seems to defy not only all the dominant trends in contemporary poetry but all the dominant notions—both American and non-American—of what is to be expected of the American poet" (86). Most telling, though, is Jay Parini's response to *An Explanation of America* in the *Chicago Review*. He rehearses Pinsky's argument about how a modernist poetics of presentation became the unexamined climate of opinion, then goes on to relate Pinsky's theory to his own career as a teacher of poets:

> Thus, elder poets will regularly advise their students: *embody* an experience, don't tell about it; avoid abstraction . . . let the shape of a poem evolve, don't prescribe a form. I have myself mouthed these truisms during writing seminars as though they fell somehow outside the realm of arguable notion. Horace, Virgil, Milton and certainly Pope would have been desperately puzzled. We may be grateful to Pinsky (as to Winters and J. V. Cunningham) for pointing out the historically anomalous nature of our current suppositions. (18)

Here we see the persistence of New Critical poetics into the 1970s and early 1980s, when the "elder poets" still preached the gospel of the poem that must not mean but be. *An Explanation of America* provided an example of a counterpoetics, and for that, readers such as Parini were grateful. Parini's gratitude went further than a good review in a prominent journal, too: he was among the first editors to elevate Pinsky to that highly coveted status, the anthologized poet.[1]

1. "Why," I imagine the reader of these last few paragraphs asking, "would discursive poetry seem liberating in the 1970s, when it had been around for decades? Isn't the poetry of Charles Olson statement-oriented to the point of pedantry and discursive to the point of outright prosiness? Isn't David Antin the discursive poet *par excellence*? And what about Ed Dorn? Isn't *Gunslinger* 'talky' enough?" These questions have been answered, I think, by Jed Rasula in his sociopoetic study, *The American Poetry Wax Museum*. Here, Rasula notices the blind spots in *The Situation of Poetry*—which coincide with the Olson-Antin wing of poetry—and accounts for

The demand for a poetics of statement explains, at least to some degree, the popularity of Robert Pinsky's poetry, both in absolute terms and in relation to the much less popular work of Yvor Winters. But in order to fully understand why Pinsky's work has had such a large public impact, we need to look at the state of American poetry's public sphere in the 1970s, when he was launching his career. That sphere became increasingly fragmented over the course of the decade, producing conditions that created a further demand for a poetry such as Pinsky's.

A Broken Field: American Poetry in the 1970s

"American literary culture," wrote Alan Golding in 1995, ". . . no longer has a center" (114). If we search for a watershed moment in the decentering of American poetry, we inevitably arrive at the shattering of the public sphere of poetry in the 1970s. This was the decade that saw poets, editors, and anthologists invent not only new identity-based publics for poetry but also new identity-based poetries for those publics. It is the decade of both identity politics and identity poetics.

David Kellogg's essay "The Self in the Poetic Field" provides the best model for understanding the emergence of identity poetics and

---

them by explaining that they are the product of poetic assumptions shared by Pinsky and the majority of readers at the time:

> Pinsky advocates an embrace of discourse ("prose virtues"), yet avoids any mention of poets who have aroused suspicion *because* of their discursivity (Olson, Duncan, Spicer, Dorn, Whalen, Oppen, Rich, Kelly, Eshleman, Antin), and who may have been more pertinent figures with which to discuss the "situation" of 1975 than many of those Pinsky chooses instead. . . . [But] Pinsky is neither a sloppy researcher nor a careless chronicler. He simply represents the predominant critical stance, which is to conflate poetry with *lyric.* (325)

For adherents of "the predominant critical stance," the discursiveness of poets such as Antin or Olson, with its radical rejection of lyric norms, was simply off the charts. Pinsky, though, offered a more acceptable discursive alternative to internalized, leftover New Critical norms. His form of making a statement in poetry, unlike, say, Antin's, appealed to the mainstream.

the decentering of the American poetic field. Kellogg proposes a field of poetry charted along two axes, one running from tradition to innovation, the other from self to community. It is within this matrix that poets take positions through their various actions (writing poems, giving readings, pursuing or spurning certain audiences, seeking or declining to seek honors, displaying or downplaying antecedents).

> The total configuration loosely resembles Bourdieu's model of the cultural field; that is, the actual possibilities are on the inside of the field and the abstract value-identifications on the outside. . . . There is an effect in the field made by each successive position-taking. I have assumed that the independence of each position-taking is compromised by the presence of other, adjacent position-takings, so that a cluster of position-takings congeals into a stable position within the field. The space of poetry as such is measured by the distance between the center and the four possible sources of poetic value. As these named sources are on the outside, critics have all too easy access to them and critical position-takings in the service of canonicity are predictable. The structure is an open one, and its capacity for change is rather high. . . . The novel feature of this structure for poetry is the manner in which the two axes are each informed by the formal and social loci of value. The loci of each axis repel each other. The axes join together in the center so that the two axes map a four-sided field when represented on a two-dimensional plane. One axis maps a set of social possibilities and the other a set of formal possibilities. (98–99)

Kellogg's field or grid can be visualized as a simple square with the four value-identifications (self, community, tradition, and innovation) making their claims from the outside:

While position-takings are rarely, if ever, matters of pure identification with one principle alone to the exclusion of all others, there are identifiable positions that come close to one or another value-identification. Poetry that, for example, emphasizes its continuity with the past (such as the New Formalist work of poets such as Dana Gioia) represents a position close to the "tradition" value-identification. In contrast, avant-garde writing represents a position near the "innovation" value-identification. The confessional poetry of poets such as Robert Lowell, Sharon Olds, or Louise Glück, with its emphasis on individual experience and a distinctive authorial voice, represents a position by the "self" value-identification. Community, though, proves the most difficult of the value-identifications to define.

"The mirror image of self," as Kellogg puts it, the community value-identification, has to do not only with matters of subject and voice but also with the audience that a poet defines for him- or herself. While the poetry of self produces authors, says Kellogg, the poetry of community produces audiences (101). "Less important than ethnic, regional, religious, or sexual identity per se," he continues, "is whether a certain poetry participates in, or is read as participating in, the social claims of one or more of these identities" (101). Adrienne Rich may well be the community-poet extraordinaire, claimed as she is by feminist, gay, and disabled communities, all of whom she seeks to gather around her by her various position-takings.

What we see in the 1970s is, in terms of Kellogg's model, the consolidation of a number of community-based positions, supported by a massive set of poetic position-takings by women and members of minority groups. Such a massive concentration of position-takings near the community pole does not take place, of course, by mere coincidence. It is a function, rather, of the poetic field (like the cultural field in general) responding to and taking part in changes in the larger field of power-relations within society. Bourdieu describes this relationship in *The Field of Cultural Production*, where he tells us that, despite its "relative automony with respect to [the field of power]," the cultural field nevertheless reflects and participates in changes in that larger field (37–44). The shifts in the poetic field in the 1970s, then, stemmed from the creation of large and vital feminist and gay-rights movements combined with the full radicalization of the black-power movement.

That great radical of the 1960s and 1970s, Tom Hayden, supplies one vivid image of the shift to identity politics when, in his memoirs, he describes a major disruption in the plans of the Red Family, a radical group for Marxist revolution. The leadership's plans for political action often became disrupted by demands for an end to "male power plays" and by what Hayden called interminable "torture sessions" in which confessions of previously unexamined male chauvinist assumptions were wrung from dazed Che Guevara wannabes (see Berman 114). Paul Berman, in his "Moral History of the Baby Boom Generation" in *A Tale of Two Utopias*, captures the mood of the era when he writes:

> The New Left in America in the early and middle sixties was notorious for its old-fashioned sexual division of labor, which made men leaders and relegated women to the rank and filing cabinet . . . But as the years advanced, the division of labor blossomed into a division of political opinion, until by the movement's final days, New Left thinking came in two versions, one for straight men, the other for women (and soon enough for homosexuals). The retreat into left-wing antiquity, the turn toward Marxism-Leninism, the celebrating of totalitarian leaders around the world, the lurch toward guerrilla war—those impulses were primarily the business of men . . . The new ideas about sex roles were not, however, the business of males, anyway not the straight ones. By the early 1970s . . . the straight males would talk about the Young Marx and the Old Marx . . . and the women and the gays would talk about elitism and male chauvinism and the division of responsibilities within the organization. It was leftist antiquity on one side, gender-role ultra-modernity on the other. (113–14)

What Berman reports is really a shift toward community-value identification in the field of power. This shift was to be of central importance to the development of poetry in the 1970s.

As the field of poetry, responding to these shifts, was being redefined, a problem arose for poets who did not find a place for themselves in any of the newly defined identity communities. The formation and consolidation of poetic communities based on historical grievances was, at times, disorienting for heterosexual white male poets, in ways they often could not fully understand or name. Many seemed, like Berman's radicals, to have been marooned by the tides of history.

This is not to say that heterosexual white men were not still selling books, getting into the anthologies, and winning the important prizes. (Indeed, six of the eleven Academy of American Poets fellowships given in the 1970s went to white men, as did nine of the ten Pulitzer Prizes for poetry.) But for those most attuned to issues of publics and public discourses, there was a creeping sense that something had happened to the idea of a common public, and it would no longer be an easy matter for them to assume the privilege of speaking of, for, and to a presumably general community. Straight white-male privilege remained, but its legitimacy had been deeply undermined. A public who shared certain presumptions about identity could no longer be assumed.

At least one critic, Peter Middleton, sees this disruption of poetry's public sphere behind Robert Lowell's growing despair over the efficacy of poetry in his works of the 1970s ("1973" 57–58). Middleton also suggests that language poetry had its genesis in the sense of crisis following the shattering of the poetic field in the early 1970s: "The story that language poetry often tells of its necessary emergence tends to create an earlier prophetic narrative of reified language in crisis, to which the poetry was an inevitable response." But this theory ignores the changing relation of poet to audience in the early 1970s. The crisis that created language poetry, says Middleton, "revolved around deficiencies in the illocutionary force of literary practice in specific political contexts, when the only accessible fields were created by anti-war movements and later the African-American and feminist movements" (65). That is, the fragmenting of the field created a need, among certain poets, to create language writing. After all, language writing was a poetry that explored the conditions of communication and audience. Charles Bernstein would describe it as a "poetry [that] explores the constitution of public space as much as representing already formed constituencies; it . . . refuses to speak for anyone as much as fronting for a self, group, people or species" (*My Way* 304). One could read the (largely white, largely male) first wave of language writing as the expression of a new self-consciousness among poets who saw the audience changing in ways that did not, in any simple way, accommodate them.

Identity politics and identity poetics sent shock waves through the whole field of culture in the 1970s, producing a vast array of consequences, some intended and some unintended. Among the latter are the creation of language poetry and another phenomenon we would not usually link with it: the creation of conditions in which the poetry of Robert Pinsky would come to national prominence. While the 1970s did not give birth to neo-Augustan poetics, they did create anxieties that those poetics resolved.

General Nature, American Nature

Just as every motion in physics generates an equal and opposite countermotion, so does every movement in culture generate some form of contrary motion. The turbulence of the culture wars of the 1980s was largely brought about by the continued force of 1970s identity politics. Allan Bloom's 1987 neoconservative *The Closing of the American Mind*, for example, is a reaction to the force exerted by identity politics. It looks with nostalgia on "the old view that, by recognizing and accepting man's natural rights, men found a fundamental basis of unity and sameness" in which "class, race, religion, national origin all disappear or become dim" (27). Clearly, identity politics had a polarizing effect. It was Pinsky's good fortune, though, to inherit both an Augustan intellectual position and a set of assumptions about modern identity that allowed him to bridge the gap between identity politics and positions such as Bloom's. The Augustan idea of general nature helped to inoculate Pinsky against the seductions of identity politics. His later position, involving a dynamic sense of modern American identity, appealed to a large audience that felt alienated from both identity politics and neoconservative positions. By appealing to such a constituency, he became a kind of unofficial laureate of the American center, a status that would soon enough become official when Pinsky was named the first-ever three-time U.S. Poet Laureate.

One of the classic articulations of the Augustan theory of general nature that Pinsky inherited had been made by Samuel Johnson, in *The*

Rambler of October 13, 1750. In an essay that starts out as a polemic on behalf of the art of biography, Johnson meanders, in his typical fashion, into larger profundities about the nature of man:

> there is such an uniformity in the state of man, considered apart from adventitious and separable decorations and disguises, that there is scarce any possibility of good or ill, but is common to human kind. A great part of the time of those who are placed at the greatest distance by fortune, or by temper, must unavoidably pass in the same manner; and though, when the claims of nature are satisfied, caprice, and vanity, and accident, begin to produce discriminations and peculiarities, yet the eye is not very heedful or quick, which cannot discover the same causes still terminating their influence in the same effects, though sometimes accelerated, sometimes retarded, or perplexed by multiplied combinations. We are all prompted by the same motives. (*Selected Writings* 169)

Yvor Winters was attracted by Johnson's universal notions of man, and Pinsky, too, has shown sympathies with the idea of general nature, especially in his first volume of poems, *Sadness and Happiness*. Unlike Winters, though, Pinsky saw the problems inherent in the Augustan position and developed a more nuanced sense of identity.

"Poem about People," which opens *Sadness and Happiness*, takes us through a four-part progression, from a naïve belief in general nature, through complications of that view, and finally to a reaffirmation of the initial position, albeit a darker and less naïve version of it. The poem begins by depicting a seemingly random pair of people seen in a supermarket:

> The jaunty crop-haired graying
> Women in grocery stores,
> Their clothing boyish and neat,
> New mittens or clean sneakers,
>
> Clean hands, hips not bad still,
> Buying ice cream, steaks, soda,
> Fresh melons and soap—or the big
> Balding young men in work shoes

And green work pants, beer belly
And white T-shirt, the porky walk
Back to the truck, polite . . .

Each character differs from Pinsky himself, and from the presumed
speaker; the first by age and gender, the second by social class. But
despite these differences, it seems possible to identify with them on the
basis of some commonly shared humanity. It is, apparently,

    possible
To feel briefly like Jesus,

A gust of diffuse tenderness
Crossing the dark spaces
To where the dry self burrows
Or nests, something that stirs,

Watching the kinds of people
On the street for a while—

Despite their variety, the crowds seen on the street consist simply of
"kinds of people," with which another person could identify. "There is
such an uniformity in the state of man," one can imagine the speaker
rhapsodizing, echoing Doctor Johnson. "We are all prompted by the
same motives." But the speaker's sense of universal identification shatters quickly in the first of the poem's turns:

But how love falters and flags
When anyone's difficult eyes come

Into focus, terrible gaze of a unique
Soul . . .

. . . .

The hideous, sudden stare of self,
Soul showing through like the lizard

Ancestry showing in the frontal gaze
Of a robin busy on the lawn.

The recognition of the horrible alienness of other people with their individual needs and desires disrupts the Jesus-like sense of a universal brotherhood. This is followed by a second disruption of general nature, this time based not on the apparently irreducible alienness of individual subjectivity but on the cultural identities that divide us:

In the movies, when the sensitive
Young Jewish soldier nearly drowns

Trying to rescue the thrashing
Anti-semitic bully, swimming across
The river raked by nazi fire,

The awful part is the part truth:
Hate my whole kind, but me,
Love me for myself.

These stanzas give us a complex system of group divisions: Nazis versus American soldiers, then an anti-Semitic American versus a Jewish American. Within these hostile differences lies yet another division, one that separates the individual, with his emotional needs, from his identity group. But the abandonment of his identity group is as "awful" as it is real, and the individual who thinks he can free himself from group identity knows only a "part truth." Group-identity difference is as real as the individual differences revealed in the "sudden stare of self."

The poem's final turn, though, brings us back to a sense of general nature, of an identity shared despite the differences of individual need and group identity. "The weather/ Changes in the black of night," we are told,

And the dream-wind, bowling across

The sopping open spaces
Of roads, golf courses, parking lots,

Flails a commotion
In the dripping treetops,

Tries a half-rotten shingle
Or a down-hung branch, and we
All dream it, the dark wind crossing
The wide spaces between us.

In place of the initial "gust of diffuse tenderness" we feel a dark wind, and the spaces between us have widened in light of the recognition of individual and group divisions. Still, the wind crosses those gulfs, and we share a universal dream of its passing across the spaces that divide us. The initial vision of general nature has become more tentative, but it nevertheless remains, cautiously affirmed.

Another poem from *Sadness and Happiness,* "Discretions of Alcibiades," ends with a less tentative affirmation of the general nature of human identity. The poem moves through a series of permutations and combinations of eros, human and divine, to end with an image of hedonism in which all differences meld:

people, on Cape Cod, the Costa Brava,
Borneo, emulate gods and goddesses:

Rubbing their skin with oil, they sun it brown
Until they are all Spaniard, Jew or Greek—
Wear sandals; ply their boat; keep simple house

Cooking red meat or fish on open fires;
Market for salt; and dance to tinkly music.

Cape Cod Yankee or Borneo tribesman; Spaniard, Jew, or Greek: all are one, and human activity becomes a single set of customs shared along the shores of world-ocean.

The ending of Pinsky's "Essay on Psychiatrists" also affirms a general human nature. Here, Pinsky's speaker tells us: "I have failed//To discover what essential statement could be made/About psychiatrists that would not apply/To all human beings." Conversely, the speaker cannot discover "what statement//About all human beings would not apply/Equally to psychiatrists." Psychiatrists, in effect, become figures for universal human nature, because, like psychiatrists, all people "try tentatively//To understand, to find healing speech. They work/For truth and money." Psychiatrist becomes synonymous with human, for everyone is "into//Truth, into music, into yearning, suffering,/Into elegant machines and luxuries." These are not the words of a man afraid of saying something about human identity in general.

Not only is Pinsky drawn to ideas of general human nature, but he also shies away from engaging in identity politics or poetics based exclusively on his own religious and ethnic heritage—an engagement that would take him away from ideas of general nature and toward a sense of the irreducible differences of various subjectivities. In contrast to poets who create a Jewish-American identity poetics, Pinsky turns toward a more broadly conceived cultural context. In fact, in his own assessment, his minority-group identity leads him not to identity politics, but toward a sense of general nature, in which humanity is conceived as *homo faber*. As he put it in a 1996 interview,

> Possibly being raised as an Orthodox Jew, which is to say with considerable separation from the majority culture, has contributed to my interest in making. Not sharing such creations as Christmas or Easter or the—our, your—Savior, and at the same time having other creations like the kosher laws or the prohibition against saying or writing the word for "God": this is a richly interesting conflict. It may have increased the impact upon me of the fact that we creatures—we mammals, we colony-insects, whatever we are—have invented not only language, but Christianity and Judaism and the United States of America and the violin and the blues and so forth. (83)

Pinsky's position between cultures gives him insight into their constructed nature. He is far from alone in such a recognition: it is, for example, one of the major themes of postcolonial writing. But Pinsky goes further. "We mammals, we colony-insects": whatever we are, we are universally united by our nature as makers.

In the same interview, Pinsky imagines a kind of general *American* nature, a majority culture that unites the country. It was, as he describes it, the object of his youthful yearning, from within the very specific confines of his early religious education:

> As the oldest child, the oldest son, I was expected to go to synagogue every Saturday. The *musaf*, the orthodox service, lasts three, maybe three and a half hours. Imagine for a moment you're eleven years old: you don't like school; it's Saturday morning; you spend nearly four hours every Saturday morning in the company of old men, chanting prayers in a language you don't understand, in a prolonged, accreted liturgy that is not dramatic. . . . You look over at the Church across the street, and you say to yourself, *hmmm*, Catholic girls and communion dresses and Jerry Lee Lewis and Jackie Robinson: it's the whole world out there, the splendid *triaf* [nonkosher] cookie jar of the world. So you just turn to the world as soon as you get a chance. Or so you do if you are a child like me then. (84)

"I *chose* it," Pinsky says of this majority culture (84). But what exactly did he choose? The figures here—Catholic girls, the southern Baptist Jerry Lee Lewis, and the African-American Jackie Robinson—could more easily be read as figures of division. Not too many years after the eleven-year-old Robert Pinsky sat in the synagogue yearning for majority culture, many southern Baptists would refuse to vote for John F. Kennedy on the sole basis of his Catholicism; and those New Jersey Catholic girls and their husbands, worrying about the property values of their first houses, would oppose the racial integration of their neighborhoods. And a few years later, African Americans for whom the integrationist dream of Robinson seemed an unattainable myth would riot across New Jersey and around the country. Another kind of poet would use Pinsky's characters to stress the forces that divide us. But these divisions pale, for Pinsky, beside the light of a common American majority culture and a common American identity.

The impulse toward similarity (human and national) is strong in Pinsky, and it represents one of the more Augustan elements of his poetics. It is also, in substance, not too different from the position about American identity outlined in Bloom's *The Closing of the American Mind*, although blessedly free of that book's ugliness, smugness, and spite. In the final analysis, though, Pinsky's overall position on American identity differs from that of Bloom and his ilk.

Along with the idea of general (human or American) nature in Pinsky's work we find something else, something that allows him to take up a middle position between general nature and identity politics. This is an idea of subjectivity that the anthropologist Jonathan Friedman has called the self of modernity,[2] and it informs Pinsky's work, especially the major book-length poem *An Explanation of America*. This poem, coming at the end of a decade of identity politics and identity poetics, articulates an idea of American identity that is both compelling in itself and comforting to those who find identity poetics narrow and excessively divisive. It is an ideal poem for a national poet to have written, and the very stuff of which laureateships are made.

The Self of Modernity

In Jonathan Friedman's important model of cultural logic, modernity, primitivism, tradition, and postmodernity express the poles of capitalist civilization's cultural space (447). The self of modernity is essentially a self that is addicted to the idea of *more* and cannot allow itself a moment of restful wholeness. It is self as perpetual *bildung*, self as continuous accumulator of wealth, knowledge, experience, what have you. It is, in Friedman's words, "an identity without fixed content other than the capacity to develop itself, movement and growth as a principle of selfhood" (448). The idea of the self of modernity, unlike the Augustan idea of general nature, does not assume the fundamental sameness of humanity. Rather, it sees a world full of different cultures and identities, all of which may be accumulated by, or assimilated to, the modern subject.

It is a notion of self necessarily opposed to both the primitive and the traditional. Friedman defines the primitive as the kingdom of

2. Friedman also, and with greater frequency, uses the term "modernism" in discussing the self of modernity. Because of the literary associations of "modernism," though, I have avoided the term in this context as much as possible, to avoid confusion.

infantile desire. Primitivism, he says, "harbors all that is uncontrolled: the confusion of eating, sexuality, aggression and pleasure . . . but also the impulsive and compulsively superstitious relation to reality; [and] religious fetishism" (448). The self of modernity sublimates the forces of the primitive into culture-building, so self-control and the accumulation of knowledge and culture go hand in hand. Traditionalism consists of culture "defined as a system of rules and etiquette pegged to a totalistic cosmology that provides an ultimate meaning to existence" and defines "man's place in the universe as well as the significance of all his activities" (449). It insists on an unchanging structure of legitimate authority and belief. The self of modernity, committed as it is to change, syncretism, and the accumulation of cultures, can accept neither the stasis of traditionalism nor its totalizing cosmology. The self of modernity must keep its cosmology open, ready to assimilate more beliefs and ideas. Since, in Friedman's view, postmodernism represents the return of both the primitive and the traditional, it too must be rejected by the self of modernity.

While the self of modernity is also "the dominant or 'normal' identity of capitalist civilization" (450), it is vulnerable to crises. It is a version of selfhood that "depends on expanding horizons, the possibility of individual development, mobility and liberation from the fixed and concrete structures of surviving non-capitalist forms" such as "family, community, religion" (451). This expansiveness, in turn, depends on an expanding modern sector of the whole global system, a growing "hegemonic center," to use Friedman's term (451). When the center goes into decline, modern selfhood becomes difficult to maintain, and other types of self—the primitive, the traditional, and the postmodern—rise to fill the gap. "Modernist identity," writes Friedman, "dominates in periods of hegemonic expansion and trifurcates in periods of contraction or crisis" (452). The European crises of the first part of the twentieth century can, in this view, be seen as the decline of the self of modernity and the rise of traditionalism and primitivism in forms particularly virulent and deadly.

The late 1960s and early 1970s certainly presented a similar crisis for the self of modernity. The year 1968, for example, marked the rise of a traditionalist threat to modernity in the form of Alabama governor George Wallace's popular, segregationist third-party presidential campaign. Examples of primitivism challenging modernity in the late 1960s are legion, ranging from Yippies hurling handfuls of dollar bills down onto the floor of the New York Stock Exchange (a reversal of modernity's accumulative imperative), to Country Joe leading the crowd at Woodstock in a chant that went "Give me an F, Give me a U, Give me a C, Give me a K, what's that spell?" (an unleashing of the infantile and sexual impulses sublimated by modernity). That the events of May 1968 represented a crisis of modernity was evident to leaders facing the disruptions on both sides of the Atlantic. Columbia president Grayson Kirk, for example, aware that their protest had less to do with particular political demands than with a fundamental loss of faith in modernity (see Witcover 188), called the students occupying the university's administration buildings "nihilists." French prime minister Georges Pompidou described the student/worker uprisings in his capital as a moment in which "our civilization is being questioned—not the government, not the institutions, not even France, but the materialistic and soulless modern society." To Pompidou this was a world-historical event, comparable in significance to the "hopeless days of the fifteenth century, where the structures of the Middle Ages were collapsing" (Witcover 215).

In the wake of this international crisis, Pinsky affirms the embattled self of modernity. He upholds all major elements of the self of modernity: the goal of accumulating different cultures into a syncretic whole, the ideal of self-control, the distrust of primitivism, and the distrust of traditionalism. More important, he defines American identity as the self of modernity, allowing him to offer a vision of the nation more open than that of neoconservatives such as Allan Bloom, and less focused on division than that of the proponents of identity politics.

One of the most powerful images of syncretic culture comes in Pinsky's "The Figured Wheel," with its depiction of an immense, symbol-covered wheel rolling through the world. It is of a culture with no specific content other than the ability to pull disparate elements together in an ongoing accumulation:

Artists illuminate it with pictures and incised mottoes
Taken from the Ten Thousand Stories and the Register of True
  Dramas.

They hang it with colored ribbons and with bells of many
    pitches.

With paints and chisels and moving lights they record
On its rotating surface the elegant and terrifying doings
Of the inhabitants of the Hundred Pantheons of major Gods
Disposed in iconographic stations at the hub, spoke and
    concentric bands,

And also the grotesque demi-Gods, Hopi gargoyles and
    Ibo dryads.

This is not the world of Augustan general nature, where humans are
essentially the same: what we have here is a display of radical variety.
But the poem is not so much a celebration of difference as it is a celebration of coming together, more melting pot than carefully subdivided
museum. Along with the overtly syncretic coming together of different
mythologies, we have a cross-pollination of cultures at the level of diction: Hopi figures are seen as Gothic, northern European "gargoyles,"
while Ibo carvings appear as Hellenic "dryads."

    The panmythological poems of *The Want Bone* are also instances of
Pinsky's syncretic sense of culture. Here, Daniel and Jesus and Shiva
and Parvati and Buddha and Thor rub shoulders. Even when the poems
are not overtly mythological, they show us cultures coming together
into a whole. In one remarkable poem, "Window," Pinsky's narrator
begins as Irish, then becomes Chinese, Jewish, Cuban, and Russian in
rapid succession, reveling in the "bright confusion" of cultures as they
come together in an immigrant America.

    "Ginza Samba," from Pinsky's subsequent collection, *The Figured
Wheel: New and Collected Poems, 1966–1996,* is perhaps the best example of a poem of syncretic culture in his oeuvre. It traces an imagined historical process that made a Belgian invention, the saxophone,
into a fundamentally African-American instrument. Through "the
unfathomable matrix" of genealogy and the interchanges of the market where fates are "changed and exchanged/As in the trading of
brasses,/Pearls and ivory, calicoes and slaves,/Laborers and girls," we
see the saxophone come into the hands of Charlie Parker, whose music

is made of elements from places as disparate as Rio and Tokyo. The coming together of culture, the marketplace where various goods are exchanged, the melding of international influences: all of this is the stuff of modernity's ideal self.

Another element of the self of modernity—self-control—is present in "Samurai Song" from *Jersey Rain*, a monologue in the voice of a samurai and almost a pure expression of will. "When I had no father I made/Care my father. When I had/No mother I embraced order," runs one stanza. "When I had no friend I made/Quiet my friend. When I had no/Enemy I opposed my body," runs another. The parallel structure reinforces the sense of the lines, with their Spartan resolve. The self at the heart of this poem is relentlessly under its own control, removed from any possibility of abandonment. One suspects that Winters would have approved, as would the work-ethic-obsessed Protestants at the dawn of the self of modernity.

This sort of self-control is a close cousin of modernity's rejection of primitivism as the unleashing of desire. We see such a rejection early in Pinsky's poetry, in the "Essay on Psychiatrists," with its reading of Euripides' *The Bacchae* and his horror of the "dark/Urgencies" the play reveals. Here, Pinsky shows sympathy for the sublimations necessary for the maintenance of an acceptable modern self, the "strategies, civilizations" that "le[t] a man consciously/Desire girls of sixteen (or less) on the street,//And not embrace them." "The culture of Freud," says Friedman, ". . . is modernity" (449), and the culture of "Essay on Psychiatrists" is, in no small measure, a Freudian one.

Pinsky also upholds the self of modernity by the rejection of narrow traditionalism. In "Memoir" from *The Want Bone*, for example, he gives us an image of traditionalism first as a prison, then as an act of self-delusion. The poem begins with an image of religious orthodoxy of the kind that Pinsky grew up with, a version of traditionalism defining one's place in the cosmos and the significance of all activities. Its rigidities are confining rather than comforting:

The iron cape of the Law, the gray
Thumb of the Word:
Careless of the mere spirit, careless
Of the body . . .

The "sealed words" of traditional religion make an unequivocal assertion: "It was like saying: I am this, and not that" (43). But the absolutism and exclusivity of traditionalism are, at the end of the poem, doomed to failure, where we return to a synagogue changed beyond recognition:

> The sandstone building converted now
> To a Puerto Rican Baptist church,
> Clerestory and minaret.
> A few blocks away, an immense blue
> Pagan, an ocean, muttering, swollen:
> That, and not this.

Not only has traditionalism been displaced, but it has also been displaced by the syncretic culture of modernity, where traditions mix and accrete. The original synagogue, now with the addition of a minaret, houses Muslims as well as a Baptist congregation of converted Catholics. The final line—"That, and not this"—undoes traditionalism's emphasis on eternal sameness and revels in modernity's xenophilia.

A Cosmopolitan Patria

Traditionalism, that bogeyman of the self of modernity, appears as an ominous force in the "Bad Dreams" section of *An Explanation of America*, where it is not only confining and deluded but also dangerous to the point of potential genocide. The section, one of the longest and most vividly imagined in the poem, begins by contrasting a "shrewd Odysseus" with a figure of rootedness and tradition, "a hick/A tribesman who never made his wander-year." Pinsky then envisions the vastness of America and worries over the kind of culture that the immigrants (tribesmen all) may produce, what the "frightened settlers may invent." The fear, or "bad dream" of the title, is that, overwhelmed by the vastness of the new place, they may invent a too-rigid tradition,

> set up a brazen calf,
> Or join a movement, fanatical, to spite

> The spirit of assembly, or of words—
> To drown that chatter and gossip, and become
> Sure, like machines and animals and the earth.

This is an interesting variation on a Wintersian theme: the great land-scape of the West endangers the minds of the settlers, making them less than human. But here the danger takes on a social or cultural form, the cult of the brazen calf with its biblical resonance. And the certainty sought by the people has the whiff of traditionalism's total-izing quality: in their absolutism and their claim to the whole truth, they would snuff out the "chatter and gossip" of true interchange and inquiry. Xenophobic as well as absolutist, the people of Pinsky's bad dream are opposed to the more humane and cosmopolitan "Greek adventurer/With his pragmatic gods."

Pinsky does not overly romanticize his Odysseus, who is capable of violence based on such ordinary human frailties as vanity and avarice. But the violence of such a figure pales next to the horrors that a people drunk on traditionalism's absolutism can perpetuate. Their violence goes beyond vanity and greed: it draws on the darker energies of a people assured of their absolute rightness. Theirs is a violence that longs for the total annihilation of the other.

> The ordinary passion to bring death
> For gain or glory, as Odysseus
> Might feel, would be augmented and inflamed
> By the harsh passion of a settler; and so,
> Why wouldn't he bring death to Indians
> Or Jews, or Greeks who stop for food and water,
> To bustle and jabber on his tangled plain?

The enemies, for the traditionalists, are the nomads, the many-tongued cosmopolitans, who freely mingle with one another in their "bustle and jabber." Traditionalism would destroy the human interchange that threatens to soil its pure totality.

Pinsky hints at a connection between traditionalism and the ter-rible genocides of the twentieth century. This implication becomes explicit when he compares his imaginary settler to the poets who contributed to the invention of fascist traditionalism in the 1940s. Writing of traditionalism as "the accumulated prison of the past," Pinsky says:

> My imaginary man is in that prison,
> Making himself less free.
>   Then let him rest;
> And think instead of the European poets
> Posed thoughtfully with cigarettes or scarves,
> As photographed for a fascist anthology
> Of forty years ago, above their verses
> About a landscape, a tribe, a mystic shadow:
> Caught in the prison of their country's earth
> Or its Romantic potential, born of death
> Or a pure idea. ". . . *Italy*
> (Germany, Russia, America, Rumania)
> *Had never really been a country,"* a book
> Might say, explaining something.

Such books would explain how a tradition could be imagined and then made real. That Pinsky moves from Italy and Germany (where traditionalism in all its absolutist atrocity became real) to America only makes the passage more terrifying, implying as it does the ever-present possibility of totalitarian traditionalism everywhere.

While some poets may wish to explain the need for traditionalism and give it "a landscape, a tribe, a mystic shadow," Pinsky wants something different in his *Explanation of America*. At the end of "Bad Dreams" he invokes Nietzsche, who turns out to be surprisingly effective in explaining the kind of virtues admired by those who tremble at the thought of traditionalism:

>   Nietzsche says
> We should admire the traffickers and nomads
>
> "Who have the freedom of mind and soul
> Which mankind learns from frequent changes of place,
> Climate and customs, new neighbors and oppressors."

These traffickers and nomads, it turns out, are ourselves, the implied readers of Pinsky's poem. We are the ones ready to learn new customs from our travels. We are, in fact, the selves of modernity. As the section's concluding lines have it,

> We accumulate the customs, music, words
> Of different climates, neighbors and oppressors,
> Making encampment in the sand or snow.

This is surely the self of modernity. It is also, in *An Explanation of America*, the true self of America.

Pinsky's first step in buildng toward this definition is to establish that the nation is a valid unit of identity, despite people's claims of irreducible individuality. At the start of the second section, Pinsky writes that "A country is the things it wants to see./If so," he continues, "some part of me, though I do not/Must want to see these things." There follows a catalog of distinctly American "things," contrasted to sights more typical of other nations. The list ends with a disturbing image he recalls seeing in England, where, he tells us,

> I saw a traveling carnival
> And fair with Morris dancers, and a woman
> Down in a shallow pit—bored looking, with bored
> And overfed, drugged-looking brown rats lolling
> Around her white bare body where it was chained
> Among them: sluggish, in a furtive tent.

His own reaction to the sight convinces him that national differences, and therefore national identities, are real:

> And that was something, like the Morris dance,
> Which an American would neither want
> To see, nor think of hiding, which helps to prove
> That after all these countries do exist,
> All of us sensing what we want to see
> Whether we want it separately, or not.

Pinsky, at least, is glad. "I want our country," he writes, "like a common dream." But that common dream comes under threat a few pages later, when the specter of race manifests itself. Racial division makes America, "as Malcolm X once said,/A prison." "Living inside a prison,/Within its many other prisons, what/Should one aspire to be? a kind of chaplain?" (168), he asks. The role of chaplain, the comforter of the people, appeals to him, but only momentarily: "But chaplains, I have heard, are often powers,/Political, within their prisons, patrons/And mediators between frightened groups." But intervention seems beyond reach:

> No kind of chaplain ever will mediate
> Among the conquering, crazed immigrants
> Of El Camino and the Bergen Mall,
> The Jews who dream up the cowboy films, the Blacks
> Who dream the music, the people who dream the cars
> And ways of voting, the Japanese and Basques . . .

This seems, at first, like despair, a downward, pessimistic movement in the poem. But just here, Pinsky introduces a contrary motion. With the phrase "the conquering, crazed immigrants," he holds together the divided communities he presents: Jews, blacks, Japanese, Basques. At the very moment when a common American identity appears to dissolve, it is revived. We are all immigrants, mad in our pursuit of conquest. He drives the point home a few lines later, when he refers to classical Greece:

> The Dorians too were conquering immigrants,
> And hemmed in too by their anarchic spirits
> And new peninsula, they too resorted
> To invented institutions, and the vote.

Pinsky sees the Dorians as proto-Americans, with their inventions, their democracy, even their possession of the land.

The genius of Pinsky's particular version of American identity is its openended inclusiveness. There is no specific content to American identity as Pinsky figures it here: we do not need *Mayflower* pedigrees, nor do we need to subscribe to the principles of any particular pledge of allegiance. We do not need to follow in the traditions of the Founding Fathers. We can be part of any identity subgroup, but we are all subsumed within the category of "conquering, crazed immigrants," whether our ancestors migrated over the Bering Straits millennia ago, or through O'Hare International Airport last week. All we need is to be the acquisitive, accumulating selves of modernity. American identity is not traditionalism of any kind (that is its "bad dream," its nightmare antiself). Its essence is its refusal of limits. As Pinsky puts it,

> Denial of limit has been the pride, or failing,
> Well-known to be shared by all this country's regions,
> Races, and classes; which all seem to challenge
> The idea of sufficiency itself.

If traditionalism is a circle, centered on an unwavering center, then this idea of the American self is a parabola, opening ever wider to its future. It can begin in any identity division (of region, race, and class), but it transcends them in its commitment to limitless accumulation and change. Published in 1981, after nearly a decade of identity politics and at the beginning of more than a decade of culture wars, *An Explanation of America* offers a vision of unified national identity.

Pinsky is not, of course, so naïve as to think that all American circumstances are equal. Far from it; and his sympathies lie with the underdog:

> White settlers disembarked here, to embark
> Upon a mountain-top of huge potential—
> Which for the disembarking slaves was low:
> A swamp, or valley of dry bones, where they lay
> In labor with a brilliant, strange slave-culture—
> All emigrants, ever disembarking. *Shall these*
> *Bones live?* And in a jangle of confusion
> And hunger, from the mountains to the valleys,
> They rise; and breathe; and fall in the wind again.

Whether beginning from the highest peak of privilege or the swamp of injustice, these "emigrants" all take part in the same desire to rise. One is not only one's identity subgroup, explains Pinsky, nor is one bound to a universal and unchanging human identity.

Fifteen years after *An Explanation of America*, Pinsky returns to its theme, this time in prose. Invited to contribute to a collection of responses to Martha Nussbaum's essay "Patriotism and Cosmopolitanism," Pinsky rejects the binary of Nussbaum's title. Instead, he speaks of the American *patria* as a form of cosmopolitanism. The self of modernity lies just beneath the surface of his comments:

> The conflict between home and marketplace, hearth and agora, known and unknown, may have some special poignancies for the United States. Genres we invented, like the Western and the gangster movie, appeal in an almost formulaic way to rapid change across generations that migrate outward and away from what was home. The forms of jazz and rock embody the eclectic, syncretic interchange of colliding origins. Never united by being a single folk culture, still less united under any ancient aristocracy, we have at our best improvised an ever-shifting culture palpably in motion—a culture, I would say, that clarifies the fact that all cultures are in motion. Insofar as the chauvinist refers to any human group or making as a static purity, the chauvinist elevates an illusion.
>
> At our best, we contain multitudes—multitudes not merely of souls, but of *patrias*: the paradox of a culturally polyglot, ever more syncretic homeland—a cosmopolitan *patria*. ("Eros against Esperanto" 86)

We are not a traditionalist culture, a "static purity" such as Pinsky envisioned in the "Bad Dreams" section of *An Explanation of America*. Indeed, we are syncretic, accumulative, in motion. The idea of a cosmopolitan *patria* takes us beyond the conflict of a purist patriotism, on the one hand, and the bloodless "Esperanto" of universalism, on the other. We can be attached to our nation without being attached to limits.

In "Culture," a lecture that he delivered at Princeton in April 2001, Pinsky also elaborates the vision of American identity that we have seen in *An Explanation of America*. Here he speaks of two fears evoked by the very idea of culture. "On the one side," he says, there is the nightmare of undifferentiation, a loss of cultural diversity comparable to the loss of biodiversity. . . . This vision of destruction by an all-consuming dominant culture reminds us of the etymological link between "culture" and the *"colon"*: the one who cultivates or scratches the soil, the colonialist. (*Democracy, Culture, and the Voice of Poetry 3*)

Setting aside the slightly desperate etymology, we can grant Pinsky his point. In the world at large, there is a fear of Western, particularly American, cultural hegemony, often perceived as a threat to the prevailing indigenous culture. And in America itself, we tend to fear pop or mass culture as "a dominating uniformity that threatens to macerate distinction and level terrain until all are the same" (3–4). On the other side, there is an opposite fear, not of encroaching uniformity but of cultural fragmentation. This dread, says Pinsky,

is of a vicious, tribalized factionalism, the coming apart of civic fabrics through fragmentation, ranging from the tremendous, paranoid brutalities of ethnic cleansing and ruthless terrorism to the petty division of mass culture into niches. . . . In this disturbing area, the etymological ghost is culture's relation to "cult," a word denoting arcane forms of worship: the perceived sinister difference of strangers, its ultimate evolution a zeal for extermination. (4)

Arcane forms of worship, and a zeal for extermination—this is recognizably the traditionalism of *An Explanation of America*'s "Bad Dreams" section. It is the essentialism or ethnocentrism at the heart of many versions of identity politics.

American poetry, says Pinsky in a fascinating and frustratingly brief passage, has tried to address these fears in two ways. Proposing "a theory of American poetry itself could be based on the polarity of cult and *colon*" (9), Pinsky first describes what can only be language poetry. "The fragmentation, ellipsis and implosion of referentiality that have been presented as an experimental or avant-garde style for nearly a hundred years resist the *colon*," he says, and so they resist "the complacent central uniformity" (9). Such fragmented, elliptical, nonreferential writing cannot easily be assimilated or commodified: it is a monkey wrench thrown into the gearbox of the culture industry. A more surprising idea follows: that other kinds of poetry (the New Formalism and the anecdotal *vers libre* of the MFA programs) constitute a kind of resistance to the phenomenon of "cult" fragmentation. "The styles of an often desperate, Anglophile urbanity or an amiable middlebrow accessibility," says Pinsky, "conduct an equally heroic—or at least embattled—resistance to cultural dissolution, a breakdown into provinces and cults" (9). It is less clear how this sort of resistance works, unless it is through refusing to recognize the claims of identity poetics, instead preferring a voice that is either traditional to the point of the impersonal, or blandly folksy to the point of deracination.

Where would Pinsky's own poetry fall in the matrix? Certainly not in the category of "fragmentation, ellipsis and implosion of referentiality": Pinsky is nothing if not a poet of clear, discursive statement. Nor would his work fall in the category of Anglophile urbanity and the "amiable middlebrow." He constantly revels in crossing Anglophile, professorial diction with low-status and despised language from the streets and from pop culture and advertising: he loves "mixing the allegedly high and the supposedly low," as he told an online interviewer in 2003 ("The People's Poet"). He has said on several occasions that he never trusts a poet who has not found a way to put a shopping mall into his or her poetry, and, while this is clearly meant as a joke, it is nevertheless indicative of his aversion to pure urbanity. Instead of falling into either of the categories he describes, Pinsky's work occupies a third position. The self of modernity, appearing as the American self in *An Explanation of America*, takes Pinsky beyond the polarities of his own matrix. It allows him to acknowledge difference enough to resist the homogenizing forces of "*colon*," while providing a unified national self that will not be destroyed by the forces of "cult." Two solutions for the price of one, and in a sophisticated yet reader-friendly package. I do not mean to sound ironic: it is a lot to offer, and Pinsky deserves the recognition that all this has brought him.

And bring him recognition it has: by almost any measure of poetic prestige, he comes out near the top of the list. Of the seven categories of poetic dominance listed by Christopher Beach in *Poetic Culture*, Pinsky ranks high in all but one (172–73). In the first category, popularity of book sales, he ranks higher than most of the living competition, and

Beach lists him as one of the eight leading figures in the second category, membership on the boards and committees of the poetry establishment. As a full professor in the English M.F.A. program at Boston University, Pinsky belongs at the top of the third category, membership in highly ranked Creative Writing departments. And as the author of the critical books *Landor's Poetry*, *The Situation of Poetry*, *Poetry and the World*, *The Sounds of Poetry*, and *Democracy, Culture, and the Voice of Poetry*, all published by top presses, Pinsky clearly ranks near the top of the fourth category, status as poet-scholars and poet-critics. Beach's fifth category, inclusion in *The Norton Anthology of Modern Poetry*, seems somewhat arbitrary, but there, too, Pinsky makes the grade, and he appears in more anthologies than most of the top poets whom Beach puts in here (Rasula 510–11). Critical reception in the academy is Beach's sixth category, and any good MLA search will show you how well Pinsky ranks there. Only in Beach's final category, "ability to sustain an important avant-garde practice," does Pinsky not rate as a dominant force in American poetry. As James Longenbach put it, "Since the death of Robert Lowell in 1977, no single figure has dominated American poetry in the way that Lowell, or before him Eliot, once did," but then again, "among the many writers who have come of age in our *fin de siècle*, none have succeeded more completely . . . than Robert Pinsky" ("Figuring Multitudes" 25).

In the same essay, Longenbach tells us that one of Pinsky's perpetual projects is to "imagine a community" (26). Both the way he imagines a community in *An Explanation of America* and the way he imagines an inclusive American identity have a great deal to do with Pinsky's dominant position. Jay Parini's praise for Pinsky is nearly ecstatic in the *Chicago Review*, and it has everything to do with Pinsky's defense of an inclusive idea of American identity: "The poet risks speaking for us all here, but the risk pays off; Americans do, in fact, live with an eye perpetually trained on the future. . . . Americans are a people of process and adaptation, and, perhaps, instability" (23). Parini acknowledges the risk involved in trying to speak for the nation as a whole after a period of national crises and the rise of identity politics. But he is glad the risk was taken. Not only does he warmly join in the celebration of the idea of an American self as the self of modernity ("process and adaptation"), but he also implies that the very troubles that threaten to tear America apart are only a sign of our unity: they reflect our shared nature as "a people of process." The genius of Pinsky's version of American identity is clear: it can turn its opposition into its allies.

While Alfred Corn is slightly more reserved in his praise of *An Explanation of America*, he, too, lauds the poem's assertion of a shared community. "We can doubt that [*An Explanation of America*] does . . . in fact, explain America," he says, in *The Metamorphoses of Metaphor*, "but not that it defends the humane values of reason and communitarianism" (153). He finds Pinsky's values "reassuring," and he sees Pinsky's poem as a continuation of Whitman's tradition of national poetry.

This sense of Pinsky as a poet with a vision of (and for) the nation as a whole, beyond allegiance to any narrower identity group, flows over into the popular perception of him. PBS, for example, refers to him as "America's Wordsmith" ("NewsHour with Jim Lehrer," April 2, 1997), and Amazon.com calls him "the people's poet." Not only that, but the website describes him as "the most regular guy yet to occupy the post of United States Poet Laureate"—a guy, it seems, reassuringly uninterested in being *irregular*, or a part of a separate, unsettlingly different identity-group. He is also, it seems, reassuringly *not* an urbane Anglophile elitist or an incomprehensible experimentalist—irregular guys both, by popular standards.

Pinsky seems to know that his prominence has to do with the sense of American identity articulated in *An Explanation of America*. It is from that poem, for example, that he read at a news conference in the Poetry Office at the Library of Congress, not long after first being named Poet Laureate (see *Library of Congress Information Bulletin* October 1997). He included one of the more overtly nation-themed passages, too, with the lines "The Founders made/A Union mystic yet rational." Pinsky deeply believes in the vision of *An Explanation of America*, and critics praise that vision sincerely. The things the poem offers are important because so many people seem to need them.

Chapter Three

James Mcmichael

Caging the Demon

Apprentice and Rebel

"Who's a better poet, Robert Frost or Edwin Arlington Robinson?"

"Frost."

"I don't think you understood the question."

It was a spring day in 1966 in Palo Alto when that exchange took place. Twenty-six-year-old James McMichael was defending his doctoral thesis at Stanford, and Yvor Winters, the director of the thesis committee, was asking what should have been an easy question. Any good student of Winters' idiosyncratic view of American poetry knew that the right answer was Robinson. Frost, for Winters, was the worst sort of poet, one who failed to provide a proper context to justify his dark emotions. Winters maintained that Frost took us too close to madness, to a paranoid sense of the world as irrationally malevolent. McMichael knew the answer the Old Man was looking for, too. In fact, he had all but provided it in the dissertation he was defending, "Rhetoric and the Skeptic's Void."

McMichael had been a favorite of Winters during his graduate-school years at Stanford. After all, McMichael had arrived at Stanford with his Wintersian credentials already in order: he held a

B.A. from the University of California, Santa Barbara, where he had been mentored by Edgar Bowers and Alan Stephens, Wintersians both. McMichael shared a great deal with Winters, including an attachment to California landscapes and many assumptions about literature. But, most important, both men shared a certain psychological disposition regarding the restraint of emotional extremes, a disposition that made similarities in their poetic practice all but inevitable. Perhaps it was his very closeness to Winters that made McMichael rebel at his thesis defense in a fit of Bloomian-influenced anxiety. The rebellion continued in the years that followed, as McMichael took up the Surrealist-oriented poetics then popular in some circles. But his rebellion was eventually to reverse itself. The two poets were too alike. Like many a son who needs to break away from a strong father, McMichael discovered over time the full extent of his resemblance to that father.

Whether McMichael had planned to break from Winters at his thesis defense or simply acted impulsively under pressure, he certainly did not jettison his Wintersian heritage along with his chances of staying on at Stanford. Only a year later, in 1967, he would publish his first book, *The Style of the Short Poem*, which popularizes Winters' ideas about poetry for an undergraduate audience. While McMichael tells us at the outset that he wishes only to "provide a brief but accurate vocabulary for discussing the style of the short poem" (vi), the book is subtle yet relentless in its Wintersian polemics. Without dragging Winters or Cleanth Brooks by name into the book, McMichael takes Winters' side in the debate over the heresy of paraphrase, saying simply that he "has assumed that the student will from the first be endeavoring to paraphrase each poem that he reads" (vi). Moreover, he embraces Winters' call for authorial control and a poetics of statement, saying that he has selected only poems "that are carefully controlled" (vi) and that, "when a poet writes a poem, he isn't talking *to* you, but rather to *you*" (1).

Whatever the distinction between talking "*to* you" and talking "to *you*," in both cases the poet treats poetry as an orthodox Wintersian "statement in words" (*In Defense of Reason* 363), not as Wimsatt and Beardsley's "verbal icon," and still less as the young, Imagist Yvor Winters' "permanent gateway to waking oblivion" (*Uncollected Essays* 195). McMichael even betrays a Wintersian prescriptiveness when he tells us that a poet should not "use language in so private a way that its meaning remains inaccessible" (4). At times these self-assured prescriptions can sound a great deal like Winters, as in the following passage, a condemnation of poetic solipsism:

> Insofar as a poet is not clear, he will be talking not to you but to himself. The temptation to talk to oneself is very great, and it is as easy to give in to the temptation in writing a small poem as in writing a big one. It is more difficult to write a clear poem about a tiny subject than to write an unclear poem about a very big one. And it is harder still, of course, to write a clear poem about a big subject. (4)

One could, of course, go on pointing out the Wintersian qualities of *The Style of the Short Poem*, from its penchant for "rarely anthologized" poets (vi) to its defense of meaningful "abstract categories" (13). What is certain, though, is that any force that worked to drive McMichael out of Winters' orbit had to contend with some very strong gravitational forces.

The metrics of McMichael's early poems can also be taken as a sign of how long a shadow Winters cast over his student. The poems are often in strict syllabics, as in "Corn" from *Against the Falling Evil*:

> I am the corn quail.
> What I do is quick.
> You will know only
> The muffled clucking,
> The scurry, the first
> Shiver of feathers
> And I will be up,
> I will be in your
> Head with no way out,
> Wings beating at the
> Air behind your eyes.

Like many of McMichael's early poems, the lines here show a modest variability in stress count but are consistent in terms of syllables (in this case, five in a line). There is nothing revolutionary about writing in syllabics in the late 1960s and early 1970s: it could even seem somewhat conservative in the context of the times. But among those who had taken Winters seriously, syllabics had a special meaning. As Pinsky wrote, looking back on his years with McMichael at Stanford, "in this atmosphere, it was considered quite daring to write in syllabics. Syllabics were in a way the official daringness of the Wintersians" ("Robert Pinsky" 246). "Official daringness"—this says it all. Even in his rebellion against a strict Wintersian formalism, McMichael takes the official path of rebellion, the semi-heresy of syllabics. He was clearly defining himself in relation to the Old Man.

The real rebellion came with his first book of poems. Robert Bly's Surrealism-inflected *The Light around the Body* won the National Book Award in 1967, and the years that followed saw the popular success of such Surrealistic books of poems as Ted Hughes's *Crow* and Galway Kinnell's *The Book of Nightmares*. McMichael's 1971 debut collection, *Against the Falling Evil*, is a close cousin of those more famous volumes and a descendant of the European and Latin American Surrealists published in translation in Bly's various magazines. While milder than Kinnell's book and significantly less violent than Hughes's *Crow, Against the Falling Evil* draws on the same set of poetic energies and possibilities of the neo-Surrealist idiom. This idiom made use of the notion of the "deep image," the archetypal and unparaphrasable symbol at the core of the poem. Almost twenty years earlier, Bly had begun his crusade for an American Surrealism by calling for poems "in which everything is said by image, and nothing by direct statement at all." For Bly, "the poem *is* the images, images touching all the senses, uniting the world beneath and the world above" (14).

McMichael's experiments with Surrealism were clear departures from the poetics of Yvor Winters. A glance at the table of contents of the 1971 anthology compiled by McMichael and Dennis Saleh, *Just What the Country Needs: Another Poetry Anthology*, reveals the direction he was taking: poems by Michael Benedikt rub up against those of Robert Bly, W. S. Merwin, Charles Simic, Charles Wright, James Tate, and Mark Strand. Included, too, are the poems of McMichael's own oddly disturbing sequence, "The Vegetables." The poem "Asparagus" is typical:

She sent packs of great beasts to pass
Over him, trailing belly-fur and dust,
Bending their nostrils to his frail spear.
This was to toughen him. For what?
Stupidly, like a squirrel, standing up,
Looking here and there, looking to all sides,
He is cut down and taken away.
She can smell him steaming, his crowns
Already tender, his spine giving in.
Now he is threatening to wither terribly,
And slip from the water altogether,
And billow through the kitchen like prayer.

McMichael's poem accords with Bly's prescriptions. After all, what could a reader do with it, if charged to paraphrase it? The results are bound to make a very strong poem seem somewhat ridiculous. One might say, "in this poem it seems that a woman, perhaps maternal, perhaps a lover, in a vaguely sexual yet possibly violent way, seeks, for reasons unknown, to toughen up a man who, in an act with strongly sexual connotations, mistakenly makes himself vulnerable and is destroyed by unknown forces, yet somehow he survives to be placed in another sexual situation where he surrenders to his urges, possibly fails, loses his sense of identity, and perhaps in a postcoital moment drifts off in a vaguely religious yet sensuous fashion, which may be sublime and perhaps also destructive." That would be my paraphrase, but, like the interpretation of ink blots, it probably tells you as much about the interpreter as it does about the interpreted. As the 1970s began, then, it seemed as though McMichael was to leave Winters behind and embark on the same uncanny ship as Kinnell, Hughes, and Bly.

Even the McMichael of "Asparagus," though, with his commitment to an image-based poetics, shares Winters' attraction toward dangerous emotional impulses. "If Winters found unreason either destructive or dishonest or both, he did so because he knew its power from inside," writes Thom Gunn ("On a Drying Hill" 684). Donald Hall is even more insightful, noting how the force of Winters' work derives from the friction between his Augustan convictions and the persistent tug of dark forces of unreason. "The power or energy in Winters' best poems," said Hall, "derives from conflict between form and reason, on the one hand, and an opposing dark chaos (demonic possession, madness), on the other; form and concept strive mightily to overcome a powerful enemy" (235). For Hall, many of Winters' more doctrinaire students are uninteresting because they adopt his precepts without having any true need to do so. Winters required order to hold back his inner demons, but, says Hall, "for the imitators, the cage that they fabricate, with inch-thick reinforced steel walls, incarcerates one mouse" (235). Unlike these poets, McMichael had good reason to be drawn to the Old Man's poetics, though his demons took a slightly different form from those of Winters.

In McMichael's case, these were not so much demons of madness or possession as of eros and desire. In "Asparagus," for example, one need hardly knock on Freud's door to note that the "frail spear" of the asparagus is phallic, both when it is "standing up" and when it is "threatening to wither terribly." Although the poem resists denotative paraphrase, the patterns of connotation strongly suggest eros as dangerous, and desire as a force that makes one vulnerable. When the spear "stupidly" stands, there is a sense of a failure to resist desire ("his spine giving in") and a sense of an impending disaster, as the spear is soon to be "cut down."

This kind of attraction/repulsion dynamic is everywhere in McMichael's early poems. Consider "The Artichoke," where repulsion and danger take a slightly different form:

> She bore only the heart,
> Worked at the stem with her
> Fingers, pulling it to her,
> And into her, like a cord.
>
> She would sustain him,
> Would cover his heart.
> The hairy needles
> And the bigger leaves,

These she licked into shape,
Tipping each with its point.
He is the mud-flower,
The thorny hugger.

Like "Asparagus," this poem is an odd one: a strange combination of erotic lyric (all that licking and penetration) and botanical illustration. The eros of the poem takes on connotations of danger in the final line, where the male-female embrace is "thorny"—difficult at the very least, probably priapic, and something more, too: dangerous for the woman. The danger here comes from the desiring male, whose embrace is, if not exactly predatory, then at least unhealthy for the desired woman. In a way the eerie distancing that we get from crossing botany with erotic lyric is a mirror for the poem's emotional qualities. It is a distancing device, just as the final line distances us from the eroticism that precedes it.

Danger and eros are constantly linked for McMichael, but in one sense, "The Artichoke" is a more representative example of this dynamic than is "Asparagus." In "The Artichoke," as in most of McMichael's early poems, the danger involves a woman threatened by an erotically obsessive man. This kind of danger hovers near the surface, for example, of the poem "Herbs":

Before fog leaves the scrub-oak
Or the grasses of the downland,
Take dragonwort under the black alder,
Take cockspur grass and henbane,
The belladonna, the deadly nightshade.
Free them as you would a spider's web,
Singing over them: Out, little wen,
Out, little wen.
Sing this into the mouth of the woman.

Shades of seduction come into contact with the nocturnal herb-gathering and chanting of witchcraft. The poet knows both the force behind the arts of seduction and the dangerous, manipulative element of those arts.

Revised in South Hadley

Given his psychological similarity to Winters, it is unsurprising that McMichael would return in large measure to the poetics he had studied so carefully at Stanford. At John Peck's house in South Hadley, Massachusetts, McMichael and Pinsky met with Peck, Matthias, and Hass to discuss the forthcoming Carcanet Press anthology, *Five American Poets*, which would contain selections from their work. It was 1978, and Matthias insisted that a large collection from McMichael's most recent book, *The Lover's Familiar* (1974), should appear. He particularly wanted to see included a good-sized selection from "Itinerary," the book's longest and most ambitious poem. McMichael was amenable to the idea, but he and Pinsky were adamant that they come not from the version published in *The Lover's Familiar* but from a revised manuscript. This manuscript, it turned out, was the result of conversations between Pinsky and McMichael about the poem and Pinsky's comments on "Itinerary" in his review of *The Lover's Familiar* in the January 1974 issue of *Poetry*. "Is this a special version of the poem for the anthology?" Matthias asked. "This is *the* version of the poem," McMichael and Pinsky responded, nearly in unison (Matthias, letter to the author). Pinsky's intervention, at this juncture, spurred McMichael's return to the Wintersian orbit from the deep space of American Surrealism.

"Itinerary" begins in the present-day Pacific Northwest, described in the poet's own voice, and moves eastward. As it does so, it also moves into the past, shifting seamlessly into voices culled from historical texts, most prominently those of Lewis and Clark on their westward expedition. It ends with an early settler in his Virginia garden, thinking on the prospects of the New World. In its original version the poem runs some 347 lines, almost 100 lines longer than the version that Pinsky and McMichael brought to South Hadley. With almost no exceptions, the lines excised are descriptions of landscapes. From a Wintersian viewpoint, description can be a vice insofar as it stands in the way of judgment and statement. For Pinsky, description was "the great rhetorical burden" of contemporary poetry, "so pervasive that to avoid it may demand an act of intervention." "'Itinerary' is partly given over to description," wrote Pinsky, "too much of it" (*The Situation of*

Poetry 159). The problem, for Pinsky, is that the contemporary rhetoric of description leaves out precisely what Winters considered the most important element of poetry—indeed, its very essence—the "statement in words": "'Statement' is one term which tempts me here. I have been using the flat, colorless word 'description' partly in order to counterbalance another mild term: discourse, discursiveness, the sound of the poet ambling or running through his subject and speaking about it. . . . [I]t is this declarative, prose quality which seems cramped or excluded by the conventions at hand" (*The Situation of Poetry* 117). Judging from the scale and locations of the omitted passages, McMichael found Pinsky's argument convincing. Pinsky had nudged him toward a poetics of statement, and McMichael seems to have been grateful for the intervention.

While attacking descriptive excesses, Pinksy praises McMichael for his more Wintersian qualities. While Pinsky finds fault with "Itinerary," he says that in other poems McMichael has been a properly discursive poet, capable of writing work that is "a statement, made in the tone of a human being speaking of and to other human beings" (162). This sociability is singled out for praise in "Itinerary," too, when Pinsky refers to that poem's engagement with "a complex world of human affairs" and its "humane or social" element. He also praises the quality of emotional "balance," its "detachment," and its "absence of hysteria" (156, 161). The real drama of the poem is Wintersian in that it "includes the nominalist dilemma as one historical part of its sensibilities among others." In fact, Pinsky argues, "that inclusion may be the poem's subject" (160).

The overt topic of "Itinerary" is the exploration and settling of the New World, but the act of coming into dominion over the virgin land is highly sexualized. The land itself inspires a desire for possession that McMichael infuses with eroticism, making it a matter of sexual as well as geographic importance. His attitude toward this desire is, however, ambivalent. This ambivalence is disclosed most fully at the end of the poem, when we have voyaged back from the twentieth-century Pacific Northwest to the Virginia of the early settlers. Here the speaker walks in his garden, thinking about the "saints of New England" and their doctrine of *contemptus mundi*:

> I am told
> such things as bring men to ill terms,
> told of those who seek congress with the earth
> that they shall have her in their time forever.
> That her places sing their love-song for no man.
> That I am not the suitor whose betrothed
> awaits him, but some unwelcome third
> with God alone her lover. And yet I would
> look upon such country as will show me
> nature undressed, the strata of the land,
> her lays and beds and all her privacies.
> For my wonder tells me I should be
> promiscuous, should learn by all the
> laws of bodies and by where they are
> the joyful news from out the new found world.

The "love-song" of the earth (figured by our male speaker as female), the man's presentation of himself as the earth's would-be suitor, the undressing of the land, the longed-for lays and beds and privacies, and the urge to promiscuity all read as erotic here. McMichael's reservations about this eroticism are based both in theology (those who love mere sublunary things love things that perish) and in a sense of himself as an intruder, as an "unwelcome third." The erotic anxiety here, as in many of the poems in "The Vegetables," is manifested as the seducer's doubts about the morality of his own impulses.

The Poet Bereft

When McMichael's next long poem *Four Good Things* appeared in 1980, Robert Hass praised it fulsomely, but he seemed to have a hard time finding the poem's focus. "It is a new, remarkable long poem about—of all things—Pasadena," he wrote, "it is about worry, death, taxes, planning, probability theory, insomnia, stamp collecting, cancer, domestic architecture, sex manuals, the Industrial Revolution, real estate" (*Twentieth Century Pleasures* 161). Hass is not alone in having trouble finding the threads that hold together McMichael's long poems. Even McMichael's best and most appreciative readers have sometimes struggled to understand the relation of part to whole. But McMichael is too much the Augustan in his long poems to welcome any dispersion of formal unity, and Hass is too good a reader not to catch on to this at some level. He intuits the true organizing principle of *Four Good Things* when he says that "all the excitement" of the poem comes "in watching McMichael take up one unpoetic subject after another and illuminate it by turning it back on the emotions of the child who is watching the city take shape around him" (162). In the end, nothing in the poem, no matter how apparently exotic, escapes the orbit of the evolving self.

The growth of the poet's mind depicted in *Four Good Things* takes the form of a story about powerful emotions and the strategies of intellectual reserve that he develops to contain them. Where the powerful impulses in "Itinerary" were erotic, here they are feelings of bereavement and vulnerability. The eventual counterbalance is a capacity to restrain and examine the self, to find its predictable patterns, and to plan around them. The habits of perpetual analysis and planning provide the materials for the cage with thick reinforced steel walls that McMichael builds to protect himself from unrestrained emotion.

The opening section is about the early death by cancer of McMichael's mother, and it is her death that opens the child's emotional register to the depths of worry. McMichael depicts himself alone as a child, his father away running a business and the housekeeper having left to marry her boyfriend.

> After she died, his business kept him longer.
> Florence had moved away with Glen, and I was
> there alone through the afternoons and early
> evenings, into the hours when I'd listen
> to the radio and wait to hear him drive in,
> late. After ten, after my shows were over, I'd
> worry every way he might be killed, would give it up
> only and completely when his car was there.
> With that exhilaration I could put on
> all the calmness I thought he wanted —

    pretend to be asleep or answer tiredly
    that I was there.

The boy cannot control his emotions, but he hopes at least to give the appearance of someone untroubled, a kind of faux stoicism.

    After this early childhood trauma, though, the poem takes a turn that has puzzled many of its readers: it presents a short history of the Industrial Revolution beginning with Richard Arkwright's invention of the water-frame loom. But there is a point to the digression: after he depicts the tremendous anxieties and vulnerabilities of all classes of people during the Industrial Revolution, McMichael tells us about the capitalists' solution to these anxieties and vulnerabilities, a solution that he transfers to his own insecure life. The entrepreneurs of the late nineteenth century, says McMichael, developed habits of self-restraint and looked for predictability, for an understanding of market cycles and the repeatable processes of standardized production. Their habits of self-control and careful planning were ways of finding safety. The exploration of the industrial past leads McMichael back to himself and toward an understanding of his own means of dealing with uncertainties and vulnerabilities. He turns panic into planning, worry into caution and carefulness. This is not exactly a recipe for ecstasy, but it is a way out of trauma. The poem is one of the purest examples of McMichael writing a clear, restrained statement in the style of analytic discourse. Mary Kinzie, exhibiting an understanding of the poem if not a sympathy to its project, goes so far as to claim in the *American Poetry Review* that it is written "in prose" (18). The poem is rivaled in this respect only by McMichael's other long poem, *Each in a Place Apart*.

Poem Degree Zero

The discursive quality of *Each in a Place Apart* (1994) is closely linked to its emotional reserve and its distrust of emotional impulse. The poem chronicles the breakup of the poet's first marriage, an affair with a much younger woman, and the troubles leading to the end of his marriage to the second woman. It is, as one might expect, a poem of relentless self-examination. The emotional impulses that McMichael addresses here are closer to the erotic drives of "Itinerary" than they are to the anxieties of bereavement examined in *Four Good Things*. Since the period he discusses in *Each in a Place Apart* includes the one in which he composed "Itinerary" and depicts that period as a time of intense emotional and erotic turmoil in his marriage, one suspects that both poems are responses to the same events.

Be that as it may, *Each in a Place Apart* shows us a McMichael whose distrust of his own most powerful emotional impulses grows from deep within his character. In one early scene, for example, he depicts himself as a fourteen-year-old on a train, sitting next to a pretty young woman, conversing with her tersely while possessed by a "tight / stultifying fear that I would touch her." He already is alarmed by the power of his erotic impulses. When he encounters Linda, the woman for whom he will leave his sons and first wife, the distrust of impulse is even stronger. As he looks back on his first interactions with her (an eighteen-year-old student in his Sunday School class), McMichael's anguish is palpable. This is not the anguish of Nabokov's Humbert Humbert, for whom lust was only limited by external necessity. It is the anguish of a man who fears that his most intimate impulses are terribly immoral, of a man familiar with self-loathing:

> Nor was it even then too late. I was the
> married, reliable sponsor of her youth group,
> I had to keep it to myself. Away from her, inside me
> it would suffocate, I thought, if I stayed busy.
> My body kept it alive. What if she weren't
> there again for the third straight week? I should
> want her not to be there. Love meant wanting her to be
> comely, prized and occupied, light-spirited, it meant
> wanting her not to want me. Another Sunday and she
> wasn't there. If I told her, would she want me then?
> I couldn't tell her, couldn't not, and did.

The anguish does not go away once the romantic relationship begins: "she hates loving to be with me," writes McMichael, and "I with her."

Affection and eroticism are at odds with judgment. As in "Itinerary," where erotic urges were linked with the possession of the land, *Each in a Place Apart* treats these urges as unreasoningly jealous.

The discursiveness of *Each in a Place Apart* and *Four Good Things* has long puzzled reviewers. But it is entirely explicable: the attitude to emotion is restrained, and the form—discursive, distanced self-examination—grows out of that restraint. There is an irony to this: one of the features of Augustan or neoclassical writing, according to Roland Barthes, is that it is, in a way, invisible or unremarkable as a style. It draws no attention to itself because the poetic, in the days of classicism, strove to avoid eccentricity. Barthes maintains that classicist poetry eschewed the display of any unseemly emotion, staying close to the level of polite conversation. This kind of writing, and the modern prose styles that most resemble it, constitute what Barthes calls "the zero degree" of writing (76), a neutral style in the indicative mood that shies away from emotive gestures. We sometimes accept such a style in prose—Barthes, for example, cites Camus' *The Stranger* as the modern *locus classicus* of writing degree zero. So far have we come from Augustan norms in poetry, though, that this kind of restraint seems eccentric and perhaps confusing. Poetry critics look for and celebrate stylistic eccentricity, but when it takes the form of a classical restraint—a *poem degree zero*—it defies easy classification. The style is so invisible that it becomes prominent. The critic does not know what to do, save to furrow his brow.

Robert Pinsky has been a lonely McMichael ally in the presence of all these furrowed brows. Asked about his favorite long poems by contemporaries, Pinsky once said that *Four Good Things* stood above all others as "a great poem, a great book, certainly the most neglected book of contemporary poetry, in relation to its merit" ("Syncopated Things" 166). Pinsky offered an economic explanation for the poem's lack of recognition, blaming Houghton Mifflin for letting it go out of print in less than a year. But such an explanation raises a question: Why was demand so low that the publisher did not see the need to keep the poem in print? One way to explain the poem's lack of popularity, despite the backing of prominent poets such as Pinsky, is to place it (and the equally uncelebrated *Each in a Place Apart*) in the context of American poetry about the self and our expectations for such poems.

When we look at contemporary poetry of the self, though, we begin to see just how thoroughly McMichael's work confounds those expectations. For several decades the benchmark for personal poetry has been the style of Robert Lowell, a *vers libre* lyricism of unrestrained revelation. I do not mean to say that McMichael's work does not reveal intimate personal details in the manner of the confessional Lowell: family trauma of the kind recounted in *Four Good Things* and *Each in a Place Apart* is the bread-and-butter of confessional verse and the very stuff of the great work itself, *Life Studies*. But consider Lowell's "Skunk Hour," and the profound differences between Lowell and McMichael become clear. "My mind's not right," Lowell writes in "Skunk Hour"; "I hear / my ill-spirit sob in each blood cell." These emotions are not only uncensored but also unexplained. McMichael could never let those lines lie on the page, unanalyzed, unexplained; he has to leash the madness. What McMichael's work has, and Lowell's lacks, is an emotional reserve bred of a deep-seated mistrust of emotional impulse. That is to put the matter in positive terms for McMichael, but with expectations for poetry of the self set by Lowell, Berryman, and Plath, the matter is much more likely to be put in negative terms: what Lowell has, and McMichael lacks, is emotional heat, lyric force, a bareness of raw feeling—put it as you will.

McMichael's constant, rational doubting and examining of his feelings, then, places him beyond the horizon of readerly expectations. Let me cite just one example of how deep-seated this expectation had become for any poetry dealing with the matter of the self when McMichael was writing his major poems. In 1977, while he was working on the poem that would be published three years later as *Four Good Things*, the *New York Times* sent a reporter to cover a reading by Allen Ginsberg and Robert Lowell at St. Mark's-in-the-Bowery. The two poets, according to the *Times*, represented "opposite ends of the poetic spectrum" ("Allen Ginsberg Will Share the Stage with Robert Lowell" 36). While this is in some respects true, it is much like saying that the Democratic and Republican candidates in a presidential election represent opposite ends of the political spectrum, a statement that ignores and makes invisible the significant territory to the left of the Democratic candidates and the disturbingly significant zone to the right of the Republican ones. That is, while there were very real differences between a Ginsberg and a Lowell, both were very much poets of emotional expression, not emotional reticence. If they represented extreme ends of the 1977 poetic spectrum to mainstream readers, then where does that leave a poet such as McMichael? Ignored and invisible and, for the moment, running a campaign that seems as certain to end in noble, principled obscurity as that of any third-party candidate.

Chapter Four

Robert Hass

Statement and Image

A *"Wynged Wondre"*

Robert Hass's career seems almost to have been designed to disprove Chaucer's claim that poetic fame is a "wynged wondre faste fleen." Critical and popular favor arrived, for Hass, on wondrously fast wings, but they have not fled, nor do they show any signs of so doing. Hass has been one of the boy wonders of American poetry since before the appearance of his first book, and he has not yet seen a slump in the opinions of the loose affiliation of reviewers, editors, and critics who comprise the American poetic establishment. Many of the bright-eyed young men and women whose first book wins the Yale Younger Poets Award may hope, with some reason, for further validation to follow in the form of an appearance in a major anthology. Such was the precocity of Robert Hass that his poetry actually appeared in an important anthology five years before it was to win the Yale prize in 1973. Since that time he has received many of the more prestigious prizes and fellowships for poetry and kept pace with the omnipresent Robert Pinsky in terms of MLA citations and anthology appearances, earning his *Norton Anthology* stripes in 1984. He was named U.S. Poet Laureate earlier than his contemporary Pinsky, too, and served two terms from 1995 to 1997.

Why such a sudden and consistent success? Certainly, talent has something to do with it, but we all know of remarkably talented poets whose work has gone unappreciated. We have seen a certain irony in the fact that the neo-Augustan poetics inherited by Pinsky from the ever-marginal Winters made Pinsky a critical and popular success. While Hass was never so Augustan as the author of "Essay on Psychiatrists" and *An Explanation of America*, his success with the critical and reading publics has, like Pinsky's, much to do with what he learned from Winters at Stanford in the 1960s.

While Hass never took up Wintersian Augustanism, he did engage with his mentor seriously. What Hass took from Winters, though, was not a coherent set of poetics, and still less was it a coherent and prescriptive moral philosophy. What Hass took from Winters was instead a set of recurring themes and oppositions, more or less in their original Wintersian form. The most important of these are a concern with the distinction between realist and nominalist views of language as well as a concern with the competing claims of the physical world and the individual intelligence. Winters had very definite opinions about these matters, choosing in his late career a dogmatically realist view of language and an equally dogmatic view of the claims of the individual intellect (with its acts of moral judgment) over the claims of the physical world. Hass took up this Wintersian matrix of thought but did so without adopting his mentor's opinions and dogmas about these themes. In fact, it is often difficult to determine Hass's exact positions on the themes that he took from Winters. He is in this sense something of a poet of negative capability, able to negotiate "uncertainties, mysteries, doubts, without any irritable reaching after fact and reason," as Keats put it in his famous letter of 1817 (494).

How Hass was able to take up Winters' characteristic themes without any irritable reaching after dogma or certainty is by no means obvious. Dogma and certainty were, after all, the fundamental attractions of Winters' thinking for many, if not most, of his followers. The answer lies in Hass's lack of the kind of early trauma that Winters suffered during his convalescence from tuberculosis and the period of isolation that followed. Winters developed his ideas about language and the morally active intellect while he was feeling acutely the possibility of the loss of meaning and identity. His hardened positions were the products of a deeply disturbing experience from which he may never have fully recovered. Hass, in contrast, encountered Winters' ideas in a far more congenial and social environment. Moreover, Hass has by his own admission led a remarkably fortunate existence—he once even wrote that he has "had it easy" in life (*Twentieth Century Pleasures* 276). Because of this, he was able to fully absorb Winters' key themes and ideas without needing to take up Winters' hardened positions. He could become a kind of soft-line or agnostic Wintersian.

If it is true, as Gertrude Stein had it, that things "are only important if unexpectedly somebody happens to need them," then we should ask just who needed an agnostic Wintersian over the course of Hass's career. The answer, as it turns out, is just about everyone. Hass was relevant in the 1970s because his explorations of the realist/nominalist divide played into contemporary concerns about image and statement, or showing and telling, in poetry. And it was the same sophisticated negotiation of the realist and nominalist positions that made Hass relevant in the theory wars of the 1980s and early 1990s. Again, his negative capability in exploring the theme made it possible for both sides of the debate to claim him as their own. Moreover, his agnostic Wintersian view of the competing claims of the judging intellect and the potentially overwhelming physical world also turned out to be something of great importance to our times.

As Charles Altieri has argued, one of the most important contradictions of postmodernity has been the conflict between two imperatives: to be open to the other, and to resist being absorbed into it. Hass inherits Winters' rich treatment of the theme of self and other, but he inhabits the matrix without any need to reach for any certainty. Instead, he provides detailed and nuanced treatments of a theme of great importance to those who experience firsthand the postmodern condition. In corresponding so well to so many of the contradictory claims heard in the poetic field over the past three decades, Hass's poetry has an almost singular distinction: it is a central poetry of our decentered times.

Agnostic Wintersianism: World and Intellect

In elucidating Hass's unusually nonpartisan approach to Winters, it is convenient to begin with a glance at a couple of texts. The first is a stanza from Yvor Winters' 1954 poem "At the San Francisco Airport":

> The rain of matter upon sense
> Destroys me momently. The score:
> There comes what will come. The expense
> Is what one thought, and something more—
> One's being and intelligence.

Here we see the typical positions of the mature Winters regarding the relation of the judging subject and the material object, the active intellect and the physical world. The Winters we see here has turned 180 degrees from the direction of the young poet who asserted, in "The Testament of a Stone," that the poetic act must involve a "fusion of the poet with his material" (*Uncollected Essays* 195). While the young Winters sought a union of self and other in "a permanent gateway to waking oblivion," the mature poet sees the material world as a threatening other that, if not resisted with constant vigilance, will destroy one's intelligence and very being (195). The proposition of "At the San Francisco Airport" is, as Terry Comito says, a familiar one for readers of the mature Winters: that "the light of our judgments . . . serves as a bulwark or refuge from the incursions of darkness" (192).

My second text comes from a poem by that most famous student of Winters, Thom Gunn. Here are a few lines from "The Geysers," which depicts a group of people, naked and at play in the cool streams near the geysers of the title:

> Some rest and pass a joint, some climb the fall:
> Tan, black and pink, firm shining bodies, all
> Move with a special unconsidered grace.
> For though we have invaded this glittering place
> And broke the silences, yet we submit:
> So wholly, that we are details of it.

Donald Hall has said that Gunn never really fell much under Winters' sway. Gunn, says Hall, was among the few poets "for whom it was possible to work with Winters for a year or so, learn something and leave Stanford without becoming beholden" (234). In one sense, Hall is surely right: the sentiments of "The Geysers" are the exact opposite of those of Winters' "At the San Francisco Airport." Where the Old Man argued against the union of self and matter, Gunn celebrates the submission of the self to the place. Later in the poem the speaker revels in an oceanic loss of self that would have made the Winters of "At the San Francisco Airport" cringe: "bobbing in the womb, all around me Mother/I am part of all there is no other." Here, Gunn allows himself to respond to the call of the other, while in "At the San Francisco Airport," Winters resists such calls with all his might.

In another sense, though, the poem shows a debt to Winters that goes far deeper than Hall's statement would lead us to believe. We can best get at the nature of the debt by pulling a somewhat antique blunderbuss out of the critical armory, the revisionary ratios described by Harold Bloom in *The Anxiety of Influence*. The third of Bloom's ratios, "daemonization," is an apt term for the relation of Gunn's poem to Winters'. Daemonization, according to Bloom, is "a movement towards a personal Counter-Sublime, in reaction to the precursor's Sublime," in which "the later poet opens himself to what he believes to be a power in the parent-poem that does not belong to the parent proper, but to a range of being just beyond the precursor" (8). Gunn, in embracing a unity with the material world, opens himself to the power of a physical being that Winters dismissed as "the rain of matter upon sense." Gunn daemonizes Winters and celebrates an opposing ideal. While Gunn values them differently from the mature Winters, he shares Winters' set of binary oppositions: the aloof self versus the self unified with the world. Gunn, as a strong poet, revalues them in accord with his different sensibility.

Like Gunn, Hass absorbs the terms of Winters' thought, but unlike Gunn he does not set up a counter-sublime. Rather, he inhabits Winters' ideas with a surprisingly negative capability. Hass's most substantial prose statement on Winters, for example, bears a remarkably nonpartisan title: "What He Did" (*Twentieth Century Pleasures* 141). Compare this to the title of the most respected book on Winters, Comito's *In Defense of Winters*, and you will get a sense of Hass's unusual position among his mentor's readers. Hass writes what is essentially a description of Winters' work rather than a critical assessment or judgment for or against the Old Man. That is, he elucidates but steers deftly between the Scylla of orthodoxy and the Charybdis of apostasy:

> Winters, in the intense loneliness of provincial places—Cerrillos, New Mexico; Boulder, Colorado; Moscow, Idaho—decided that Imagism was a bad, dangerous method, that it could render experience but not judge experience, and that constantly calling up feelings that you couldn't understand made people crazy. . . . There is the world, and there is man; and man should not confuse himself with the world, because he is going to die. He was drawn to the poets of the sixteenth and seventeenth century who held close to this fact: and, to the end of his own life, he always praised most highly those poems that look directly and without flinching at the loneliness of human death. (146)

One simply cannot infer any particular judgment of Winters from the passage. Significantly, we find his mature ideas explained as the product of his own experiences. We are not encouraged to see them as either true or untrue.

Winters "wrote criticism to explain what had happened to him as a poet" (149), writes Hass, in the concluding paragraph of his essay. This statement performs an odd kind of alchemy on Winters' highly polemical critical writing. Work that Winters presented as being not only true about the world, but also urgently true, is transformed into a purely personal statement—true as an explanation of Winters' own work but without pretensions to a larger relevance. Hass's statement makes it possible to think of Winters without any nagging questions about whether the idiosyncratic representation of the canon in *Forms of Discovery* or the condemnation of modernism in *Primitivism and Decadence* are true or false.

Elsewhere in his prose, Hass elaborates the agnostic gesture that he made in his essay on Winters. In "Looking for Rilke," for example, he reads Rainer Maria Rilke through a Wintersian frame of reference but refuses to judge him as Winters would. Hass describes how when he first read Rilke's "Archaic Torso of Apollo," it "seemed, finally, to have only one subject, the self," a self that "stands outside natural processes" (*Twentieth Century Pleasures* 245). But while Hass at first found "Archaic Torso of Apollo" to be an exemplary poem of the Wintersian kind, placing the self over against the world of objects, he came to the realization that it is, in fact, a very different—indeed, an opposite—kind of poem. When Rilke looks longingly at the torso, Hass says, "Art answers him, but only by intensifying his desire to pass over into the country it represents" (245). Because it intensifies Rilke's desire to lose himself in an obscurely imagined union with the world of eternal art, the poem's true subject is not the affirmation of the independent self but rather an affirmation of a loss of self, tantamount to affirming "death, or if not death, death's bride, its lover and secret" (245). The terms of Hass's thought here are clearly Wintersian: self-possession versus a deathly union with the other. Hass's teacher would have recoiled from the poem and condemned Rilke for having the kind of death-wish that he found endemic to Romantic and modernist writing. Hass, though, describes his own reaction to Rilke's longing for self-loss quite differently: "I think I should report that when I first recognized this impulse in these poems, I had a very strong, divided response" (245). Unlike Winters, Hass feels no need to resolve this sort of contradiction.

Something similar happens in a number of the poems from Hass's first book, *Field Guide*. "Fall," for example, sits squarely in the matrix of Wintersian thought about the world and the intelligence, but its position within that matrix is by no means a simple one. The first stanza of "Fall" indicates a position closer to Winters than to Gunn:

Amateurs, we gathered mushrooms
near shaggy eucalyptus groves
which smelled of camphor and the fog-soaked earth.
Chanterelles, puffballs, chicken-of-the-woods,
we cooked in wine or butter,
beaten eggs or sour cream,
half expecting to be
killed by a mistake. "Intense perspiration,"
you said late at night,

quoting the terrifying field guide
while we lay tangled in our sheets and heavy limbs,
"is the first symptom of attack."

Amateur readers of the field guide had better hone their skills of interpretation if they are going to gather mushrooms and eat what they
find. Only the well schooled and ever vigilant can preserve us against
the dire consequences we face when we take the world into ourselves.
The stanza reminds us of "At the San Francisco Airport," where the
dangers of the material world and the senses are just as strong. But
the second and final stanza of Hass's poem complicates the picture:

Friends called our aromatic fungi
"liebestoads" and only ate the ones
that we most certainly survived.
Death shook us more than once
those days and floating back
it felt like life. Earth-wet, slithery,
we drifted toward the names of things.
Spore prints littered our table
like nervous stars. Rotting caps
gave off a musky smell of loam.

The danger of assimilating the world to the self remains, but it is
through the exposure to that danger that life is truly experienced. It
is also through exposure to the dangers of the material world that the
"amateurs" gain the knowledge to properly read the field guide. While
the themes of the poem are clearly Wintersian, the position is neither
that of "At the San Francisco Airport" nor that of "The Geysers." Is it
right to act like the amateurs of the poem, who seek out the dangerous
pleasures of the material world and slowly grow in knowledge through
their experiences? Or are the cautious friends, who "only ate the ones/
that we most certainly survived," the wiser characters? The issue is
undecidable.

Another poem from *Field Guide*, "On the Coast near Sausalito,"
takes up the same theme and makes a similar gesture of negative
capability:

I won't say much for the sea
except that it was, almost,
the color of sour milk.
The sun in that clear
unmenacing sky was low,
angled off the grey fissure of the cliffs,
hills dark green with manzanita.

Low tide: slimed rocks
mottled brown and thick with kelp
like the huge backs of ancient tortoises
merged with the grey stone
of the breakwater, sliding off
to antediluvian depths.
The old story: here filthy life begins.

This experience of the sea is a far cry from that of the bather in Gunn's
"The Geysers." The sea, after all, is "unmenacing," and almost the color
of milk, the *ne plus ultra* symbol of the nurturing and the maternal.
Then again, the negation of danger in the term "unmenacing" is different from an out-and-out presentation of benevolence, and the milk
is sour. Along with the Gunn-like sense of a welcoming physical world
there are traces of a Wintersian recoiling from such a world. The
balancing of these contraries continues throughout the poem, which
explores both perspectives but commits to neither.

Lack of resolution in Hass's poems is no more a failing than it is
in the poems of Keats, and from many perspectives it can be considered a virtue. It certainly seems so when seen from the postmodern
perspective articulated by Altieri. In fact, a look at Hass in the light of
Altieri's observations about the postmodern condition goes a long way
toward explaining Hass's remarkable success.

The Fourth Contradiction of Postmodernism

Most of us are aware that there are certain contradictions to our postmodern condition, but few of us have the erudition or the gusto to lay

out those contradictions in a list, name them, and cite specific examples. This is exactly what Altieri does in *Postmodernisms Now*, where he tells us that postmodernism is bedeviled by five fundamental contradictions. He argues that while postmodern theorists have "worked themselves into several paralyzing contradictions," certain poets have brought enough "intelligence and flexibility" to the table to "finesse the most severe aspects of the contradictions" and to develop positions "far more plausible and livable than current theory has managed to formulate" (24–25). Robert Hass is one of these poets.

Altieri's five contradictions are as follows:

- The contradiction between the need to show that a cultural product is a symptom of its conditions and the need to show how that cultural product creates possibilities for resistance to those conditions
- The contradiction between the celebration of diversity and heterogeneity, on the one hand, and the erasure of various kinds of difference through the construction of the identity-groups, on the other.
- The contradiction between the challenging of the bourgeois individual and the celebration of fully individuated subjectivity
- The contradiction between the imperative to escape from narrow self-regard in responding to the call of the other, and the imperative to resist the seductions of the other
- The contradiction between deconstructive antifoundationalism and pragmatic antifoundationalism.

For Altieri, Robert Hass achieves his "contemporaneity" through his deft negotiation of the first and fourth contradictions.

The first contradiction, between the artwork's status as symptom and resistance, is treated rather briefly. In essence, Altieri's claim is this: Hass, along with a rather select company of poets (C. K. Williams, John Ashbery, Adrienne Rich, Robert Creeley, and Frank O'Hara), helps us transcend the contradiction, not so much by resolving it as by refusing to accept its terms. As Altieri puts it,

> There is no way to claim that significant contemporary art can establish what can be considered symptomatic about postmodernity while also providing some plausible notion of cure. It is not even reasonable

to claim that art offers cogent general models for escaping the play of simulacra or the alienations that stem from the collapse of scene into screen and mirror into network. However, one can show how specific writers [Hass, Williams, Ashbery and company] develop imaginative energies that do not fit easily into these binaries. And one can hope to build on those examples by showing that there are feasible imaginative strategies for finessing the entire model of judgment that invites predicates like symptom and cure. (35)

Hass is, in this view, part of a group of poets whose work "recast[s] judgment so that it is no longer a matter of finding appropriate concepts" (36). Although Altieri offers no examples in support of this claim, it is surely some element of Hass's negative capability that Altieri has in mind: the refusal of certainties is also a refusal to engage in the logic of symptom and cure.

The fourth contradiction is more immediately relevant to Hass's work, and it is in his engagement with this one that we see a greater part of his importance to our time. It is here, too, that Hass's agnostic Wintersianism comes most strongly into play. The fourth contradiction of postmodernism can be described as a struggle between the imperative to own the self and an equally powerful imperative to "undo the sense of demand basic to the masculine ego" (48). On the one hand, we have the self-command that allows us to resist forces both from without (such as the manipulative discourses of the powerful) and from within (such as irrational impulses and destructive fears). One version of this heroism comes in Yvor Winters of "At the San Francisco Airport." On the other hand, we have the imperative to feel for and identify with the other and to be open to interpolation in its discourse or identity. Think of the Thom Gunn of "The Geysers," for example.

"While poetry cannot be very helpful in developing specific moral arguments that might address these contradictions," continues Altieri, "it can explore versions of agency that we then call upon for our representations of moral powers and moral responsibilities" (48). That is, it can offer us examples of how to be in the world while balancing the claims of the contradictory imperatives. Hass manages to do this by presenting a version of the self that recognizes both its own isolation and its necessary reciprocity with others.

Looking again at "On the Coast near Sausalito," we can see the agnostic Wintersian basis for Hass's negotiation of the fourth contradiction of postmodernism. Hass feels the call of the other profoundly in that poem. The "recognition" of another life felt by the fisherman in the "fierce quiver of surprise" and the "line's tension," the puncturing of the barrier between fish and fisherman in the sudden, tautological recognition that the "spiny monster['s] . . . /bulging purple eyes/ were eyes," and the identification of the fisherman with what was his prey when he sees the fish "creature to creature"—these are all instances of opening to the other. The poem knows "how deeply otherness pervades any experience of our own possible identities" (48). But Hass also knows the Wintersian truth of the value of self-possession. The holding-off from the "sour milk" of the sea at the start of the poem, the unsqueamishness of the protagonist as he plucks the legs from a prawn, the praise he offers the Italian cooks who turn the fish into a meal—these are instances of the self-possessed ego, refusing identification with the other. In showing us the possibility of negative capability in the face of competing imperatives, the poem offers a way of living with the fourth contradiction of postmodernism. It offers no moral statement per se, but it does "explore versions of agency that we then call upon for our representations of moral powers and moral responsibilities," to use a phrase of Altieri's (48). Perhaps surprisingly, agnostic Wintersianism turns out to offer a way of negotiating our postmodern condition.

Agnostic Wintersianism: Image and Statement

"The spiritual development of Robert Hass," according to Terrence Doody, is a journey "from image to sentence" (Doody 47). This is at least as right as it is wrong. What is right is this: in speaking of the use of images and statements as a matter of spiritual importance, Doody gets at the high stakes involved in the use of images and statements for Hass. What is wrong, though, is the clear line of development, from a young image-based Hass to an older sentence-based Hass. Although this version of Hass's biography would have a nice symmetry with that of his teacher Winters, the evidence points to a different story, one based less on change than on consistency. From *Field Guide* in 1973 through *Sun under Wood* in 1998, Hass has been intrigued by the contrast between image and statement, but he consistently defers from making a final choice between them.

For Winters, the difference between image and statement or sentence was surely a matter of some spiritual import. He maintained that a poetry of images went hand in hand with a nominalist philosophy of language, while a poetry of statements was the appropriate expression of a realist philosophy of language. A nominalist's poetry would be one of images and immediate physical sensations, shying as far away as possible from abstract statements or judgments. This was dangerous because, as Comito says, it would make us "helpless victims" of our experiences, without any way of fully understanding them (*In Defense of Winters* 242).

Hass, like Winters, sees the question of image-based/nominalist versus statement-based/realist writing as a question of some spiritual importance. The ideas permeate his work from his first collection of poems to his most recent and appear in many guises in his prose. In his essay "Images," for example, he writes of the poetic image as a means of connecting with the eternal, an idea not unconnected to the early doctrine of the young Imagist/nominalist Winters:

> Images are not quite ideas, they are stiller than that, with less implication outside themselves. And they are not myth, they have no explanatory power. . . . In the nineteenth century one would have said that what compelled us about them was a sense of the eternal. And it is something like that, some feeling in the arrest of an image that what perishes and what lasts forever have been brought into conjunction, and accompanying that sensation is a feeling of release from the self. (*Twentieth Century Pleasures* 275)

Here, Hass first defines the image in opposition to discursive writing, the sort of work that has "explanatory power" and does not shy away from the use of abstract categories. He then offers an idea of the image not unlike that defined by the young Yvor Winters, who wrote of the image as "a permanent gateway to waking oblivion" (*Uncollected Essays* 195).

Hass seems, at first, to be siding with the young Winters over the mature Winters. The sense is confirmed when Hass describes how his experience of his own life is a still image:

> Walking through the rooms of my house on a moonlit August night, with a sharp sense of my children each at a particular moment in their lives and changing, with three or four shed, curled leaves from a Benjamin fig on the floor of the dining room and a spider, in that moonlight, already set to work in one of them, and the dark outline of an old Monterey pine against the sky outside the window, the one thing about the house that seems not to have changed in the years of my living in it, it is possible to feel my life, in a quiet ecstatic helplessness, as a long slow hurtle through the forms of things. (*Twentieth Century Pleasures* 275–76)

Without the sense of the eternal given us by images, Hass says, we would experience only a dark forest of mere contingency. He voices the nature of such experience as follows: "I live in this place, rather than that. Have this life, rather than that. It is August not September for physical and historical reasons too boring to go into and I am a man approaching middle age in the American century . . . This is the *selva oscura*" (276).

This seems to place Hass firmly on the nominalist/image-based side of the debate. But even as he tells us about the vitally important spiritual value of image-based perception, he shies away from embracing images wholeheartedly. Thinking of the "quiet ecstatic helplessness" he felt in his quiet house, Hass recoils. "I think I resist that sensation," he says, "because there is a kind of passivity in it; I suppose it would make me careless of those things that need concentration to attend to" (276). This is not to say that he dismisses images and the kind of perception they open up in favor of "fact." "For me, at least," he tells us, "there is a delicate balance in this matter" (275). His idea of the poetic image is essentially Wintersian, but here Hass hovers between the positions of the young and the mature Winters.

Hass's poetry also manifests this agnostic view of the realist/ nominalist debate. *Field Guide*, for example, worries the theme of image versus statement in many ways. In fact, one way of reading the book is as a dialogue, sometimes between poems, sometimes within poems, about image and statement.

"Spring" is perhaps the most wholly nominalist poem in the book. It proposes an immersion in the world of the senses as a path to union with something larger than the self. It begins with a couple casually enjoying the pleasures of the senses and anticipating the pleasures of discursive language:

> We bought great ornamental oranges,
> Mexican cookies, a fragrant yellow tea.
> Browsed the bookstores.

Soon, though, an incident in one of the bookstores impresses upon them the distance between discursive language and their experience of the world:

> You
> asked mildly, "Bob, who is Ugo Betti?"
> A bearded bird-like man
> (he looked like a Russian priest
> with imperial bearing
> and a black ransacked raincoat)
> turned to us, cleared
> his cultural throat, and
> told us interminably
> who Ugo Betti was. The slow
> filtering of sun through windows
> glazed to gold the silky hair
> along your arms. Dusk was
> a huge weird phosphorescent beast
> dying slowly out across the bay.

One does not want to lean too heavily on the contrast between the raffish unhealthiness of the representative of discursive language and the bodily well-being of the couple, but it does color our perception of the bearded man. More important is the disconnect between his long discourse on Betti and the experience of his interlocutor, who attends not to the speech but to the physical world. The next few lines continue to stress the apparent emptiness of discursive language:

> Our house waited and our books,
> the skinny little soldiers on the shelves.
> After dinner I read one anyway.

The significance is in that last word, "anyway," which implies that the act of reading is essentially futile, the nature of language empty. It is very much a nominalist's "anyway." The poem ends with a further turn, in which discursive language becomes subordinate to the immediacies of the body:

> You chanted, "Ugo Betti has no bones,"
> and when I said, "The limits of my language
> are the limits of my world," you laughed.
> We spoke all night in tongues,
> in fingertips, in teeth.

The chanting of "Ugo Betti has no bones" is not only a farcical undoing of the bearded man's pedantic monologue on Betti. It is also an emptying out of the statement-content of language, because the chanted version of a statement, in emphasizing the formal qualities of sound, deemphasizes statement to the point where it becomes something other than a proposition with which one may agree or disagree.

The last two lines of the poem further enforce this dismissal of realism. The pun on tongues as both languages and parts of our bodies ultimately gives the primary meaning to the latter when "tongues" is put into the same category with fingertips and teeth. Discursive language becomes subordinate to the loss of self in the body of the other. And, driving the point home further, Hass invokes the idea of speaking in tongues, the inspired speech that surpasses our control or understanding—an ecstasy of linguistic nonmeaning.

"Letter," one of the last poems in *Field Guide*, can be read as a version of "Spring" steeped in negative capability: here, Hass explores the same themes in similar terms but defers the taking of any conclusive position. The poem begins with Hass's desire to speak to his wife about his recent experience of the world:

> I had wanted to begin
> by telling you I saw another
> tanager below the pond
> where I sat for half an hour
> feeding on wild berries
> in the little clearing near the pines

This desire, though, is thwarted. Language seems inadequate to experience, let alone to any larger understanding of experience:

> But I had the odd
> feeling, walking to the house
> to write this down, that I had left
> the birds and flowers in the field,
> rooted or feeding. They are not in my
> head, are not now on this page.
> It was strange to me, but I think
> their loss was your absence.

Language, in its abstractness and in the absence of an interlocutor, becomes empty and disembodied, a weightless thing floating above a world with which it cannot connect. This comes as a surprise to the speaker: "I have believed so long/in the magic of names and poems/I hadn't thought them bodiless/at all." In exchange for a bodiless language that cannot be sufficient, he turns to the body of his wife. Just as at the end of "Spring," where the body's tongue replaces the tongues we speak, the body displaces the insufficiencies of language:

> It all seemed real to me
> last week. Words. You are the body
> of my world, root and flower, the
> brightness and surprise of birds.
> I miss you, love. Tell Leif
> you're the names of things.

"Letter" seems at first to be another poem of nominalism, but the conclusion differs from that of "Spring" in two important ways. The first difference comes when Hass places his disillusion about language in time: "It all seemed real to me/last week. Words." The disillusion is presented as quite possibly temporary. The other difference comes in the final injunction to speak to Leif, Hass's son. Rather than ending with the body as in "Spring," we end with a return to speech, as if meaningful language were again possible after the word has become flesh. There is none of the finality of "Spring" here: nominalism is entertained as a possibility, and we feel what it is like to live in a nominalist moment, but there is no reaching for a final judgment about its validity.

One of Hass's more extended treatments of the question of whether language can be adequate to anything other than immediate impressions comes in "Maps." This poem, which consists of seventeen sections ranging in length from one to ten lines, seems at times like a small Imagist anthology. One gets a good sense of Imagist poetics at work from sections like these:

> Apricots—
> the downy buttock shape
> hard black sculpture of the limbs
> on Saratoga hillsides in the rain
>
> *
>
> Last summer—
> red berries darken the hawthorns
> curls of yellow in the laurels
>
> your body undulant
> sharp edges of the hills

Physical precision, the avoidance of abstraction, even (in "your body undulant/sharp edges of the hills") something of T. E. Hulme's visual chord—everything here comes out of the Imagist handbook that Winters would have burned as a black-hearted work of nominalist heresy. Another section of the poem, though, might meet with Winters' approval:

Musky fall—
slime of a saffron milkcap
the mottled amanita
delicate phallic toxic

The section seems concrete and descriptive enough, until the adjectives of the final line. It is not the use of adjectives *per se* that makes suspect the poem's Imagist credentials: it is the nature of the final one, "toxic," which is no longer a sense detail, but rather a judgment or analysis. If the realist believes in the validity of abstractions, and the need to make judgments in language along with impressions and descriptions, then "toxic" takes us closer to realism.

Where "Maps" really begins to find language sufficient to something larger than the presentation of physical particulars, though, is in a late section that begins with the incanting of California place names:

Chants, recitations:
Olema
Tamalpais Mariposa
Mendocino Sausalito San Rafael
Emigrant Gap
Donner Pass

Of all the laws
that bind us to the past
the names of things are the stubbornest

The names listed here "bind us to the past" with a stubbornness we may even wish to resist. There is no nominalism here, but a sense that words carry large meanings and deep historical resonances. "Maps" provides us with both realism and nominalism and lacks any conclusiveness. It juxtaposes Imagist elements with sections where language is trusted to signify beyond the immediate physical context, presenting us again with Wintersian issues without a Wintersian position-taking.

"Graveyard at Bolinas," like "Maps," finds in history a significance for language that goes beyond the nominalist realm of physical particulars, although here any such significance seems fleeting. As we wander through the graveyard, the tombstones with their carved names appear at first as mere objects:

> The markers are scattered like teeth
> or bones among wild violets
> and reedy onion grass:
> Eliab Streeter,
> Gamaliel St. John.
> At the end of their world
> these transplanted Yankees
> put down roots at last
> and give a sour fragrance to the air.

What is important here is the equation of the language-bearing stones and teeth or bones: we experience them as equivalents, and language shows little or no ability to take us beyond immediate physical particulars. In the lines that follow, though, the names on the stones bring us a vivid sense of history, taking us beyond the senses and the present: "Sarah Ransom,/all her days an upright wife," we read, or "Velorous Hodge,/done with the slaughtering of seals."

This sense of language as bearing a significance beyond the world of immediate sensation fades by the end of the poem, though:

> Afterwards I walked along the beach,
> remembering how the oldest markers,
> glazed by sea wind,
> were effaced, clean
> as driftwood, incurious
> as stone. The sun was on my neck.
> Some days it's not so hard to say
> the quick pulse of blood
> through living flesh
> is all there is.

The fading of language is quite literal; it is worn away from the stones by the elements. It cannot transcend its existence as a physical object in the world. Hass is led to a profoundly nominalist moment in which abstract categories or ideas or a sense of history are eclipsed by creaturely being, the pulse of blood and the sun on the neck. The moment, though, is exactly that: a moment. It is not a conclusion or anything approaching an orthodoxy or final position.

Praise, Hass's second book, continues to treat the theme of realism and nominalism, either remaining ambiguous or presenting us with contingent, momentary convictions rather than definitive stances. Two of the most celebrated poems from the volume—"Picking Blackberries with a Friend Who Has Been Reading Jacques Lacan" and "Meditation at Lagunitas"—raise doubts about the realist position without actually affirming the opposite position. "We have stopped talking//about *L'Histoire de la vérité*," we read in "Picking Blackberries," where discussion of "subject and object/and the mediation of desire" has ceased. As they let go of the abstractions about desire offered by language, Hass and his friend are overwhelmed by the immediate world and their desire for it:

> Our ear drums are stoppered
> in the bee-hum. And Charlie,
> laughing wonderfully,
>
> beard stained purple
> by the word *juice*,
> goes to get a bigger pot.

The substitution of physical immediacy for linguistic abstraction and the substitution of laughter for discursive speech argue for a nominalism here. The final stanza, though, is wonderfully ambiguous and polysemous: it is the word "juice," not juice itself, that stains Charlie's beard. Then again the poem does not return us to a discussion of desire: it ends with a rush to take in physical experience. Both immediate experience and the efficacy of language are upheld.

"Meditation at Lagunitas" arrives at a similar place, but instead of offering an overdetermined final image, it offers a contingent position.

It begins with a friend expounding the latest theoretical variation of the nominalist position. (Since the poem dates from the late 1970s, one may assume this to be some version of deconstruction.) He speaks with a voice containing "a thin wire of grief, a tone/almost querulous," apparently only begrudgingly accepting the new, nominalist thinking that Hass summarizes as being "about loss":

> In this it resembles all the old thinking.
> The idea, for example, that each particular erases
> the luminous clarity of a general idea. That the clown-
> faced woodpecker probing the dead sculpted trunk
> of that black birch is, by his presence,
> some tragic falling off from a first world
> of undivided light. Or the notion that,
> because there is in this world no one thing
> to which the bramble of *blackberry* corresponds,
> a word is elegy to what it signifies.

We do not long remain fallen away from the luminous world where word and thing correspond, though. Thinking first of a former lover, Hass then recalls other longed-for and absent things and is reminded of his lost childhood places, where:

> we caught the little orange-silver fish
> called *pumpkinseed*. It [the memory] hardly had to do with her.
> Longing, we say, because desire is full
> of endless distances.

First, we see Hass take up a physically immediate thing, a fish, and imply a kind of linguistic adequacy to the word that he and his child-hood friends assigned to it. Then he makes the same gesture about something abstract, the concept of longing. Whether his etymology is good or bad here is beside the point: what is important is that Hass implies that words can have some nonarbitrary relation to their referents, even if those referents are as abstract as the idea of longing. He takes us from the nominalism that opens the poem to a kind of linguistic realism.

The end of the poem acknowledges the contingent nature of this sense of realism. In the final lines, Hass articulates a powerful version of realism, but he stresses that any apprehension of that realism is momentary:

> There are moments when the body is as numinous
> as words, days that are the good flesh continuing.
> Such tenderness, those afternoons and evenings,
> saying *blackberry, blackberry, blackberry.*

"Numinous" is significant in this context, because in Hass's poem the *numen*, usually a presiding spirit of a particular place, informs words, not physical places. Here it is the physical world that aspires to the reality of words and the ideal Platonic realm of "undivided light." But this is a recognition seen only at particular moments, on certain specific days.

Human Wishes and *Sun under Wood*, Hass's third and fourth books, continue to treat the realist/nominalist question with negative capability, although it recedes in importance in the latter book. There the question appears in "Layover," which juxtaposes reified abstractions with concrete particulars; "Regalia for a Black Hat Dancer," which questions but does not discard the validity of abstract statements about "the heart's huge vacancy"; and "English: An Ode," in which the "craving" for "some pure idiomorphic dialect of the thing itself" is balanced against the historical freight carried by words. It also appears in "Interrupted Meditation," the poem that closes the volume, where Hass hears an unnamed character describe the beliefs of his friend Czeslaw Milosz in realist terms:

> *Milosz believes there is a Word*
> *at the end that explains. There is silence at the end,*
> *And it doesn't explain, it doesn't even ask.*

The familiar debate is laid out for us, with realism represented by Milosz, and with nominalism championed by our speaker (presented as a reader fond of quoting Edmond Jabès), for whom language is empty.

The poem remains dialogic in that it does not take sides in the conflict that it presents.

Perhaps we can attribute the relative unimportance of the realist/ nominalist question in *Sun under Wood* to the prominence of the question in *Human Wishes*, where Hass explores it in depth. In *Human Wishes*, for example, he not only inhabits the terms of the debate with negative capability, but he examines and ultimately defends that negative capability. We see this most clearly in "Spring Drawing," the prose poem that opens the volume. It begins with a crisis of signification, with a man unable to make a statement adequate to his experience of the vividly real world of concrete particulars:

> A man thinks *lilacs against white houses*, having seen them in the farm country south of Tacoma in April, and can't find his way to a sentence, a brushstroke carrying the energy of *brush* and *stroke*

One could imagine *"lilacs against white houses"* as a free-standing Imagist poem, but here that will not do: one wants a fuller statement, an understanding rather than a mere apprehending of the experience.

Unable to make a statement about experience, the man in the poem is forced to act as if the nominalist position were true, but the poem will not affirm this position, describing it in purely hypothetical terms. "As if" recurs as a refrain that continually reminds us of the contingent status of the nominalist position:

> As if the deer pellets in the pale grass and the wavering moon and the rondure—as they used to say, upping the ante—of heaven
>
> were admirable completely, but only as common nouns of a plainer intention, *moon, shit, sky,*
>
> as if spirit attended to plainness only, the more complicated forms exhausting it, tossed-off grapestems becoming crystal chandeliers,
>
> as if radiance were the meaning of meaning . . .

We act "as if" we believed in the radiance of things themselves, and the plain intentions of simple concrete words, says the poem, but we do so in particular moments, when we cannot find the way to make a fuller and more abstract statement about things.

"Spring Drawing" ends with a different use of the word "if," a use that makes a case for the kind of negative capability that Hass has practiced since *Field Guide*. He makes an analogy between the distance separating statement and world and the distance between two lovers after the woman turns her back on the man and begins to walk away. Linguistic displacement is envisioned as erotic displacement. Then Hass returns to the lovers:

> Only the force of the brushstroke keeps the lilacs from pathos—the hes and shes of the comedy may not get together, but if they are to get at all,
>
> then the interval created by *if,* to which mind and breath attend, nervous as the grazing animals the first brushes painted,
>
> has become habitable space, lived in beyond wishing.

Will the lovers come together? Here is another way of asking whether statement and world can coincide, whether language can carry the fullness of realism. Rather than reaching for an answer to the question, Hass looks at uncertainty itself as a kind of fulfillment: "The interval created by *if*"—the possibility of language's fullness and meaningfulness—becomes "habitable space, lived in beyond wishing."

Hass as Translator

Consider the following two passages of poetry translated by Hass:

> Apprentice's holiday:
> hops over kite string,
> keeps going.

*

Yet I belong to those who believe in *apokatastasis*.
That word that promises reverse movement,
Not the one that was set in *katastasis*,
And appears in Acts 3, 21.

It means: restoration. So believed St. Gregory of Nyssa,
Johannes Scotus Erigena, Ruysbroek and William Blake.

For me, therefore, everything has a double existence
Both in time and when time shall be no more.

The first passage is a haiku by Buson, the second a section from the
end of Milosz's "From the Rising of the Sun." Each represents a major
sphere of Hass's considerable activity as a translator—he has translated a number of Milosz' books, including the majority of the poems
in Milosz's *Collected Poems, 1931–1987*, and enough haiku to fill an anthology (*The Essential Haiku*). One could cite many differences between
the two passages, but the most important is that between the haiku's
poetics of image and Milosz's poetics of statement.

Hass certainly thinks of the difference between the passages in this
way. In his essay on "Images," he makes explicit the link between haiku
and Imagism, comparing Buson's haiku to the Imagism of William
Carlos Williams (*Twentieth Century Pleasures* 274). In another essay,
"Reading Milosz," he turns to the passage of "From the Rising of the
Sun" as a contrast to Williams's doctrine of "no ideas but in things"
where, à propos the lines above, he marvels that "this *is* an assertion. . . .
It is quite extraordinary to look at a poem that tells because it suspects it would be a profanation to try to show, asserts because it would
be impossible to embody" (*Twentieth Century Pleasures* 212). It appears
that Hass is drawn, as a translator, to works that connect with his own
concerns about image and statement. The two very different types of
poetry that he translates allow Hass to indulge quite separately in the
two kinds of poetics that are almost always held together in a dynamic
tension in his own work.

Another, related way of thinking about the two types of translations is to see them as Hass's means of poetic self-correction, a way of
balancing out any tendency to lean too far toward image or statement

himself. One certainly gets this impression when one reads Hass's account of encountering Milosz's work for the first time, when he was a student active in the antiwar movement at Stanford in 1966:

> My real teachers had been, for the most part, the American poets I was reading and studying, and I began to get a sense of just how radical the proposal of modernist poetics had been. No ideas, William Carlos Williams had insisted—but in things. And Ezra Pound had said that the natural object was *always* the adequate symbol. Pound's Fenellosa was the most extreme version of this because he called for a poetry built entirely from pictographs, as if no one had ever thought before and nothing needed to be thought that was not shot through with the energy of immediate observation. In practice, this meant that if one were to write about the antiwar demonstrations, the poem would likely end with an image: beyond the chemical plant, clouds of white gulls above the garbage dump. (*Twentieth Century Pleasures* 175–76)

The modernist tradition in which he had been immersing himself presented Hass with something of a moral quandary, being by itself inadequate to the needs of the moment. Milosz, among others, offered a way out:

> those images had a way of always throwing the weight of meaning back on the innocence and discovery of the observer . . . It made me feel vaguely ashamed when I saw it in the poems I was reading. I could not formulate the problem for myself very exactly, but I wanted to read a poetry by people who did not assume that the great drama in their work was that everything in the world was happening to them for the first time. So, during those years, like many other young Americans who were writing poetry or contemplating writing poetry, I began to read hungrily in translations of European and Latin American poets, and the same impulse sent me to [Milosz's] *The Captive Mind.* (176)

The Milosz alternative to image-based poetics was there when the radicalized Hass needed it most.

Milosz proved important to Hass for other reasons as well. He was not only relevant to Hass's Wintersian inheritance as a poet of statement who "told terrible truths . . . in the plainest of language" (*Twentieth Century Pleasures* 178), but he was also a poet who addressed the other great Wintersian theme, the relation of the self-contained intelligence to the physical world. Like Hass (who attended Catholic schools, a Catholic college, and who taught for almost twenty years at a Catholic institution), Milosz had a profoundly Catholic intellectual background. Hass picks up on this in describing Milosz's concerns with the world and the intellect:

> Milosz had had a Roman Catholic education. At the center of Christian thought in the West is the idea, or metaphor, of incarnation: through Christ, the divine had entered the world and created a bridge between matter and spirit, time and timelessness. The world was good and man could, therefore, approach the divine through the intermediary of the senses. It was possible for the mind of man to discern moral laws that underlie the universe, adapt itself to them and transcend time. (*Twentieth Century Pleasures* 194)

On occasion, Milosz follows this street until he arrives at an address not many doors down from that inhabited by the young Yvor Winters. In the second of *The Separate Notebooks*, for example, Milosz invokes the following passage by Schopenhauer, which Hass had singled out for commentary in his essay on Milosz:

> the quiet contemplation of the natural object actually present, whether a landscape, a tree, a mountain or a building, whatever it may be; in as much as he loses himself in the object, i.e., forgets even his individuality, his will, and only continues to exist as the pure subject, the clear mirror of the object, so that it is as if the object alone were there, without anyone to perceive it, and he can no longer separate the perceiver from the perception but both have become one, because the whole consciousness is filled and occupied with one single sensuous picture; if thus the object has to such an extent passed out of all relation to the will, then that which is known is no longer the particular thing as such; but it is the *Idea*, the eternal form, the objectivity of the will at this

grade; and, therefore, he who is sunk in this perception is no longer individual, for in such perception the individual has lost himself; but he is the pure, will-less, powerless, timeless subject of knowledge. (see *Twentieth Century Pleasures* 209)

Aha! you might shout, having untangled the Gordian knot of Schopenhauer's syntax. Isn't it a contradiction, holding up a passage like Schopenhauer's, yet writing what is largely a poetry of statement, rather than image? There is indeed something of this contradiction in Milosz, as Hass intuits when he writes that Milosz's "central preoccupation" is the question of whether "one should rescue being from the river of time by contemplating it or embracing it" (*Twentieth Century Pleasures* 206). The young Winters would embrace, the mature Winters would contemplate; Milosz hovers between these possibilities, and so does Hass.

With regard to the issue of the self's relation to the word, Milosz is, like Hass, a poet of negative capability. Many of Milosz's best poems, Hass says, "refuse to resolve themselves" (208). "Milosz no sooner invokes [the passage from Schopenhauer] than he answers it with a lyric" that takes the opposite view, writes Hass, "and the poem will not rest here either; it is pulled on . . . under the imperative of the need to suffer multiplicity of being, which is finally what is meant I think by dwelling in contradiction" (209). The poetry in which Milosz "comes to its full power" for Hass are the works that come after Milosz encountered Simone Weil, because "what Weil gave him . . . was crucial: the permission to dwell in contradiction" (200, 202).

Hass has been prolific and successful as a translator precisely because his translations, whether of Milosz or the Japanese haiku masters, plug directly into his most central concerns about image and statement, world and intellect, language and being. And Milosz has provided him with a model of a poetry capable of engaging such concerns with a Keatsian comfort in contradiction and uncertainty.

Paid on Both Sides

Michel Delville, in *The American Prose Poem*, writes Hass into the history of that genre on the grounds that "Spring Drawing" and the other prose poems of *Human Wishes* combine "two radically different ways of handling the poetic idiom"—the statement-based, personal, referential poetics that one finds in the prose poems of Stephen Berg; and the experimental, nonreferential, "flamboyant textual games" found in Amy Gerstler's *Bitter Angel* (246). That is, Hass merits inclusion in a standard history of the prose poem because he bridges the gulf between what we might call the realism of a Berg and the nominalism of a Gerstler. It is his agnostic Wintersianism that makes him a part of Delville's history. In its small way, Delville's inclusion of Hass is an act of canonization.

I mention Delville writing Hass into one of the standard histories of the prose poem here because when we look at the reception of Hass's work in the 1970s and 1980s, we see something similar happen in a variety of contexts. Again and again, Hass's agnostic Wintersianism allows him to straddle important divisions in the poetic field. In many cases, it even allows Hass to be claimed for competing critical agendas simultaneously. In the 1970s, for example, one of the main divisions in the poetic field was a version of the realist/nominalist conflict between statement and image. As Marjorie Perloff has described it, it was a division between "'Deep Image' or 'American Surrealist'" poetics on the one hand and "confessionalism" and "plain-talk bardic poetry" on the other (*The Dance of the Intellect* 156). Hass's persistent engagement with the issues relevant to this debate, combined with his negative capability regarding those issues, left him very well positioned to be praised by partisans of both sides.

Champions of Robert Hass, Imagist, include Linda Wagner, who praises *Field Guide* in the *Ontario Review* as "reminiscent . . . of the purist Imagists," with a concreteness and "loving emphasis on the very thinginess of his images" (89) that reminds one "only of the very best of Hemingway" (91). Not bad for a first collection, surpassing mere run-of-the-mill Hemingway to equal Papa's very best. Michael Waters is nearly as fulsome in his praise for the Imagist version of Hass. *Field Guide*, writes Waters in *Southwest Review*, is "one of the very best [books] to appear in a long time" (311). Its greatness derives from its images, its "perfect details of natural landscape" (308), and from the way that Hass's use of these images "suspends a sense of time, and the poet and his landscape become one" (309–10). Whatever its inaccuracies, this brand of appreciation for Hass was to continue right through the 1970s. Ira Sadoff, for example, in his review of *Praise* for the *Chicago Review*, reads such key poems as "Meditation at Lagunitas" as profoundly antiabstraction. "The poem proceeds to deconstruct and dismantle [the] abstract ideas . . . and to combat those ideas with moments of eternal pleasure," writes Sadoff (134), who goes on to tell us that *Praise* "might even be the strongest collection of poems to come out in the late seventies" (133).

Even as some critics set out to canonize Hass as a great imagistic poet, others praised him as a great poet of discursive statement. Robert Miklitsch tells readers of *The Hollins Critic* that *Praise* has forced him to "be blunt" and admit that the book "marks the emergence of a major American poet" (2). The best poems of the volume, the ones that mark Hass as a major poet for Miklitsch, are those "of discursive meditation" (13). Such discursive poems provide Miklitsch with a welcome contrast to *Field Guide*, where he finds that "particulars obstruct the rhythm of the poem and [result in] stasis—an inescapable condition of painting which every painter has to work against" (7). Hass, here, is the Imagist apostate, a prodigal son welcomed warmly back into the open arms of the church of discursive statement. Hass is welcomed, too, in the hallowed pages of the *New York Times Book Review*, where David Kalstone praises "Songs to Survive the Summer" for being "a larger tissue of inquiry" than most contemporary poets are capable of creating (15). Kalstone singles out the discursive and narrative elements of the poem, its "memories" and "tales," and finds some of the other discursive poems ("The Origin of Cities" and "Not Going to New York: A Letter") "particularly appealing" (43). Hayden Carruth joins the chorus of those happy to perceive a turn from image to statement in *Praise* when he writes in *Harper's* that the book is "a notable advance" over *Field Guide* and lauds it for discursive power, or for "what we—or our ancestors—used to call eloquence" (90).

Amid this cacophony of contradictory adulation, a few critics see Hass's position in the image/statement debate in more subtle terms. Peter Stitt, for example, takes the unusual position of recognizing the presence of Hass's imagistic qualities *and* his discursive qualities, and admires him for both. "In *Praise*," Stitt writes in *Poetry* (Chicago), "Robert Hass combines rather radically two complementary trends present in the progress of American poetry since the nineteenth century. In terms of imagery and statement, he is willing to include anything demanded by the poem" (229). A few years later, Alan Shapiro would look back on Hass's work of the 1970s and read it into the context of the realist/nominalist divide with a considerable degree of nuance (and, one might add, self-consciousness: Shapiro invokes the term "nominalism" in his discussion). In his *Chicago Review* article, Shapiro points to both Hass's discursive intelligence and his imagistic immediacies, but he finds the emphasis on images and sense-particulars problematic: "One of the strengths of Robert Hass' work is his great ability to describe the world around him. Yet much of his interest in description proceeds from a disturbing desire (which gets complicated in his later work) to live wholly in a world of sensory experience and from a concomitant distrust of intellectuality" (84). While Shapiro admires the "prose inclusiveness" he sees in some passages of Hass (89), he faults him for relying "principally on impression and the juxtaposition of fragmentary details (literary techniques associated with Imagist and post-Imagist practices)" (90). These mixed feelings do not keep Shapiro from praising Hass, though: instead, he envisions a possible future for Hass as a major poet, if he develops "a method of composition that is not so inextricably bound up with the intensity of the marginal and the momentary" (90). The fact that Hass's poetry holds realist and nominalist elements together makes possible this chorus of praise and hopeful appreciation, where Hass himself emerges as both the Imagist hero and discursivity's great poetic hope. Circumstances conspired to make him a kind of poetic double agent, paid on both sides of one of the great literary divides of the 1970s.

A Hero of the Theory Wars

Just as Hass's agnostic Wintersianism made it possible for both image-partisans and statement-partisans to claim him in the 1970s and early 1980s, it also enabled both of the opposing sides of another debate to claim him in the 1980s and 1990s. This was the debate between those who advocated that loose agglomeration of ideas that passed under the name of "theory" in Literature departments, and those who deplored such ideas. Hass's persistent and nuanced engagement with the question of language, and his negative capability regarding any answers to that question, once again allowed him to be praised from all sides. Perhaps ironically, in a period that saw the relative decline of poets' cultural capital compared to that of theorists, Robert Hass's reputation rose as a result of the theory wars.

The story of the theory wars is by now a familiar one: it tells of how, in the wake of the translation of Jacques Derrida's *Of Grammatology* appearing in 1976, the debate over deconstruction energized literary theory, generating a huge polemical literature both pro and con; of how the early 1980s saw the institutionalization of poststructural linguistic thinking; of how such institutionalization was accompanied by a nearly simultaneous backlash; of how in the late 1980s many humanists (in Gerald Graff's words) "decided that the literature department [could] right itself only if it desists from theoretical chatter" (254); of how the zeal of the insurgent theorists and the outrage of the recalcitrant humanists became, eventually, a story that ceased to grab headlines in *The Chronicle of Higher Education*; and of how, finally, we all learned to more or less get along in the faculty lounge again.

The tempests in the academic teacup would not have mattered much for poetry (or for Hass's reputation) had the academy not become what Christopher Beach calls "the major screening mechanism for the poetry culture," not only "the single most important source of cultural capital" but also "the single most important agent in legitimating that capital" (38). As Ron Silliman put it, "The primary institution of American poetry is the university. In addition to its own practices, it provides important mediation and legitimation functions for virtually every other social apparatus that relates publicly to the poem. . . . Regardless of what we may think of the situation, the university is the 500 pound gorilla at the party" (157). Silliman's gorilla, though, is a bit schizophrenic: the university, Silliman tells us, "is not a monolith, but rather an ensemble of competing and historically specific discourses and practices" (165). The canon that it creates is therefore also an "ensemble of socially competing discourses" (154). It is a sign of Hass's good fortune that the work he was producing could be championed by both the discourse of poststructural linguistic theory and the discourse of antitheoretical humanism. No matter what the mood of our schizophrenic gorilla may have been on any given day of the theory wars, one thing is certain: he liked to stretch out under the banana tree and read Robert Hass.

The poets who benefited most from the rise of theory were, of course, the language poets, whose efforts were championed by (and in many cases made intelligible through) the work of theorists such as Andrew Ross and Jerome McGann (see Silliman 164). But Hass's work was also praised for its perceived affinities with linguistic themes that had become *au courant.* Don Bogen, for example, finds Hass an important poet because he goes beyond mere description: "The mind behind the description is analytical, probing, unsatisfied with the conventional stances linguistics provides." In this view, "Hass' awareness of the limits of language helps fuel his restless exploration of different poetic strategies." Moreover, his courage and significance derive from how he "has never shied away from the language of theoretical discourse" (722). Hass, here, is the theorists' champion on the battlefield of poetry. Similarly, in Charles Altieri's *Self and Sensibility in Contemporary American Poetry,* he appears as the poet who complicates the meditative scenic mode of lyric poignancy with a fuller comprehension of linguistic slippage.

While Hass's work was esteemed by some for not shying away from theoretical discourse, others saw in it a heroic resistance to the rise of theory in the academy. Gunilla Florby, for example, writing in 1991, tells us that Hass is "strangely heroic" in his building of a bulwark against the "threatening inroads . . . [of] French poststructuralism" (189). Viewing "Meditation at Lagunitas" and "Picking Blackberries with a Friend Who Has Been Reading Jacques Lacan" as firm statements of the antitheory position, Florby heaps accolades on Hass for how he "thumbs his nose at post-structuralist notions of alienation" (194).

"The world looks almost to have invited us," says John Matthias in "On Rereading a Friend's First Book," a poem for Robert Hass. Matthias is talking about a great deal more than poets' reputations and the reception of their works, although he is talking about these things too. ("These poems discussed by all the critics now," he said à propos of Hass's work, "as if they had been written by a poet/dead a hundred years.") In Hass's case, at least, Matthias is dead on: Hass has had what has been described as a "charmed literary career" (Kellogg, "The *Pages of John Matthias and the Future of Critical Recognition*" 16). Hass's particular take on the Wintersian inheritance positioned him in such a way that he could be claimed by many constituencies in the decentered poetic field. The quality of his work is beyond question, but, unlike many other excellent poets, he has had the good fortune to appeal to the (sometimes opposing) forces shaping our literary world—the world that has most certainly welcomed him.

Chapter Five

John Matthias

Homing Poems

Applause in South Bend

It was fall in South Bend, Indiana, when Robert Pinsky appeared
at the University of Notre Dame to read from *The Figured Wheel*
and to discuss his new translation of Dante's *Inferno*. The year 1997
had been a good one for Pinsky, who had taken to his role as U.S.
Poet Laureate like a newly tenured professor takes to a sabbatical,
and he walked on stage to applause considerably more heartfelt
than the mere polite smattering given to most visiting poets. A
good portion of the applause was, no doubt, offered up in defer-
ence to the title of laureate, and a few further decibels were probably wrung from the heavily Catholic crowd at Notre Dame due
to a certain home-team feeling for the translator of Dante's great
Catholic epic. For a few members of the crowd, though (mostly
graduate students in the English Department), the applause was as
much in appreciation of the man who had introduced him as it was
a welcome for the laureate himself. That man was John Matthias,
Pinsky's classmate at Stanford and the senior poet on the faculty
at Notre Dame. After the reading, while Pinsky was being mobbed
by an appreciative crowd, some of those graduate students clus-
tered in a corner of the reception room and disparaged the famous
man, comparing him unfavorably to their own relatively unsung

poet. ("Graduate students of many years standing," the Canadian writer
David Arnason once observed, "speak only in easy insult" [102].) None
of the disparagers was among the authors of the articles soon to appear in *Word Play Place*, a collection of essays on the poetry of John
Matthias, but their somewhat prickly defensiveness about Matthias was
a sentiment not uncommon among the contributors to that volume, at
least in private conversation.

The scene in the theater after Pinsky's reading can be seen as em-
blematic of the different kinds of recognition that Matthias and Pinsky
receive. While Pinsky is valued by a fairly general readership by the
standards of American poetry at the turn of the twenty-first century,
Matthias's reception is in some ways similar to that of Yvor Winters.
Like Winters, Matthias has few readers; but like Winters' readers,
Matthias's support him with an uncommon intensity. It is significant in
this regard that despite Pinsky's considerable renown and his triple-
crown laureateship, there has yet to be a book dedicated to the study
of his poetry. Viewers of, say, PBS's *NewsHour with Jim Lehrer* may
be familiar with Pinsky as a commentator and deliverer of ceremonial
poems (as, for that matter, are viewers of *The Simpsons*, on which an
animated Pinsky once gave a reading of "Impossible to Tell"). But this
kind of recognition is as different in kind as it is in degree from the
devotion to Matthias shown by the writers of the essays of *Word Play
Place*, many of whom were once his students, just as Winters' primary
critics have been his former students. While Matthias would never
want to offer anything as doctrinaire as the later Winters' version of
literary history and morality, there is a certain intensity about his
readers: they do not enjoy his work so much as they believe in it. If
Pinsky has a broad-church following, based on an appreciative but
relatively casual engagement with his work by a great many readers,
then Matthias has a small band of passionate heretics, few in number
but producing a great deal of text and commentary per capita.

Why is there such a difference in the degree and kind of esteem
offered to Pinsky and Matthias? What differences in career, disposition, habitus, and poetics make for such different kinds of appreciation
as well as such different trajectories through the American poetic field?
To understand these differences, we should begin by looking at what
Pinsky, Matthias, Hass, and the other Stanford poets of their genera-

tion have in common. Jeremy Hooker gets to the heart of the matter when he writes:

> It seems to me that John Matthias and the American poets (all students of Yvor Winters) with whom he is most frequently associated, Robert Hass, James McMichael, John Peck, and Robert Pinsky, all feel the need both to create a covenant between word and world and to defend an idea of integral human personality. Consequently they all devise different poetic strategies to these ends, but without falling back on outworn notions of a correspondence between word and thing or a naively conceived ego. (110)

Hooker sees the mark of Winters on the brow of each poet-student. But the Wintersian concerns take significantly different shape in the work of Matthias than they do in either Hass or Pinsky, and an examination of the differences takes us a good way toward an understanding of the different kind of recognition that Matthias has received.

Unlike Pinsky and Hass, Matthias interpolates both the self and language into history in order to find them meaningful. That is, he finds the integrity of the word not through any affirmation of the inherent meaningfulness of words or abstractions (realism, in Winters' sense) but through a powerful invocation of their historical origin and efficacy. He finds, too, an integrity of the self, but not through any policing of its boundaries, as Winters does in "At the San Francisco Airport." Rather, he finds the self to be the product of history, and the authentic self to be the self-aware agent who acts from within a history that he or she has come to understand. The self is real, for Matthias, and language is meaningful, but neither is understandable without a working-through of the textual and historical contexts in which they are interpolated.

The abiding interest in history on Matthias's part is sometimes casually attributed to the influence of Ezra Pound, an observation not without some measure of truth. But to understand Matthias too thoroughly through Pound is to misunderstand him and to kidnap him from the contexts that give his work meaning. Matthias's real context, as it is for any poet, is the confluence of his own time, place, and circumstances. In Matthias's case, the times to begin with are the 1960s and 1970s; the places, America and England; and the circumstances, a profound alienation and a deeply disillusioned radicalism. It is the convergence of these things that compelled Matthias to choose what I call a poetics of interpolation, and it is, to a large degree, this choice that makes him both obscure within, and important for, American poetry. The grumbling graduate students in South Bend may, I think, have been on to something.

"This World Did Not Invite Us": The Habit of Alienation

John, I am dull from
thinking of your pain,
this mimic world

which makes us stupid
with the totem griefs
we hope will give us

power to look at trees,
at stones, one brute to another
like poems on a page.

What can I say, my friend?
There are tricks of animal grace,
poems in the mind

we survive on. It isn't much.
You are 4,000 miles away &
this world did not invite us.

So ends "Letter to a Poet," Robert Hass's poem to John Matthias. The poem was included in *Field Guide* but written in 1966, when both Hass and Matthias were in the graduate program at Stanford and Matthias had, in the wake of a divorce, gone to England on a Fulbright. What is interesting about the poem is the way it reveals the contrasting dispositions of the two poets. Hass appears as the consoler, mindful of the "tricks of animal grace" that can sustain us. He is very much the poet whom Stanley Kunitz was to describe a few years later as a man who "sits easy in his skin" ("Foreword" xvii). The Matthias we see in the poem is displaced, expatriate, pained, looking for a way to be sustained—in a word, alienated.

If this was true of Matthias in the late 1960s, then it was to become even more true of him over the decade or so that followed. His poetry of the period is filled with characters uprooted from their proper contexts and removed to places alien to their dispositions. "Bakunin in Italy," "Alexander Kerensky at Stanford," "Zurich to London, Tzara to Trotsky": one need look no further than the titles of Matthias's poems from the 1970s to see that displacement and alienation rank high among his concerns. His peripatetic life in that decade also indicates a certain restlessness and alienation from his own time, place, and circumstances. He spent several years in England and returned there almost every summer "seeking refuge," as he put it, from an America seen as violent, unmanageable, and impossible to love (*Reading Old Friends* 53).

The roots of Matthias's alienation run deep, and we can find them even in his adolescence. One incident from the summer of his senior year at Ohio State University just before he left for Stanford is particularly important in that it graphically foreshadows the form that his early poetry of radical liberation was to take. That summer, Matthias found himself, through his family's political connections, working in the State of Ohio's Auditor's Office typing up report after report in a painstakingly precise format, until one day he decided to insert a line of Wallace Stevens' poetry into one of the reports. No one seemed to notice, so he began to insert longer and longer passages of Stevens, and eventually whole poems, into the precisely delineated tabs and margins of a State of Ohio auditor's report. None of this was uncovered until his reports had consisted of nothing but Stevens for some time. The playful manipulation of the language of state power was not just an act of adolescent rebellion by an alienated kid in a stuffy office in Columbus; it was also an early articulation of the poetics that would inform the most important poems of *Bucyrus*, Matthias's first and most politically radical volume of verse.

So when Matthias arrived at Stanford in 1963, he had already formed a habitus of alienation: alienation from his family and from conservative politics, the two being inextricably linked (his Republican father sat on Ohio's Supreme Court). Almost to a poem his early works demonstrate an alienation that the political tenor of the era could only exacerbate. As Michael Anania said of the poems that the young Matthias submitted to him at Swallow Press, "they treat always a disjunctive breach between affection and the exigent world" ("John Matthias' *Bucyrus*" 22). Some of the poems work out their alienation fairly conventionally, as in "Chicago: The Cops" (where the alienation is political), or "Triptych" (where the alienation is romantic, stemming from the end of Matthias's first marriage). In "Triptych," as in many of his poems, Matthias presents the act of artistic creation as an ambiguous liberation from alienation:

> He doesn't sleep. He sits.
> He looks around.
> Afraid of quiet, bits
> Of dust and sound,
> He doesn't sleep. He sits.
> And looks around.
> He was in love, he thinks.
> He cannot smile.
> He reads his early poems
> To learn his style.
> He doesn't write. He was
> In love. He thinks.
> He scribbles at a pad
> With colored inks.

The artistic act is a kind of therapy for the dispossessed, although its efficacy remains ambiguous. The same sort of thing can be said of "Independence between Christmas and New Year's Day," an antiwar poem written at Stanford in 1966:

> Sixty-six in the year
> of our war and on earth peace
> bad winter weather. . . .
> This, among the dishes seen:

Daily news. Also, a faustian fox
of a fellow, fed:
    Below the eye
A time of adjustments.
In broken Asia, blood.
"In a cosy room
I'll paint my
beard a regal
blue for the sake
of delight . . . no hand
of mine will end, my
love, my warrior brother,
War . . ."
"Is the weather wrong?
Am I scribbled out?
Season of hibernation forced,
A time for the painting of beards!"

The political weather was certainly wrong that year, and the poet out
of step with his times. But what to make of this painting of beards?
Something must be done in the face of historical wrongs, but Matthias
knows too well that "no hand of mine will end . . . War." The artistic
act comes from political alienation, but its effectiveness here, as in many
of Matthias's short poems of the period, is deeply suspect. It was only
when he began to realize the potential of the method of textual intervention that he had stumbled on in the Auditor's Office that he creates
a poetics in which art takes on the aspect of a true political and personal liberation.

Poetics of Liberation

Between Matthias's earliest poetic efforts and his mature work of historical and linguistic interpolation lies an intermediate body of work
made up of the longer poems of his first book of poems, *Bucyrus*. In
these poems a heroic figure intervenes in a situation of repression (political or otherwise) and, through a kind of verbal or artistic virtuosity,

reshapes the oppressive discourses of power. Call it a poetics of liberation. Or call it the poetics of a radical's hopes in a season that ever-so-briefly seemed to hold out, in Matthias's words, "millennial expectations" (*Reading Old Friends* 41).

Here is the ending of the long prose-poem "Statement," which depicts Henri Gaudier-Brzeska, the sculptor and friend of Ezra Pound, jailed by the powers that be:

> So then Gaudier. Gaudier choosing craft and consciousness, choosing freedom. So then Gaudier—Gaudier refusing to be enslaved by refusing to know, Gaudier refusing imprisonment. But they tried, the governments and their jailors, the governments and their jailors unconscious and therefore unfree, to jail, in the war, this conscious spirit, this Gaudier. But Gaudier loved freedom, and because he loved freedom he learned craft. Because he loved freedom he learned craft so perfectly that he became a craftsman of genius. And his medium was stone. Stone were the jails of the governments and the jailors. Stone was his medium—a genius with exquisite perfectly trained controlled and controlling hands. Free hands. Free because they knew their craft. Jails, Penitentiaries, Sanatoriums, all made out of stone. Stone walls, many feet thick. Stone jails, Jail-thick stone walls where they put him, craftsman and free, they—the governments making their wars.

> Minutes after they threw him there in his cell, minutes after they locked him in that cage of stone, Gaudier, Pound's friend the vorticist, took, with his bare hands, an eight-foot-thick wall apart and went home.

The confining stone is not just stone, here: it is the repressive instrument of state power, the discourse of the jailors and the war-making governments. Like any discourse, it is most powerful where it is accepted least critically: it affects those who are "unconscious" but not the free and conscious Gaudier, who liberates himself by re-shaping it. As Anania puts it, "Matthias means Gaudier's 'statement' to be understood as his own, as well. Language is the poet's medium, as obdurately textured and compacted as granite. Like stone, also, it is confining." Anania continues, pointing to stone's symbolic value as "the basic material of the confinements of family, culture, and the state"

("John Matthias' *Bucyrus*" 21). The very fact that discourse appears to Matthias as repressive, rather than as a comforting home for subjectivity, is itself a sign of his alienation. And the fact that discourse can be reshaped by the conscious and skilled individual can be taken as a sign of his radical hopes and his millennial expectations. Bliss was it in that dawn to be alive.

Where "Statement" treats repressive discourse by picturing it as stone, "Bucyrus" and "Poem in Three Parts" take up the subject of repressive discourse as language. Both poems hold out the strong hope that we can be liberated from discourses of repression by intervening in and mastering them. Alienated yet hopeful, they bear the marks both of Matthias's habitus and his circumstances during a brief window of radical hope. With their faith in the liberating force of imaginative interventions in the discourse of power they bear, too, the recognizable mark of the young man who reworked State of Ohio auditor's reports into the poetry of Wallace Stevens.

In 1995, when Swallow Press republished "Bucyrus" as part of *Beltane at Aphelion: Collected Longer Poems*, it bore the dedication "For a Class of 1968." That inscription underlined the importance of the prose poem's era to its politics of liberation and hope. In "Bucyrus," these politics take place in a very odd imaginative context, a tale about three aunts who keep prisoner two sixteen-year-olds in their house and force them to recite by rote the tenets of Dianetics, the puritanical theology of Richard Baxter, and, of all things, the rules of Anglo-Saxon grammar. The aunts seek to keep pure a story they relate about their father, Bucyrus, whose disembodied spirit still haunts the house. In the aunts' story, Bucyrus, a middle-aged virgin of set habits, was the victim of Becky, a waitress who invaded his house, cooked for him, raped him nightly, and bore him three daughters before being banished. If Ada and Aben (the adolescents in the aunts' charge) deviate from this story in retelling it, they are punished, as they are if they fail in reciting the rules of Anglo-Saxon grammar or the tenets of Baxter and L. Ron Hubbard. The opening lines give a sample of the poem's unusual texture:

> "Don't do that," said Aunt Ooney.
> "Don't do that," said Aunt Olley.

"Don't do that," said Aunt Oam.

Don't do what? asked the midnight darkness pierced by Olley's flashlight beam. *And why not do it?* asked Bucyrus, dead Bucyrus, uncle of drawn curtains and tar-papered windows. *And why not do it, Aunts?*

"Your law forbids," said Oam.

"And Baxter rests," Olley whispered. "He rests everlastingly."

"As dianetical truth reveals, " added Ooney. "As truth reveals."

But don't do what? asked Bucyrus through the night again. *Tell me Aunts of shadows.*

"Thou shalt not copulate upon the floor at midnight," they all sang. "Up, Aben, Up, Ada. Get up. Thou shalt do thy Anglo-Saxon Grammar."

Outside of this closed world of incanted discourse—a discipline "both arbitrary and mysterious, so . . . exactly suited to tyrannical authority" (Anania, "John Matthias' *Bucyrus*" 23)—there hovers an unknown force, threatening to break into the closed system. This manifests itself via a refrain running through the poem: "Here, there was an insistent, violent knocking at the door." The refrain appears more and more frequently toward the end, its source unknown, although the return of the exiled Becky or of a possible fourth aunt is suggested.

As in "Statement," though, liberation comes from within the system, not from without. The agent of liberation will be Ada, the cause will be a change in consciousness, and the means will be an intervention into the discourse of power. Ada simply refuses to believe that Becky raped Bucyrus, choosing instead to say that Becky was his willing lover, and he, hers. Any revision in ritual or narrative is, of course, resisted by the aunts, who punish Ada:

"And so [said Ada] . . . Anglo-Saxon grammar changed when Aben asked me for a difficult declension. I knew it, I gave it to him, and he kissed me for the gift. That's when Ooney came with therapy, she said, to restore the worship of our discipline. Olley came with her, bringing Baxter's prayer books, and she took Aben from the room. Ooney asked me to recite some fifteen paradigms, which I did. Then she told me to relax and to imagine Aben's face in front of me. She told me I should spit in Aben's face and when I refused, she spat in mine. She told me again to spit in Aben's face and then I did. Ooney gave me two heavy texts to hold—a dictionary and a lexicon. I held them at arms' length, with weary arms, and she told me I should imagine Becky's face in front of me and spit in Becky's face. I didn't do it, but she didn't spit in mine this time. Instead she took off all my clothes, and while with weary arms I held a lexicon and a dictionary in the air as though my hands were nailed to a cross, she kissed me in three places, here and here and here. I wish Aben were allowed to kiss me there, but Aben, who told me so himself at midnight, had to kiss Aunt Olley while he recited grammar and while she repeated Baxter's prayers."

A cult-like act of imaginative reprogramming in the name of therapy: Michel Foucault, one thinks, would approve of the depiction. A Christ-like martyrdom, not to the political power of Rome but to the discursive power of a language system used only for control: Noam Chomsky would have liked this. And a perversion of eroticism by the repressive forces of power: Herbert Marcuse, whose *Eros and Civilization* was enjoying its paperback vogue, would have been pleased. The poem certainly earns its dedication to the generation of 1968. And it ends hopefully too, with Ada denying the aunt's version of events and swaying the timid Aben to her side, even as the walls shake with an insistent pounding from outside. Millennial hopes of radical liberation flash before us.

"Poem in Three Parts" follows a slightly different pattern of liberation through discursive intervention. Where "Statement" and "Bucyrus" show us heroic figures intervening in the discourses of power and through intervention ending them, "Poem in Three Parts" works by revealing to its readers the nature of repressive discourse. We see no hero here, but are given insights that imply that we ourselves can become heroes of discursive liberation. The insights are best characterized in terms spelled out by Claude Lévi-Strauss in his *Structural Anthropology*. Here, Lévi-Strauss makes a distinction between normal thinking and pathological thinking, and he describes the traditional shaman's role as a socially necessary intermediary between the two modes of thought:

In a universe which it strives to understand but whose dynamics it cannot fully control, normal thought continually seeks the meaning of things which refuse to reveal their significance. So-called pathological thought, on the other hand, overflows with emotional interpretations and overtones, in order to supplement an otherwise deficient reality. . . . We might borrow from linguistics and say that so-called normal thought always suffers from a deficit of meaning, whereas so-called pathological thought (in at least some of its manifestations) disposes of a plethora of meaning. Through collective participation in shamanistic curing, a balance is established between these two complementary situations. (181)

Societies, in this view, will tend to create "stable fabulations" (Anania, "John Matthias' *Bucyrus*" 25) in which our excess anxieties are attached to somewhat arbitrary objects or beings in the world. One might describe these fabulations as ideologies. In "Poem in Three Parts," Matthias takes instances from several such ideological formations and puts them side by side in a kind of archaeological layering, to expose their artificiality and thereby show that they can be changed.

The three parts of the poem's title take up sixteenth-century witchcraft trials and the Cold War arms race in the first; alchemy in the second; and the Bogue Banks trials (in which the claims of traditional and legal rights to land ownership were decided) in the third. The unlikely pairing of topics in the first part serves to underline the pathological nature of the reasoning of both the witch trials and the arms race. It begins by quoting found texts from the testimony of those involved in witchcraft. This highly erotic testimony reveals that the imagined or half-imagined rituals of devil-summoning serve as an outlet for the unresolved sexual energies and anxieties of the women involved. They suffer, our narrator tells us, from:

Boredom? mainly.
(white monastic walls—daughters were immured
and mortified)
boredom, mainly
leaden ennui
languid dreary melancholy days.

In a society that inadequately recognized female sexuality, that sexuality sought something to which it could attach itself—the something, in this case, being witchcraft.

In contrast to the witchcraft itself, the legal discourse of the trials seems at first to be what Lévi-Strauss would call normal thought: an inquiry to understand the meaning of a poorly understood phenomenon. The language of reasonableness and patient inquiry, though, soon changes into something every bit as pathological as the discourse of witchcraft itself. The investigators attempt to order, record, and control anxieties about female sexuality, while at the same time exploiting and abusing it within the containing form of an investigation. The shamanistic mediation of which Lévi-Strauss writes comes to pass in the union of normal thinking (the act of investigation) and pathological thinking (the need to attach anxieties about female sexuality to something concrete). Then, quite suddenly, the poem shifts, and we are in the modern world, working through found texts from another context: reports of Cold War-era congressional hearings:

> The army told congressmen yesterday it has enough of a single nerve gas in its chemical biological warfare arsenal to kill the world's population many times over. But Russia, one lawmaker reported, may harbor an even more lethal capability in this little discussed and highly secret field. The substance is labeled by the army "G.B." and the world's population is estimated at around 3.4 billion. Rep. Robert L. F. Sikes, D.-Fla., said he thinks the U.S. is not doing enough in this field. Sikes said it is estimated the Russians have "seven to eight times" the capability of the United States. The U.S. has enough "G.B." to kill the world's estimated population about 30 times. Russia, on the other hand, has enough to kill the world's estimated population,

> say

> 160 to 190 times.

Like the witchcraft trials, the congressional hearings show a shamanistic mixing of normal and pathological discourse. While cast in the form of a rational inquiry, the procedures become a venue in which

pathological anxieties about a hostile other attach themselves to something concrete: the quantity of available "G.B." By laying the witch
trials and congressional hearings side by side, Matthias shows how
one is no more rational than the other. The second and third parts of
the poem, which show both alchemy and the legal system as pathological discourses, repeat the process. We see pathologies clearly by
seeing them laid side by side, so we can hope to escape them. "Poem in
Three Parts," though, was to be the last strong manifestation of this
radical optimism in Matthias's work. In the context of doubt, fear, and
emotional exhaustion that followed the Democratic National Convention in Chicago in 1968, Matthias' millennial hopes, like those of so
many others, died.

"I See America Closing In on My Friends"

Many of the poems in Matthias's second book of poetry, *Turns*, express disillusion, hopelessness, and political paranoia. Some also reflect
a loss of faith in linguistic mastery as a means of radical liberation.
Whereas language once appeared to Matthias as the means of social
liberation, there were moments in the early 1970s when it seemed
empty to the point of meaninglessness.

Gassed by Mayor Richard Daley's rioting policemen at the Chicago
Democratic Convention and forced to watch them viciously beat the
students he had brought with him, Matthias was understandably
shaken. The first and last stanzas of "Halfdream after Mandelstam:
Who Spoke of the Language Itself" capture his fear and lack of hope:

> I see America closing in on my friends.
> Once I was angry; once I protested in poems.
> Mandelstam: May 13, 1934: I see
> The Kremlin's mountaineer in America.
> . . . .
> They will murder us, simply.
> They have been elected to do it.
> There is no motivation at all.
> Our documents are simple and in order.

The radical's hopes have been replaced by alienation, not just from the police who sought to "preserve the existing disorder" (in Mayor Daley's unforgettable phrase) but also from the nation as a whole. In "Three Around a Revolution," Matthias's sense of linguistic mastery as a means to liberation falls apart. After meditating on the fate of the failed revolutionaries Babeuf (in France) and Gracchus (in Rome), Matthias offers an image of himself as a political speaker for whom the language of liberation goes suddenly wrong:

> There must be lawsuits. There must, moreover
>
> And eventually, be justice. There must be words.
> I write down words. Are we lost in our names?
>
> Yesterday I spoke for hours and nobody stirred.
> Rapt. They cheered. I am a hero.
>
> I said words like *action, money, love, rights*
> And was moved to elegance, alliteration,
>
> Saying, apropos of what I did not know,
> *Palfrey, palindrome, pailing, palinode, palisade.*

"If poetic art begins this passage as a language of the new social compact," writes Vincent Sherry, then "that compact is subverted in the last line: words as weapons of class warfare have been sold out" (27). The potentially transformative words of radical politics have been replaced by a string of words chosen for their alliterative qualities rather than their political import: a kind of aesthetic betrayal of politics. Sherry goes on to point out that radical politics are replaced by "emblems and implements of an antique martial aristocracy, a foregone order invoked by a language out of key with our time but rhyming with itself and with the poet's delight in the repeated sound" (27). Even "palindrome" and "palinode" connote counterrevolution: a palindrome goes forward by going back, and a palinode is a formal retraction (Sherry 27–28). Not only does liberation face resistance from without, as it does in poems such as "Halfdream after Mandelstam," but it also faces corruption from within, as its leaders forget the motives for their actions and, high on the applause of the crowds, speak from impure motives and to dubious ends.

Homing Poems

"'I must have savagery,' a wealthy British/poet told me, leaving for the States," wrote Matthias in "For John, After His Visit: Suffolk, Fall." America harbored savagery enough for any aristocrat looking to go barbarously native, but Matthias could not relish it and went the other way across the Atlantic. His turn to England, and to a new poetics inspired by English modernism, would save him from alienation and lead him down paths to both obscurity and importance.

Here is the first section of "Homing Poem," from *Turns*, written while Matthias was in England:

An acre, a rod,
and eleven
perches of land

The stone walls
The thirteen towers

And all tithes
& corn & hemp & flax

The stone walls
The thirteen towers

The second and final section then reproduces this first section word for word. The repetition shows a kind of willful insistence on owning and belonging to the place. This is a poem for a detached man in an alienating time, not at home but "homing," willing himself toward a sense of belonging. It is significant that the place is clearly English rather than a part of the America that Matthias saw "closing in on [his] friends." The archaic features of the landscape appear here as consolations, as signs of the rooted and the established. This homing sentiment occurs in many of the poems of *Turns*. Here, Matthias turns away from radical hopes of political change and seeks an inner transformation that will allow him to live in an unreformed world. British places, British Romanticism, and, most important, British modernist poetry would all prove essential for his quest for a home in the world and in discourse.

Matthias's fortunate situation in a Suffolk house suffused with history did much to calm his American anxieties. "A rambling house pieced together by joining three Elizabethan cottages made of mud and horse hair," the house in the village of Hacheson in East Anglia became, in Matthias's words, "as numinous for me as Howards End for Margaret Schlegel." Settling here amid the visible past, he "slowly opened [himself] to the full geological, topographical, natural, historical, and social context of the region" (*Reading Old Friends* 47).

Matthias's home-making in Suffolk was made possible in no small measure by his reading of Wordsworth. He reached for the great Romantic "as one might reach for the right medicine in the medicine chest" (*Reading Old Friends* 41), remembering what Wordsworth had done to restore the spirits of both John Stuart Mill and Matthew Arnold. Every writer reads a different Wordsworth, and Matthias's version is in many ways a doppelgänger of Matthias himself: a disillusioned radical looking to regain his balance by settling in a particular place. Matthias senses this when he writes, in "Places and Poems":

It's not that I exactly abandoned "present objects, and the busy dance/Of things that pass away" for "a temperate show/Of Objects that endure" by turning to Wordsworth at this time, and eventually he led me neither to a Natural Supernaturalism, nor a Via Naturalitar Negativa, nor a Burkean Second Nature, nor an Established Church, but simply to a place—and not *his* place either, but a place of my own. Perhaps I misread him . . . In any case, [I turned] in my postactivist consternation first tentatively to standard anthology pieces and then in earnest to "Home at Grasmere" and *The Prelude* for whatever therapy they could provide. (*Reading Old Friends* 42)

If Matthias's reading of Wordsworth helped him to "cas[t] off a persona from the late 60s" (*Reading Old Friends* 42), it was the discovery of British experimental poetry that gave shape to his new sense of self and place. He had first encountered this tradition when he was in London on his 1966 Fulbright, arriving just in time for the Fulcrum edition of Basil Bunting's *Briggflatts* and for the conversation about David Jones and other neglected British modernists in the pages of *Agenda.* Having been told by Donald Davie that there was no indigenous British modernism, Matthias delved deeply into the very tradition that Davie had denied existed, editing *23 Modern British Poets* as a wake-up call to those who felt that, in poetry, "'British means *old* or *tired* . . . Philip Larkin rather than Tom Raworth" (*23 Modern British Poets* ix).

"Matthias," says Jeremy Hooker, "is one of the few . . . on either side of the Atlantic to show an appreciation of the modernist tradition in postwar British poetry" (107), a tradition that builds on the works of Bunting and Jones and includes such poets as Roy Fisher and Jeremy Prynne. What these poets have in common, besides their interest in formal innovation, is a concern with the particular context of the poet in geography and history. This, Romana Huk tells us, is what separates them from their peers in postwar American experimental poetry for whom the emphasis lies more on linguistic disruption than on the locatedness of the poetic subject (118). The British experimental tradition promised a poetics of location for the dislocated American poet.

The most overt use of the British experimental tradition in *Turns* comes in what David Jones scholar Kathleen Henderson Staudt has called Matthias's "Jonesian discipline of 'digging down' through the strata of place and history as a way of situating the modern poet's own experience" (155). Matthias used the archaeological poetics of Jones and his peers to great effect in situating himself, most notably in "Epilogue from a New Home."

This poem, written in 1972, places Matthias's experience in the context of the history of the place from which he writes. He peels back the archaeological layers until past and present become interfused:

> There's a plague pit
> just to the edge of the village.
> Above it, now mostly covered with grass,

    a runway for B-17s: (American
  Pilots back from industrial targets). Tribes
    gathered under my window;
  They'd sack an imperial town: I'll wave
    to my wife at the end of the Roman road.

We can view the final image in two ways at once: the sight of his wife on a Roman road could be the sight of her on a newly built road at the edge of the Roman Empire. Then again, it could be a more literal image of his wife in the present, standing on an ancient road that has endured. The correct interpretation is undecidable, and we are left having to suspend any clear distinction of past and present.

As the poem continues, we see it register Matthias's "postactivist consternation." Considering the town's medieval plague pit, he says:

  Enclosed within a boundary of stones
    they died in isolation. All of us have
  Colds; we visit the parish church and read: "Names.
    The numbers of persons who died of bubonic plague."
  Grey-stone cottages across the road,
    a stream at the end of the church-yard,
  Giant harvesters working the mechanized farms. . . .

  Yesterday I walked to see the black,
    malignant huts that held the bombs.
  After the war, nobody tore them down. Some
    are full of hay. Mechanics counted, standing
  There, the number of planes that returned.

The very fact that "the war" here could only refer to the Second World War, while in the San Francisco Bay Area of the early 1970s those two words could only refer to Vietnam, is significant. It is a sign that the immediacy of the crisis that had so alienated and disillusioned Matthias is fading for him in his new context. The juxtaposition of the bomb huts of the 1940s with the plague pit of the fourteenth century also helps to put current crises in context. Both war and plague had their counters enumerating the dead (churchmen in the plague, mechanics in the war); both have left their monuments on the landscape. And Matthias, as a war protestor and as a sick man with a sick family, feels his connection to both tragedies. But neither tragedy is immediate, and Suffolk has endured both of them: the perspective of history opens up, and present crises no longer appear with the same urgency. Detachment, it seems, is a close cousin of historical consciousness.

The parallels between past and present here resemble those we see in much modernist writing, but only to a point. Hugh Kenner described the modernist sense of history as one of synchronicity. In poems such as Pound's, Kenner claimed, "no felt continuum reached back to [figures from the distant past], with dimming aerial perspective, as it did for instance in the age the Pre-Raphaelites favored. Time folded over; *now* lay flat, transparent, upon *not-now*. . . . Nor would any evolutionary curve pass through them" (*The Pound Era* 30). There is some of this sense of synchronicity in Matthias, derived for the most part from the work of David Jones, of whom Anania writes:

> Jones is aware of the resonance of place in the significant past . . . it is a part of the synchronistic present. This sense of synchrony is part of Jones' Christianity, in which all time is present in the eyes of God. . . . For example, when a soldier falls in Jones, and his helmet falls down over his face, Jones associates that with the vision of the visor worn by knights at war over the same ground long ago. The excitations in Jones' poetry are excitations of those things that are deeply embedded in place—as are the excitations in Matthias' poetry. ("Talking John Matthias" 4)

This is spot-on about Jones, and also about the shared source of the excitements in Jones and Matthias in the concern with the archaeology of place. But Matthias differs from Jones in the sense of the timeless, of the identity of *now* and *then* in the eyes of eternity. For Matthias, there are significant rhymes between different historical moments, but these do not open out into a sense of the eternal. Rather, they stress the continual turbulence of history. One effect of this view of history, as filled with ruptures and moments of tragedy, is to transform any apparent millennial aspect of the present into something more ordinary, something precedented rather than singular. We feel we have been here before.

Detachment from the sense of crisis, and from the language of protest and activism, was exactly what Matthias needed if he was to regain
his sense of balance and well-being after the political disappointments
of the late 1960s and early 1970s. In "East Anglian Poem," which sits
next to "Epilogue from a New Home" in *Turns*, Matthias strives to teach
himself just such a detachment. His method will be the archaeological
poetics of the British experimental tradition. The first of the poem's
six sections catalogs the artifacts left in the Suffolk soil from the period
when the Romans began to displace local tribal leaders. These "Materials of Bronze and Iron" are both ceremonial and martial in nature:

> linch-pins and chariot wheels, nave-bands
> and terret-rings: harness mounts, fittings, and
> bridle bits: also a sword, an axe: also a
> golden torc.

The second section depicts the people who created these artifacts as
well as the social and political relations and anxieties of the tribe and
its different classes:

> They herded oxen and sheep They hunted the deer
> They made a simple pottery, spun yarn They scratched
> in the earth to little effect
> > They were afraid
>
> > of him
> here, with his armor
>
> > thigh and skull unearthed
> > > beside the jawbone of his horse
>
> Afraid of him who
> > feared these others, Belgae,
> speaking Celtic too, but building oppida, advancing,
> turning sod with coulters and with broad-bladed ploughs.
>
> > (Caesar thought them civilized—
> > > which meant familiar

They minted coins

They made war on a sophisticated scale)

Class divisions, difficult economic conditions, international power politics, the great arrogance of power—these are just the kinds of concerns
that had occupied the young radical poet of *Bucyrus*. They are also the
same obsessive concerns that Matthias describes as having exhausted
him in the years after *Bucyrus*. But here they no longer present themselves as urgent crises: the archaeologist's detachment allows Matthias
to consider them dispassionately. This is not to say that the perspective is apolitical, but rather that it becomes more nuanced. The civilization he reconstructs from history and artifacts appears to him not
merely one of oppressive, warlike barbarism. On the contrary: its artifacts manifest both its civilization and its barbarity, its aesthetic and
spiritual aspirations as well as its political conditions. Moreover, the
relative detachment of the historical perspective implies a sense of the
present crisis as merely one among many.

The third section of "East Anglian Poem" elaborates these themes.
It begins with the arrival of the Romans and their mercenaries, who
displace the existing tribal order. The unnamed tribal leader we encountered in the second section witnesses this arrival:

He saw them on parade:

> their elegant horses, their leathers
> studded with gilt, their silvered pendants and
> the black niello inlay of their fittings
> and their rings

> their helmets made an apparition
> of the face: apertures for the eyes. Their
> jerkins were embroidered, their yellow plumes and
> scarlet banners sailed in the wind.

So they'd propitiate their gods.

The replacing of an old dispensation by a new one furthers the poem's depiction of history as a layered archaeology of old crises. In addition, the richness of the Romans' material and aesthetic culture, along with their gesture toward the spiritual in the propitiation of their gods, gives a nuanced portrait of their society. It is a society bent on domination and power, but not one defined only by those desires. Unlike the malignant aunts of "Bucyrus" and the arbitrary, warmaking jailors of "Statement," the powers-that-be in "East Anglian Poem" are more than simply forces of oppression.

Sections four and five of "East Anglian Poem" historicize and deromanticize the indigenous tribal society that was displaced with the coming of Rome, and in so doing further decrease the sense of crisis surrounding the Roman invasion. "Consider what they were before," urges the fourth section, with regard to the hard labors of the indigenous people in their pre-Roman economic underdevelopment. Then, all was not a matter of noble savagery. Rather, existence was generally nasty, brutish, and quite probably short. The fifth section envisions the slow development of the tribal societies from their beginnings to the coming of the Romans, seeing it as a constant state of flux, from "the first tamer of horses" to the full flower of druidic culture. Here we see that the Romans did not disturb a pristine and unchanging culture. They were merely the latest and most dramatic phase of an always-changing, always-hybrid British culture.

"East Anglian Poem" ends with depictions of both ceremony and "the Forward Policy of Rome"—with, that is, both civilization and a policy of barbaric violence. Here again we see the forces of power as more than mere oppression. Where the longer poems of *Bucyrus* sought to transform a world of oppressive powers, *Turns'* "Epilogue from a New Home" and "East Anglian Poem" seek to bring about a revolution in the poet's own consciousness.

Goodbye to All That

In 1979's *Crossing*, Matthias bids a final farewell to his early radical self. Two sequences of poems from *Crossing* give the strongest expression to this parting of the mature Matthias and the young Matthias: "The Stefan Batory Poems," written on a ship heading from England to America, and "The Mikhail Lermontov Poems," on a ship heading in the opposite direction. Together the sequences free Matthias from any lingering ties to his old self.

As the Watergate affair slouched toward its sordid end in 1974, Matthias was on board a Polish ship, crossing the Atlantic with his wife and two daughters to resettle in the United States. His view of himself as a returning refugee is clear at the outset when he conjures up one Mr. Katarsky, a Polish political refugee who had once lived near Matthias's part of Suffolk but had returned to Poland with his family after the Second World War, never to be heard from again. The shadow of Poland's tragic history in the twentieth century falls over the first section of "The Stefan Batory Poems" and casts doubts over the wisdom of Matthias's return to America. The sections that follow seek to dispel these doubts and to shape ways of thinking about the return that make it a viable option. These ways of thinking include both the historical-archaeological viewpoint we have seen in *Turns* and a conscious resolution to abandon the radical muses that inspired *Bucyrus*.

"How much did you know?" Matthias asks in an apostrophe concerning the political machinations of Stefan Batory, the elected king of Poland in the late sixteenth century. That question, in the days leading up to Richard Nixon's resignation, could not fail to resonate with the great national refrain of the country toward which Matthias's ship was steaming: "What did the president know and when did he know it?" The importance of the question, and the sixteenth-century political minutiae with which Matthias surrounds it, lies in the connection between Batory's and Nixon's machinations in realpolitik. In finding a large historical rhyme for the present circumstances, Matthias repeats the technique of the archaeological poems of *Turns*. The Batory poem takes a current crisis and introduces a detachment derived from historical perspective. The present crisis is revealed as simply one more instance of history's perpetual state of crisis, something normal, which both we and our civilization are likely to survive.

Something similar happens later in the Batory sequence when Matthias considers the economic consequences of the American crisis of state under Nixon. Reading the mimeographed news gazettes in the ship's library, he observes:

> The banalities of rhetoric and power
> Dovetail with the mathematics
> Of the market: Soon the brokers,
> As in 1929, will sail nicely
> From the upper stories
> Of the highest buildings in New York,
> Their sons will pluck the feathers
> From their hair and look for jobs
> A thousand miles from the ethnic
> Bonfires of their dreams, the
> Poor will stand in bread lines . . .

Everything here is about distance. The flippancy we hear, so at odds with the subject matter and its pessimism, is Byronic in both tone and intent: it allows one to experience the turbulence of history without becoming so close to it that one risks emotional injury. Distance, too, is what we get from the invocation of 1929 to describe America in the mid-1970s. Matthias's skill, or lack thereof, as an economic prognosticator is less important than his skill in creating a context for current crises: again, they suddenly seem precedented and even normal. The sense of distance becomes an important part of Matthias's farewell to his young, radical self. "I, a curio from 1959," he writes at the end of the section, deliberately bracketing out his persona of the 1960s, ". . . return/To Indiana—the only place/Save Utah where the Sixties,/ Though Peter Michelson was waiting,/Failed to arrive."

Matthias also finds other, subtler ways of bidding adieu to his former self. Observing that we live in an age of pastiche and creative exhaustion, he goes on to write of himself in the third person, saying:

> With total serenity
> He abandoned pastiche for patchouli
> For patchouli and panache
> He abandoned his panto-panjandrum

With utter contempt for panache
He abandoned patchouli
He abandoned himself with unspeakable simplicity
To pastrami

Sometimes poetry—like history, as Karl Marx so famously described it in *The Eighteenth Brumaire of Louis Napoleon*—repeats itself first as tragedy, then as farce. The passage above is in a way a repetition of the ending of *Turns'* "Three Around a Revolution," where the language of political emancipation goes badly awry. In "Three Around a Revolution" the slip into alliteration is tragic: hopes for revolution are perverted by human fallibility. Here, though, the slip into alliteration is pure farce: the move is not from revolution to reaction but from pastiche to antipasto. Matthias drops the heavy burden of political anxiety for a purely ludic activity meant to dispel the ghost of the man he had once been.

The long goodbye to 1960s radicalism continues in "The Mikhail Lermontov Poems." Returning to England after "two years of sincerely trying to come to terms with America" (*Beltane at Aphelion* 158), Matthias continues to write in the farcical, Byronic idiom of the earlier sequence, complete with touches of virtuosic comic rhyming and invocations of Byron and his Russian disciple, Pushkin. The Lermontov poems allow him to see his times in a broader historical context in which they appear far less menacing than they seem at first. The technique, once again, is a consideration of history conditioned by place. As the ship *Lermontov* approaches the mouth of the Thames, the poem begins to take on the matter of the river's mouth through history. While that history appears appealing at first, at just the moment when Matthias presents himself as ready to prefer the past to his own time, we begin to see it soaked in blood:

Tippling pints in Whitby's Prospect or in Ramsgate's Town we
think we'd like it better in the past. When they flushed the virgins
down the drain at Leche, floated heads in rivers or impaled them
ornamentally on pikes—when oh they hung the pirates low beneath
the tide. We'd drink we would
we'd

go pursue them durste
supply the victualles and munitione
write immortal doggerel we'd fight for Gloriana
Boudicca Victoria Regina choose your time
by Kitchener do your bit
. . . .
But you do not choose your time

Lucky, guilty—
exiled or pursued,
some at least can choose a place

The past appears as a long story of violence, graft, and patriotic gore, and "you do not choose your time." By contrast, in Matthias's own time, he invokes a figure recognizable from "The Stefan Batory Poems"— himself, fortunate and complicit (a man with "children/and a wife/who is middle class for life"), who chooses his own place.

At Home in East Anglia, at Home in Indiana

Place, for Matthias, is always a matter of accreted history, and choosing a place necessarily means writing oneself into the history of that place. Finding the continuity of present and past in geography is the project of his "An East Anglian Diptych," found in *A Gathering of Ways*. As the title indicates, the poem consists of two parts, the first considering history with reference to the ancient trails, or ley lines, that cross East Anglia, and the second considering history in the context of East Anglia's rivers.

The poem seeks out historical continuities, often through a strange converting of time into place or place into time. In the following passage, for example, a bird's flight along the seashore becomes a flight from the past into the present, as if history were as coherent as a walk along the beach:

The men who work the maltings
and the bargemen line up for their pay.

The bird that flies about them angling toward
the Orford Ness they call a *mavis*;
by the time it reaches the sprawling spider-webs

of early-warning radar nets it's lost its name,
and anyone at Chantry Point
looking with binoculars for avocets or curlews
would only see, if it passed by, a thrush.

The sight of the same kind of bird over the centuries knits together the discrete moments of history, from nineteenth-century bargemen to turn-of-the-millennium radar installations. Change seems cosmetic, a mere shift of names, while continuity seems substantial.

Something similar happens in the way the poem reads modern and Romantic-era events as manifestations of the same ancient forces. In the first section of "Ley Lines," for example, Matthias invokes Belus, the ancient Celtic god of the sun. He describes the Beltane fire line, a forty-mile ancient trail marking the angle of the sun on May Day, the feast of Belus. While a connection between the Neolithic makers of the Beltane fire line and the British sailors who fought the French under Admiral Nelson at the Battle of the Nile may not be at first apparent, Matthias draws one. He establishes the connection first through place (some of Nelson's ships were built at yards near the Beltane line), then through treating the later event in terms of the earlier one. He describes the ships as "belching a thousand years of Beltane fire at French sails on the Nile," which puts Nelson and the Neolithics participants in the same story. Later in the poem the contemporary world is also folded into the history of Beltane in East Anglia, when Matthias tells us that "along the ley-alignment point/at Sizewell, Beltane fires in the reactor//are contained by water drained out of the sea." Beltane presides over the history of the place, and it secures the coherence of that history from the earliest times to the nuclear age.

Two artists appear in "An East Anglian Diptych," the Edwardian writer Edward Thomas and the Romantic painter John Constable. Their love for East Anglia explains their presence, but it is the formal parallels of their presentation that are of most interest here, because these open the way for Matthias to include himself in the poem. Each artist is described in two prose paragraphs and two verse stanzas, with the prose portions introducing them without naming them. The first verse stanza in each treatment relates each artist's values through a series of parallel statements (following the basic form "it's better to be . . . than to be . . ."), while the final one asks us, in each case, a question from a friend ("*And what are you fighting for over there?*" in Thomas's case, and "*And what are you drawing landscapes for out here?*" in Constable's), to which the answer is the same:

> he picks a piece of dirt up off the path
> they're walking and says *This!*
> *For this*, he says
> *This this this*
> *For*
>
>   *this*

The form not only underlines the parallels between these two artists but also, by implication, the kinship of all artists taking on the matter of East Anglia. One could imagine another two paragraphs and two stanzas in this format for the poet of "An East Anglian Diptych," where the final question might be, "For what have you fled your violent country?" And the answer, from a man stooping to pinch soil between thumb and forefinger, would be, "*For this.*"

But the importance of "An East Anglian Diptych" in Matthias's career comes less from the way it inserts him into the history of East Anglia than from the principle of understanding history through place. If such an understanding can make one at home in East Anglia, then is there anything to prevent it from making one at home elsewhere? Can the poetics of place be translated to the country that Matthias had fled after two failed years of sincerely trying to come to terms with it? This is the question that he takes on in the next section of *A Gathering of Ways*, "Facts from an Apocryphal Midwest."

In 1984, family difficulties made it impossible for Matthias to spend long periods of time in his adopted England, and he found himself returning to the American Midwest that he had fled on the *Lermontov*. His long poem of this period, "Facts from an Apocryphal Midwest," begins with a great deal of trepidation. It was, in Matthias's words, "an act of will," an investigation of a place and a history that might, he thought, have stimulated "another kind of poet," but not him (Note to "Facts from an Apocryphal Midwest," *Beltane at Aphelion* 199). His anxieties about the poem can be traced back to the previous year when, in an omnibus review covering books by Wendell Berry, Gary Snyder, and other poets associated with their regions, he considered writing about northern Indiana. The prospects for what will clearly become "Facts from an Apocryphal Midwest" do not look good:

> Why not a poem about the St. Joseph [the principal river of northwest Indiana]? I think the reason is that while the St. Joseph is rich with associations that might stimulate another poet—La Salle came down this river, the Potawatomi lived nearby, the continental divide split it from the Kankakee and created a famous portage, Francis Parkman wrote about it, etc.—for me it is associated entirely with the kind of daily grind that prevents poetry from being written. . . . I know and love the Suffolk rivers—have loafed and invited the soul on their banks—but have no feeling at all about the St. Joseph . . . on the banks of the St. Joseph I sought, I think, to summon back emotions I have felt on the banks of [Suffolk rivers called] the Alde, the Deben, and the Stour. (*Reading Old Friends* 67-68)

Matthias seems to have the poem fairly clearly planned out and merely to be balking at the American setting. The poem, when he does write it, mirrors "An East Anglian Diptych" not only in the emotions in which it traffics but also in its construction. Matthias quite consciously imitates the techniques of "An East Anglian Diptych" in this attempt to ground himself in the Midwest. "Facts from an Apocryphal Midwest" has a tougher task than its precursor, though: while England had always been a refuge for Matthias, America had constantly appeared as a threatening and alienating presence.

The first section of the poem bears the title "Seven Moves toward Embarkation on the Local River," indicating a hesitancy about beginning the textual and literal exploration of the terrain. The whole first section exudes pessimism about the poem's mission of home-finding or grounding, which still appears to Matthias as an act of will and determination rather than a spontaneous, Wordsworthian delight. In some ways the opening section echoes the pessimism of T. S. Eliot's *Waste Land*: it begins with fragmented quotations in French, and it contrasts an apparently heroic past with a debased, banal, and infertile present, whose figure is a stagnant river. In contrast to the exploits of René Robert Cavelier, Sieur de la Salle, we find the diminished world of the present, where the St. Joseph River runs through South Bend. But what begins in pessimism and a High Modernist sense of entropy turns, at the end of the section, to a kind of tenuous hope. While the poem began with a foreign language, spoken in fragments, and dealing moreover in alien measurements (the "arpents" of French colonialism), the first section ends with a system for converting arpents to miles and with a lucid translation of the Belgian explorer Louis Hennepin's fragmentary French into English. Initial hesitations have been overcome, and Matthias has embarked on his river and his poem.

There can be no real sense of homecoming, though, until Matthias addresses his early concerns about American power and violence, and the role of discourse in perpetuating them. He comes at the problem directly in the fourth section of the poem, where we hear the language of power from the mouth of Nicolas Perrot, an agent of the French king during the age of exploration. His language, like that of the malignant aunts in "Bucyrus," is the enactment of an ideology of domination, which the assembled shamans of the Winnebagos and the Potawatomi recognize as a "spirit-power":

> *Vive le Roi, and hail*
> *the highest and most mighty monarch and*
> *most Christian King of France and of Navarre*
>
> *for whom I take possession of this place Sault St. Marie*
> *and also lakes Superior and Huron also*
> *Manitoulin also all the countries rivers lakes and*
>
> *streams contiguous adjacent thereunto both those dis-*
> *covered and the ones we will discover*
> *in their length & breadth & bounded only by the seas*

declaring to the nations living there that they
from this time forth are vassals
of his Majesty bound by laws & customs which are his.

This is an alchemy of sorts: the conversion of what power would deem mere lead (free people in an undiscovered land) to pure gold (subjects of his Majesty, "bound by laws & customs which are his"). In this poem, though, it is a language that fails. Immediately after Perrot's words, Matthias turns to Parkman's commentary on Perrot, which asks:

"What remains of sovereignty
thus pompously proclaimed?

Now and then
the accents of some straggling boatman or
a half-breed vagabond—

this and nothing more."

This is what we might call an "Ozymandias" moment. Look on Perrot's works, ye Mighty, and despair, for little remains of the French ambitions along the Mississippi and its tributaries. As in the archaeological poems of *Turns*, "Facts from an Apocryphal Midwest" cures anxieties about power through a kind of distancing. The difference between this poem and the poems of *Turns*, though, is that here Matthias takes the technique out of England's shires and back to the country that had so thoroughly alienated him.

At Home in the World

If the first two poems of *A Gathering of Ways* were about being at home in particular places, then the third one, "A Compostela Diptych," is about making oneself at home ontologically. As John Peck, one of the poem's most sensitive readers (and one of its dedicatees) says, the poem's true goal is not to add France and Spain, the territories it describes, but rather to enact "an inner regrounding" for both poet and reader ("Petitio, Repetitio" 220).

Although the poem is set out in three parts, "France," "Spain," and an intermediary section called "Intercalation," one might also think of it as divided into a long section, spanning most of the poem, and two short ones coming suddenly one after the other at the very end. The first takes on the history of the routes of religious pilgrims across France and Spain, which comes to suggest the history of the West. Like a piece of modern music, the poem hovers between imposing a unity on this theme and letting it fall into cacophony and dissonance. The history of the West here constantly promises to come into a harmony in which all its parts are embraced, but that harmony is continually undone, as the history of heretics and outsiders proves inassimilable.

The long opening sections first present the people of the West on their pilgrimages over the centuries as a kind of unified historical subject bent on a single task of mutual significance. The pronoun "they" links many disparate peoples into one subject, even as the poem's musical incantations lull the reader into a kind of rhythmic repetition:

> Via Tolosona, Via Podiensis.
> There among the tall and narrow cypresses,
> the white sarcophagi of Arles
>
> worn by centuries of wind & sun,
> where Charlemagne's lieutenants it was said
> lay beside Servilius & Flavius
>
> and coffins drifted down the Rhone
> on narrow rafts to be unloaded by St. Victor's monks,
> they walked: Via Tolosona.
>
> Via Podiensis . . .

The passage goes on, with the refrain of "Via Tolosona, Via Podiensis" recurring, even as the referent for the pronoun "they" expands to include pilgrims from farther and farther afield, and separated by more and more centuries.

Among the other devices used to pull the disparate strands of history together is Matthias's repetition of significant passages in the mouths of different characters drawn from the history of France and Spain. Again, the technique is essentially the same as the passing of a musical theme from one section of the orchestra to another. This is extremely rare in poetry: I cannot think of another poem of any length where passages of half a page or more are repeated verbatim and attributed to different speakers as, say, is a certain apocalyptic dream in Matthias's poem. The passage, originally from the *Chanson de Roland,* appears first as part of a dream of Charlemagne, then as the words of Saint Bernard, and then again as the dream of Aimery Picaud, the shadowy figure to whom the authorship of the first guidebook to the pilgrim routes is often attributed. Finally, the passage is ascribed to John Moore, an English general whose expeditionary force helped to oppose Napoleon's invasion of Spain.

Running counter to the great binding-together of many peoples and many periods is a dissonance that comes in the depiction of the history of heretics in Spain and Provence. After writing of the movement of the pilgrims as a kind of song, Matthias turns to the heretics and tells us:

> there was another song—one sung inwardly
> to a percussion of the jangling
> manacles and fetters hanging on the branded
>
> heretics who crawled the roads
> on hands and knees and slept with lepers under
> dark facades of abbeys

This dissonance is an apparently inassimilable disruption of the cultural unity evoked by Matthias's repetitions. And it too repeats, the jangling of manacles being heard for the destroyed Gnostics, the hunted and besieged Cathars, the victims of the Inquisition, the displaced refugees of the Napoleonic Wars, the politically repressed Basques, and, after the Christian reconquest of Spain from the Moors, "the Jews [who]/hid their secret practices, and the Arabs [who hid] theirs." The harmony-dissonance dialectic of the poem's long treatment of history comes to an abrupt end with the great munitions blast that opens the final section. Although the historical source is the explosion at an arsenal near Santiago during the Carlist wars, the context leaves the source ambiguous to all but the most informed scholars of Spanish history and, in fact, suggests that it may have occurred during the Civil War of the 1930s. The actual date is of less importance than the location of the blast within the poem, where it leads to a stunned silence that opens up a sense of ontological belonging. Our first clue to the significance of the blast comes when we read that, when the blast shook the earth and caused the bells of faraway cathedrals to ring, "men/whose job it was to ring them stood/amazed" and "wondered if this thunder/and the ringing was in time for Vespers//or for Nones or if it was entirely out of time."

Along with this suggestion of eternity, though, comes a long chant invoking again the history of the West, taking us from prehistory up to the day of the poem's composition and presenting it as a kind of harmony that acknowledges but is not destroyed by turmoil, bloodshed, and deadly rifts in doctrine and ideology. The final chant with its repetitions and variations embraces a whole series of phenomena in a kind of Hegelian *ausgehoben*. Peck, once again, understands the poem well, writing that its final lines

> proceed to the embrace—with the silence of the ground of grounds— St. Francis's sermons and songs, the Logos and the Deunde, Ignatian propositions, the Grail legend . . . Mithraic oaths, the bellowing of dying bulls, the silence of abbeys, abbots, monks in the fields, sacristy, stores, garden and copy room, the language of Castillian *juglares*, and then Matthias' own powerful hymn to primordial silence. (221)

The history that had previously seemed riven by dissonance appears now as a whole from which nothing can be separated, and into which everything is gathered. Matthias himself is included in this gathering:

Towards Pamplona, long, long after all Navarre
was Spain, and after the end
of the Kingdom of Aragón, & after the end of the end,

I, John, walked with my wife Diana
down from the Somport Pass following the silence
that invited and received my song.

Here at last Matthias is at home, not in a particular place but in the
history of the West, with all its dissonances and troubles. It is a tremendous surmounting of the alienation that has been characteristic of so
many of his poems.

There is more at stake here than one's place in history: as the last
two lines of the second stanza above indicate, Matthias sees himself
not only in relation to history but also in relation to the great silence
that invites and receives his song. Jeremy Hooker has argued that
Matthias's attempts to find a kind of home in his poetry have, in the
end, an ontological element (104), and in these lines it is to such an
element that we are asked to turn. The silence, Matthias writes, is "as
it was in the beginning before silence," as it was long before the Christian silence of the monks, as it was:

in the stillness

before anything was still, when nothing
made a single sound and singularity was only nothing's
song unseeing . . . aphonia

before a whisper or a breath, aphasia
before injury,
aphelion of outcry without sun

One reaches, at moments like these, for the right word. The German
abgrund seems appropriate here, the originary ground of being in which
all of history is taken up, the primordial silence embracing all speech
and history. Perhaps better, though, is the Greek word *chora*, in its Platonic usage as the condition of existence itself.

In Plato's *Timaeus, chora* is a silent void that provides the space for the sensible world; it is therefore "the nurse of all becoming and change" that "provides a position for everything that comes to be" and "continues to receive all things" while "never itself tak[ing] a permanent impress from any of the things that enter it" (Plato, 66, 70, 68). Edward S. Casey, perhaps our foremost philosopher of place, writes of *chora* as a kind of vast receptacle, an *ur*-state of nature "uncontrolled (perhaps even untouched) by *eidos* or *logos*" (201). The end of "A Compostela Diptych" puts us in touch with this *chora*. Matthias incants all of history, seeking behind it the precondition of that history, the silence that has "invited and received" his song. Plato (and, in our own time, Julia Kristeva) speaks of *chora* as maternal, and what Matthias touches upon at the end of the poem is deeply maternal, the ground from which and in which everything grows.

In turning to incantation to evoke *chora*, Matthias repeats, in the final section, the resonant words "before" and "as it was in the beginning" over and over as he lists historical events. In a sense, he empties the *chora* of those things that have filled it, referring us to a time "before" or "long before" the event in question, chanting the specific forms of being out of existence to get at the *chora* that lies behind them. Incantation becomes the means of making himself at home in being, as it also, in other contexts, serves as the means of making himself at home in language.

Turns in "the Prisonhouse of Language"

In 1972, Frederic Jameson lifted Nietzsche's observation that "we have to cease to think if we refuse to do it in the prisonhouse of language" for the title of his book, *The Prisonhouse of Language: A Critical Account of Structuralism and Russian Formalism*. Jameson was not the only one haunted by Nietzsche's ghost. The year 1972 was also when Matthias composed "Turns: Toward a Provisional Aesthetic and a Discipline," in which he clearly feels the shades of the Nietzschean prisonhouse surrounding him. The poem is important not only as a sign of how Matthias, like Jameson, twigged to changes in the *zeitgeist* and anticipated the linguistic turn in criticism and poetry, but it is also important as an episode in a slightly different version of the story of alienation and home-finding that we have seen in Matthias's evolving poetics. Just as he journeyed through alienation to a feeling of at-homeness in place, he also journeyed from a sense of alienation within language to a sense of at-homeness within language. "Turns," appropriately enough, represents a turning point in this story.

If the question of poems such as "Bucyrus" and "Poem in Three Parts" was some version of "how can we liberate ourselves from the discourses of power," then the question of "Turns" is something like "given my inevitable interpolation in power and discourse, how can I relate to it satisfactorily?" Put another way, it is "how can I live in the prisonhouse?" The poem, one of the oddest in Matthias's often unconventional oeuvre, signals from the start that we will not be taking language and power for granted. It begins with a somewhat unfaithful translation of the beginning of Thomas Hardy's *Jude the Obscure* into a West Midlands dialect of Middle English. The poem continues by foregrounding the questions of translation and audience and then breaks into a long comic-Marxian gloss on itself. Having presented us with a willfully obscure text (punning on the "obscure" of Hardy's title) and having defended its obscurity, Matthias's narrator goes on to examine his own pro-obscurity position, seeing it as determined by his interpolation in the very system that those beliefs protest:

> Now some of the obscure, like some of the lucid, do not become proletarianized. . . . Perhaps they hold teaching jobs in public schools or universities; perhaps they have an inherited income. In any case, some maintain their hermetic privilege. They are not obliged to live by their art or to produce for the open market. Such unproletarianized obscure are revolted by the demands of a commercialized market, by the vulgarity of the mass-produced commodity supplied to meet it.

Our own doctrines of aesthetic resistance to power are, it seems, themselves the result of the position into which power puts us. We have met the enemy, and he is us. We find that we do not stand outside the system we wish to protest. Even as we protest it, we embody it. The system speaks its words against itself through us.

What can we do in such circumstances? We cannot charge through the language of power, as we do in the long poems of *Bucyrus*, since there is nowhere from which to charge, no Archimedian point outside of the discourse from which to take our running start. Romana Huk, perhaps the poem's subtlest reader, tells us that "the complexity of the situation . . . calls for an aesthetic of 'turning,' of looking at what one writes (or thinks one has written) from the back of one's head, or from another historical/discursive angle" (123). One must try to comprehend one's own interpolation by examining the discourse in which one is inscribed. If this won't exactly liberate us, it will at least make us more fully cognizant of our situation. And so, we see the odd translation of Hardy's novel into Middle English as an attempt to return to the origins of discourse and therefore to understand them—an attempt that acknowledges its necessary failure. The opening, Huk tells us, suggests two things: first, the need to acknowledge the historical roots of our language and system of understanding; and second, "the obvious impossibility of translating current (con)texts backward towards 'origins'" (123). This latter suggestion is signalled by Matthias's dramatization of his need to invent Middle English terms for nineteenth-century phenomena. This, Huk tells us, shows "the impossibility of viewing past texts or myths or language in anything but Jude-like ways: appropriatively, and through the present's desires and self-definitions" (123). We can only understand our interpolation through a return to origins, but no such return is possible, for we can only read our origins through the assumptions that we have inherited. There is no interpretive outside from which to take a larger view.[1]

1. One way to gloss this would be to lift a passage from Francisco Varela's gloss on an M. C. Escher etching that depicts a man at an exhibition of prints, who turns out to be standing inside the same work of art he is viewing:

> We find ourselves in a cognitive domain, and we cannot leap out of it or choose its beginnings or modes. . . . In finding the world as we do, we forget all we did to find it as such, entangled in the strange loop of our actions. . . . Much like the young man in the Escher engraving "Print Gallery," we see a world that turns into the very substratum which produces us, thereby closing the loop and intercrossing domains. As in the Escher engraving, there is nowhere to step out into. And if we were to try, we would find ourselves in an endless circle that vanishes into empty space right in the middle. (Varela 304)

In one sense, we can read the beginning of the poem as an emblem of this situation. Here, we see Jude leaving town with his goods, including a piano ("symphonye") that, in Hardy's original, he leaves behind:

> The scolemayster levande was the toun
> and sary of hit semed everuch one.
> The smal quyt cart that covert was and hors . . .
> to ferien his godes. To ferien his godes
> quere he was boun.
>
> The onelych thyng of combraunce (combraunce)
> was the symphonye
> (saf a pakke of bokes)
> that he hade boghte the yere
> quen he bithought
> that he wolde lerne to play.

The variation from Hardy's original is significant, because the "symphonye," as Peter Michelson has argued, "serves the figural transformation of the 'scolemayster' into the poet" (91). The schoolmaster/poet sets out, encumbered with his cultural baggage ("a pakke of bokes"), but his destination is unclear and remains so throughout the poem, unless it is to be the cart itself. Read this way, his condition is that of one condemned to move without hope of any arrival, always burdened with the weight of his culture's verbal discourse. His is, in Huk's phrase, a "pilgrim's progress . . . into his own 'baggage'" (124).

If "Turns" offers a consolation about the inevitability of our interpolation in inherited discourse, it is that we can to a degree become familiar with our conundrum through the contemplation and reworking of bits of text. This is the method of "Turns," and it is the method of other poems from the volume *Turns*, such as "The Great Tournament Roll of Westminster" and "The Art of Fence: A Letter," both of which rework historical texts. As Michael Anania says in a discussion of "The Great Tournament Roll of Westminster," Matthias "allows repetition to give a palpable familiarity to things that were alien to us." The process of the repetition and reworking of text "isn't liberating in the contemporary cultural critic's sense of that term, that once you notice something then you can operate as though you're free of it." Rather, "Matthias's assertion is that you're never free of the mystifications in language, you're only able . . . to familiarize or defamiliarize . . . to turn them, as in the turnings of phrases in his poem 'Turns'" ("Talking John Matthias" 4).

A Flight through Space

"Northern Summer" picks up where "Turns" leaves off, moving us further away from a sense of alienation within language. Central to any understanding of the poem, though, is another one with a much simpler and less sophisticated sense of language. "Void Which Falls Out of Void," by Göran Sonnevi, was translated by Matthias and the Swedish poet Göran Printz-Pahlson for their 1979 volume, *Contemporary Swedish Poetry*. It is short enough to reproduce in its entirety:

> *a*
> Void which falls out of void, transparent,
> cones, hemispheres,
> fall through empty space.
> Thoughtform, crescent, trajectory.

> *b*
> However relevant!
> In the infinite freedom I can
> keep back, give
> my notes resilience, in relation
> to each other, to my whole body, which also
> falls in infinity through empty space:
> e.g.
> Charlie Parker's solo in *Night in Tunisia* on May 15th 1953.

> *c*
> The flight of sentimentality through empty space.
> Through its elliptical whole

an heraldic blackbird's
black wings, yellow beak, round eyes, with the yellow
ring, which defines its inner empty
space.

The opening section introduces the idea that we have a kind of exis-
tential freedom of mind in relation to the meaningless void into which
we have been thrown. We project patterns of meaning—the "cones"
or "hemispheres" that the final line defines as "thoughtforms." The
second stanza asserts that the meanings we make work as variations
on our original act of thought, just as Parker's saxophone solo makes
variations on the initial statement of a musical theme. In the final
stanza, Sonnevi implies that our projection of discursive meaning onto
a meaningless void leads to self-definition. The pattern we project—
here, an heraldic bird—defines the limits of our inner space against
the void beyond. Rather than seeing meaning as something generated
by a system of signification larger and more powerful than the individual speaker, the poem looks at the individual as the heroic creator
of meaning in a world empty of significance. It is a far cry from the
world of Matthias's "Turns," where we inhabit not a void but an inescapable network of already-inscribed meanings. It would seem to be
an odd poem for Matthias to be drawn to. The attraction was clearly
there, though, since images from Sonnevi's poem haunt the long
poem that Matthias began a year after translating "'Void Which Falls
Out of Void,'" "Northern Summer." As a reading of "Northern Summer"
makes clear, the attraction was essentially a negative one. Matthias
was drawn to Sonnevi's poem as an antithesis to his own evolving
position.

One way to read "Northern Summer" is as a poem of place, or what
I have been calling a "homing poem." In this view, it is roughly analo-
gous to the three long poems collected as *A Gathering of Ways*. It em-
ploys some of the same archaeological-archival methods. In Matthias's
own assessment, though, it is a less successful version of these poems.
But if we look at his afterword to *Beltane at Aphelion: Collected Longer
Poems*, we see Matthias gesture toward another element of the poem
beyond its poetics of place, an element both more significant and more
wholly successful:

"Northern Summer" was begun in Fife, Scotland, on the Wemyss Castle estate in the summer of 1980 and finished three years later in the Cambridgeshire village of Trumpington. It was written at a time when my family had lost our summer home in Suffolk, the place where I had done most of my writing for fifteen years and more. The attempt to integrate myself in this particular landscape and history was not, it seems to me, successful; and the poem deals with an ultimately alienating experiece. Perhaps for this reason the most important section is the seventh, "A Voice," where in fact I hear not only my mother's voice reading from Stevenson and Scott, but also my wife's reading the same texts to my daughters. ("Afterword and Notes" 195)

Voice, or language, is the more fully realized theme.

The poem begins by taking lines from Sonnevi's "'Void Which Falls Out of Void'" as an epigraph and then breaks into lines that seem, at first, shocking in their banality. Matthias has really lost it, one thinks, reading his initial description of the castle at Wemyss. The castle, he tells us,

> *Occupies*
> a picturesque
> commanding strong position
> on the summit of a cliff some forty
> feet in height
> the base of which is covered
> up at flood tide by the waters of the Forth.
> Large, magnificent, commodious
> with rock nearby and wood and water to afford
> the eye a picture of a rare
> and charming beauty
> forming a delightful and romantic spot

To the relief of the reader, Matthias has been quoting a source chosen for its banality:

> the sight of which
> could not but amply compensate et

cetera

        the language of a tour book

threading aimlessly

through sentimental empty space.

The last line resonates with Sonnevi's poem and implicitly criticizes Sonnevi's view of language as an act of will exercised in a world void of previously inscribed significance. Language that operates as if in a void is seen, here, as unmoored and insignificant, the merest flight of sentiment. In a way it is an empty language, what Yvor Winters would call a nominalist language. Matthias's proposition for an alternative to such emptiness, though, is quite different from that of Winters or from the alternative offered by a more Wintersian student of Winters such as Robert Pinsky. Where Winters and Pinsky would fight against nominalism by affirming that abstractions have a kind of eternal reality, Matthias turns to history to give language a meaning and resonance that it cannot have in the ahistorical nattering of a sentimental tour book. Matthias suggests, in this case, the words of Edward the First, the English king who fought Robert the Bruce for dominion over Scotland:

Or build on, say, an Edward's language

to his dear and faithful cousin

Eymar de Valance

like a second generation builds upon

the ruins of a first?

        finding not

in our Sir Michael Wemyss

good word

nor yet good service and

that he now shows himself in such a wise

that we must hold him traitor

and our enemy we do command you that ye

cause his manor where we lay

and all his other manors to be burned his lands

and goods to be destroyed

his gardens to be stripped all bare
that nothing may remain
and all
may thus take warning —

Language
moving upon consequence
Consequence
upon a language: Flight
of an heraldic bird
through space that is inhabited.

In contrast to Sonnevi, Matthias sees a world comprised of space already inhabited by significance, already written over by the discourses of power ("language/moving upon consequence"). The place in Scotland where Matthias finds himself has a history conditioned by linguistic acts (the destruction mandated by Edward's words). Matthias's turn to historical text in "Northern Summer" is an act of understanding tradition, and he presents it as having saved him from the banality with which he opened the poem.

In the poem's sixth section the "inhabited space" of discourse becomes conflated with Matthias's mother's voice as he remembers it from his childhood. Here, he writes, "I hear my mother's voice reading Stevenson —/or is it Scott? Someone's wandering lost/in the heather. I must be eight or nine." As he recalls his mother reading to him, he is transported into a state where he himself becomes the characters in her stories ("Am I papered for the murder of that/Campbell back in Appin?"). He becomes the subject of the discourse, and while this experience comes with the anxieties and fears felt by the characters, the ultimate emotional quality of the experience is a kind of trust in his mother as he surrenders himself to the sound of her voice. Referencing Sonnevi, he tells us that he experiences the "flight of an heraldic bird through language,/and my mother's voice."

This is important, not as a departure from the intellectual position of "Turns" (which it is not) but as a departure from the emotional tenor of that poem. In "Turns," the emotion accompanying the revelation that we are always inevitably interpolated in discourse is best described as a kind of manic frenzy; here, interpolation in discourse is like the child's immersion in the voice of the mother. We feel a kind of comfort as well as a reverence for the voice of the comforter. The poem comes close to paralleling the ending of "A Compostela Diptych," where the experience of the maternal *chora* makes Matthias at ease on the earth. Once again a maternal presence allows him to escape from anxiety and enter into a kind of gratitude.

The way to express this gratitude, for Matthias, is to become a "paying guest —/of language of/the place." And the "cost of lodging is extracted by a pile of books." That is, the price of living legitimately is to know one's discourse, with all the complications of that project, rather than simply projecting one's will and sentiment onto the world. In a way, the need to understand the discourse into which one has been interpolated is a sort of Wintersian urge. Matthias goes farther than Winters would have permitted, though, in allowing text from the past to shape the verbal surface of the poem. This shatters the Wintersian norms of Augustan clarity and statement even as it fulfills Winters' program of saving oneself from linguistic deadness through knowing the past. This represents a very different ethic from that of those writers who perceive the world as a discursively uninhabited space, free of previously inscribed meanings. Where such writers are projective, Matthias is reflective. Where they project their sentiments outward, Matthias seeks to understand the discourse that made him and the place in which he finds himself. It is in this attitude toward historical text that Matthias breaks with his modernist forebears and makes an important (though largely unrecognized) contribution to our poetry.

"Just Modernism"?

After sizing up Matthias's oeuvre for an award, one of the judges, Helen Vendler, is reported to have said that her main critique of the work was that it was "just modernism."[2] The charge is important in

2. This was said in conversation with Michael Anania, after Matthias had been turned down for a Guggenheim (Anania, personal interview).

that it was a major impediment to the growth of Matthias's reputation, not only in the case of this prize, which was not conferred, but also in a more general sense. As Huk says, "Matthias is often thought of as a kind of 'neo-modernist,' or some such variant of writer still limited by the projects of a revered but past past, removed from our newly established 'posts' [postmodernism, poststructuralism, etc.]" (115). There are certainly a number of signs that point toward modernist sympathies on Matthias's part. He has, for example, been the most prominent American champion of the great Anglo-Welsh modernist David Jones, and he has written sympathetically of the young, still-modernist W.H. Auden, and of Geoffrey Hill. His own poetry can also seem Poundian at first glance.

The resemblance to Ezra Pound is misleading, though. While the verbal surface of Matthias's work is often similar in texture to that of Pound's most characteristic poems, the differences between the two poets are at least as profound as the similarities. Peck understands this when he says that Matthias, unlike Pound and Charles Olson, is primarily concerned with "a reflective movement" rather than "a projective one" ("Petitio, Repetitio" 214). Poets such as Pound and Olson seek to impose or reveal large patterns on history. Pound, for example, shows a vatic side antithetical to Matthias when he seeks to demonstrate mythic moments and their "repeat in history" in *The Cantos* ("Letter to Homer Pound" 93). Pound begins with a vision of history, finds the moments to demonstrate it, and layers them so as to demonstrate the "repeat" or pattern. In contrast, Matthias begins with particular moments of historical text and works out from them toward larger conclusions. Moreover, Pound has a halcyon quality lacking in the far less sentimental Matthias. The lost, historical world is, for Pound, a better world compared to which our contemporary world seems a diminished thing. Matthias adopts a critical and analytic attitude toward the past even as he acknowledges the way it has formed the present. This critical kind of historical consciousness allies Matthias with a range of British experimentalists from Hugh MacDiarmid to J.H. Prynne, but this context is largely invisible to American readers.

Despite these important differences, it is the resemblance to Pound that is most often noticed. Keith Tuma, however, recognizes the superficiality of that resemblance. He sees the apparent parallels with Pound as the great limitation on Matthias's reputation, arguing that it marks Matthias's work as too complex and demanding for an "M.F.A. culture" in American poetry characterized by "apathetic provincialism, ahistorical solipsism, and willful anti-intellectualism" (43). While Tuma's analysis is clearly a partisan one, this does not necessarily detract from its truth. In the 1990s (a crucial juncture for Matthias's reputation, since it was the decade when the two volumes of his collected poems appeared), for example, we saw a distinct bias against modernist poetics and anything that resembles them. The bias was strong enough to lead the usually level-headed critic Calvin Bedient to rant against the "antimodernist temper of the times" in the journal *Modernism/Modernity* (221). We see the antimodernist bias in Mary Kinzie's *The Cure of Poetry in an Age of Prose*, where she argues for a poetry of "clarity and dignity" based on a well-balanced "middle style" (62, 300). Echoing the Pinsky of *The Situation of Poetry*, Kinzie calls for a resurgence of the "prose virtues" in poetry (293), helping to create a taste that will elevate an Augustan such as Pinsky while downgrading Matthias.

The antimodernist bias is also clearly visible in what was perhaps the most prominent book of poetry criticism of the decade, Dana Gioia's *Can Poetry Matter?* There, he argues in favor of poetic "clarity and accessibility" and an Augustan "classical style" (232–33). Gioia dismisses what he calls "the mandarin aestheticism of international Modernism" (55) and argues that American literature must "free poets from the burden of writing the definitive long poem" (29). The climate of opinion that Gioia's book reflects could hardly be receptive to the Matthias of *A Gathering of Ways* or *Beltane at Aphelion*.

The modernism to which Matthias's work bore a strong resemblance came under attack from another position, too, besides that of neo-Augustans such as Kinzie and Gioia. As Tuma observed, there is a profound irony here, because Matthias is "likely to have every bit as hard a time finding readers among those more willing to engage exploratory writing for exactly the same reasons that M.F.A. types will ignore him, as these readers also will be put off by his historical references, which they are likely to misread as Poundian or Olsonian in the era of Stein" (43). The facts bear this out. Matthias's work is notably absent from such "exploratory writing"-friendly environments as Paul Hoover's *Postmodern American Poetry* and Pierre Joris and Jerome Rothenberg's massive *Poems for the Millenium*. It is not a topic of discussion in the pages of experimentally inclined journals, nor does SUNY-Buffalo's Electronic Poetry Center list a Matthias page. The denizens of the M.F.A. world cannot appreciate a poet such as Matthias, but neither can those poets and critics struggling to push experiment beyond the frontiers set by Pound.

If we return to David Kellogg's model of American poetry in his essay "The Self in the Poetic Field," we get a clear perspective on the difficulties faced by Matthias's reputation. Some of Yvor Winters' students have seen their reputations rise as a result of the dynamics of this field. Robert Pinsky has been claimed by traditionalists, and he also benefited from a certain kind of community-based claim when *An Explanation of America* offered a general view of a community that could be held up against identity-group-based community claims. Even more enviably, Robert Hass has been claimed by several constituencies: he is seen as a poet of linguistic innovation as well as a traditionalist resisting the innovations of poststructuralist linguistics. John Matthias has had a much different fate. Seen as a Poundian modernist, his work is rejected by traditionalists as "just modernism" and ignored by the experimental wing of American poetry for the same reason.

Where, then, is Matthias's place in the field of American poetry? Kellogg himself raises the question in his essay "The *Pages* of John Matthias and the Future of Critical Recognition." "What is the place of John Matthias' work in contemporary poetry?" Kellogg asks. "South Bend, Indiana, of course," he continues, ". . . or maybe it is in Ohio: Columbus, where Matthias was born . . . or Athens, where Swallow/ Ohio University Press publishes his work. Or perhaps we should place his work in the United Kingdom, where he has lived from time to time and written much of his work." But Kellogg is being disingenuous. He knows that "the question of a poet's place is not usually asked with such answers in mind" (15). If we look at Matthias's place in American poetry from a Bourdieuian perspective, we must acknowledge that "there is no other criterion of membership in a field than producing effects within it" (Bourdieu 42). From this perspective, Kellogg says, "it is not clear that Matthias belongs on the field at all" (15), in that he has garnered so few worldly honors of the kind granted to his more famous peers. There is another way to look at Matthias's place in the poetic field, though, best expressed by a phrase coined by Vincent Sherry and picked up by Keith Tuma: he is "way out in the center" (Sherry 29; Tuma 33).

"Way Out in the Center"

Sherry and Tuma use the idea of Matthias existing "way out in the center" differently. For Sherry, Matthias's odd and apparently oxymoronic location has to do with his relationship to the historical texts that permeate his poetry:

> On the one hand, [Matthias] the pedagogue offers from his word-hoard and reference trove the splendid alterity of unfamiliar speech; on the other, this is our familial tongue, our own language in its deeper memory and reference. It is strange only in the ways of the uncanny or, more suitably, the *unheimlich*, in the double implication of the German word's literal and Freudian meanings: not homey or not familiar but only because too intimate and well known, and strange only because repressed, or forgotten. This is the paradox that defines the enlivening conflict of Matthias' verse. Here is a poet who must work, as it were, way out in the center. He is an idiosyncratic radical who is only trying to get back to a common root . . . aiming to reclaim and consolidate a language that is already there, the true depth of our civil speech. (29)

Thinking of Sherry's statement in terms of Kellogg's map of American poetry, we could say that Sherry argues for a Matthias with legitimate claims to both the tradition-based and innovation-based poles of value. The traditionalism here is not limited to a shallowly conceived formalism. Rather, it is an appeal to tradition based on an examination of the historical roots of contemporary experience. It is a making-familiar of the apparently strange that is, simultaneously, an act of innovation, in that it is a defamiliarization of the present. Matthias, in this view, hovers at the center of the field.

When Tuma takes up Sherry's phrase, he turns its significance in a slightly different direction. Were there any reasonably good maps of American poetry, Tuma argues, "Matthias' work would be recognized as part of a viable center" in that poetry (35). In Tuma's opinion, Matthias's oeuvre belongs there for its appeal to both traditionalist and innovative poles of value. The opinion is similar to Sherry's, although Tuma, unlike Sherry, does not see Matthias as appealing strongly to both poles simultaneously. Instead, he sees the traditionalism and innovation of Matthias's work more as a matter of variety and the taking of middle paths. "Matthias' practice," Tuma says, "is Audenesque in its variety" (42), and while it uses "devices associated with various modernisms and postmodernisms," it "will not employ . . . collage-based techniques to the point where he loses sight of discursive ends or even narration" (43). Tuma's Matthias is eclectic, flexible, and various.

I am in agreement with Sherry and Tuma about the central importance of Matthias to contemporary American poetry. My reasons, though, have less to do with those articulated by Sherry and Tuma than with Romana Huk's observations. After she writes that Matthias's work has been "all about contemplating complex historical contingencies as they impact upon—*by providing apocryphal text for*—the necessary 'making' that results in . . . notions of the self" (115–16), Huk goes on to conclude that the result of this activity is the imagination of "a postmodern but 'located'" art and self. That is, the self imagined in Matthias's poetry is one that is neither taken for granted, as in so much mainstream poetry, nor erased in an "authorless art" (116), as in much avant-garde work. Rather, it is seen as the product of the historical and textual sources that make it possible, and that bequeath to us the terms in which any self-investigation can take place.

Matthias developed his poetics out of personal needs, as solutions to his various alienations. But these poetics could well answer a larger need in (and in a sense *at the center of*) contemporary American poetry. At least one of America's more interesting and ambitious younger poets, Kristin Prevallet, has seen this need and has sketched the general outline of a poetry that would address it. In "Writing Is Never by Itself Alone: Six Mini-Essays on Relational Investigative Poetics," Prevallet quotes Ammiel Alcalay on how we must "brin[g] knowledge and history back in at the point where they have become almost non-existent in our [American] poetic culture" (25). This turn to history and knowledge represents the "investigative" part of the "Relational Investigative Poetics" of her title. Looking back at Charles Olson, Prevallet admires his interest in history and historical texts and sees them as politically valuable: "History is what connects a person to space and time; it is not a force that acts upon the individual from outside. . . . So, instead of allowing larger power structures and forces to act upon you as a passive, helpless object, you act upon them subjectively by expanding your knowledge" (21).

The problem with Olson, though, is the drive to totalization, to the projection of patterns upon the past. What is called for is a poetics that can be what Prevallet (following the Caribbean poet Édouard Glissant) calls a "relational" orientation toward history and knowledge. The special sense of "relational" here involves a nonappropriative relationship to the other, a relation that does not seek to bend the other to one's own ends. A relational poet, in this view, would accept "wandering, polylingualism, multiplicity" in "his or her thinking and interactions with the world" (24). According to Glissant, once we accept a relational view of the other, "we no longer reveal totality within ourselves by lightning flashes"; rather, "we approach it through the accumulation of sediments . . . lightning flashes are the shivers of one who desires or dreams of a totality that is impossible or yet to come" (Glissant 32). Prevallet glosses this, saying:

> This emphasis on the accumulation of sediments implies an apprehension of the world not as an unshaped bundle of materials waiting to be formed, but rather as a diverse and extensive patterning that is already formed and transforming, already imbued with a logic. . . . the relational poet is concerned with respecting what already exists and translating the content of the borrowed truth into a form that usefully complicates apparently simple truths. This . . . is the crucial difference between appropriation (stealing from the Other in order to complete oneself) and relation (recognizing that one's self and one's poetics are mutable forms, moving among the multiplicities that constitute the world). So, the poet is not writing above the larger environment, but through encountered and known materials. (24–25)

The relational investigative poetics that Prevallet finds largely absent from an American poetic scene that badly needs them constitute the central project of Matthias's poetry. His archaeological poetics have emphasized "the accumulation of sediments" both geological and textual, and his working of obdurate texts has been a reflection on materials "already formed." He has "mov[ed] among the multiplicities that constitute the world" without placing himself in a vatic position "above the larger environment"—in fact, he has appeared (in, say, "Turns" and at the end of "A Gathering of Ways") as the product of the very environment he investigates. That Prevallet, whose reading seems quite broad, is unaware of the affinities between Matthias's work and the project that she sees as vital for American poetry is a sad testament to the way that his poems have remained off the radar of a generation that could benefit from them. Working a variation on Gertrude Stein, we might say that we happen to need something that we do not know that we have been refusing. Having mistaken it for something else, we have yet to see how important it can be.

Chapter Six

John Peck

The Road to Zurich

"Mere Amusements"

Let me begin by going back to Robert Pinsky's "Essay on Psychiatrists," with its depiction of Yvor Winters addressing his graduate students circa 1963:

> *you will grow up*
> *To become happy, sentimental old college professors,*
> *Because they were men of genius, and you*
>
> *Are not; and the ideas that were vital*
> *To them are mere amusements to you.*

Those of us who entered the academic job market in the 1990s faced long odds in our quests to become happy, sentimental old college professors. The job market was desperately anemic, especially in the humanities, so when one of our number landed a decent tenure-track job in his or her field of studies, we were torn between celebration and envy. We all harbored a fear that our fate would be to serve as the part-time replacements for a slowly retiring generation of tenured, tweedy dinosaurs. Happy, sentimental old college professors? We should be so lucky. We were terrified at the prospect of ending up as embittered, disillusioned, old diploma-mill adjuncts. In the gallows-humor atmosphere of the hotel lobbies of late-1990s MLA conventions, though, among the newly purchased navy-blue blazers and the leather portfolios full of sample syllabi, there was one consolation: we were not alone in our misery. We had been preceded by a generation that faced a market even more benighted, an MLA job list even more barren and stricken than ours.

Back in 1970, when John Peck was still three years from finishing "Pound's Idylls, with Chapters on Catullus, Landor, and Browning," his enormous 700 page dissertation, the chairman of the MLA's Commission to Study the Job Market reached the "melancholy conclusion" that the new generation of Ph.D.s faced a situation that "could turn grim indeed" (Orr 1185). His sad prophecy soon came to pass. Peck confronted a job market that was rapidly coming to resemble the sterile, Eliotic wasteland that so many of his fellow Ph.D.s had spent years annotating and explicating. He, unlike so many others, did well, starting with a visiting position at Princeton and moving on to a tenure-track job at Mount Holyoke, where he made tenure after three years. Had he been cut out to be a happy, sentimental old college professor, he would have stayed put and been the envy of all the young English Literature Ph.D.s of the 1970s, who found themselves eking out uncertain livings teaching huge survey courses at obscure institutions in states devoid of coastline. Instead, Peck left.

In 1982, one of the bleakest years for academic employment on record, Peck resigned his associate professorship and went to Zurich, Switzerland, where for the next dozen years he studied at the C.G. Jung Institute. It is a move almost beyond understanding for a happy, sentimental, college professor such as myself. Beyond understanding, that is, until one realizes that Peck's writing of a 700-page thesis (such overkill, from an institutional standpoint) and his quitting an enviable tenured post are symptoms of the same condition. We might call this *intellectual seriousness,* a condition shared by Yvor Winters.

Winters experienced intellectual imperatives as personal imperatives. When he arrived at the conclusion that modernist poetics led to mental instability and moral decrepitude, he abandoned them to become a neo-Augustan. To understand just how strange this is, you may ask yourself whether you or any of your colleagues have ever felt a moral

imperative to change your writing style and, if so, whether you devoted decades to carefully developing and defending your new style. Is
style that *serious* to you? For most of us, the answer would be *no*. Peck's
deepest affinity with Winters—an affinity deeper than the subscrip-
tion to any particular tenet of Wintersian doctrine—comes through
the sharing of this disposition, and this conflation of the intellectual
and the personal. When Peck left Mount Holyoke for Zurich, he did
not do so for professional reasons or in response to any familial or romantic developments. He did so because he sensed an urgent need to
understand more fully his own poetics, and he found in Carl Jung a mind
that had thought deeply on the matters most urgent to him. Unlike his
more conventional colleagues, Peck did not wait for a sabbatical, scan
the back pages of the *New York Review of Books* for a house exchange,
and study Jung for a semester or two before returning with a somewhat improved understanding of the man and his works. The intellectual imperative, not relative to any practical concerns, was absolute.
Just as Peck felt compelled to write a mammoth dissertation (would
his committee really have denied him the degree if he had left out the
chapters on Catullus, Landor, and Browning?), he also felt compelled
to understand Jung at a profound level. That he did, and he returned
to the United States in 1992 wearing the mantle of a fully licensed
Jungian analyst.

Why Jung, one wonders? The answer, I think, lies in the deep
affinity between some of Jung's insights and Peck's own early sense
of the possibilities of poetry. In a way, Jung proved a more amenable
mentor figure for Peck than Winters. Although Peck underwent what
Pinsky called "a period of total conversion" to Wintersianism ("Robert
Pinsky" 246), he soon parted ways with his graduate-school mentor,
because his own orientation toward poetry was fundamentally at odds
with that of his teacher. Even in Peck's earliest books of poems we find
evidence that he did not want to make statements about experiences in
the Wintersian manner; rather, he saw the poem as an instrument of
augury. That is, the poem was a manifestation of truths not held wholly
in the conscious mind. Instead of speaking through the poem, as the
mature Winters did, Peck set out to listen to its multiple voices. Where
Winters saw the irrational as a threat and the conscious rational self as
the only legitimate self, Peck saw the irrational and unconscious self

as important and essential parts of the legitimate self, which could never be fully conscious and rational. This view, along with an early intuition that collective cultural experience shapes and conditions the self, led Peck to Jung.

Peck has been absolutely serious about his project, and so has his publisher, Michael Schmidt of Carcanet Press, who refers to him as "the most difficult and powerful poet" of the generation who studied with Winters in the 1960s (768). Peck is fortunate in having such a dedicated publisher: his very limited popular success would have long since put off a less principled director of publications. Reviewers (whom Peck has never lacked) frequently note and lament his unpopularity, his near-invisibility in the field of poetry. They usually explain this with reference to Peck's difficulty, his formal complexity, and, most important, his penchant for arcane references. "Too often," writes Jules Smith in the *Times Literary Supplement*, that forum for the educated and erudite general reader, "Peck is operating beyond the level of erudition that most readers would be prepared to tolerate" (22). While Peck certainly is a challenging poet, his status as the least-read Stanford poet of his generation is not just the product of difficulty. It is also the product of the changes in the American poetic field over the course of his career—in some cases, the very changes that lifted Pinsky's work to such great popularity and official acclaim. The result is an obscurity that would not much matter if the poetry did not, in fact, have something vital to offer us.

Pound versus Winters, Judge Davie Presiding

The English poet Clive Wilmer, perhaps Peck's best reader and no stranger to the works of Yvor Winters, sees Peck's *Shagbark* as "a debate between Pound and Winters with [Donald] Davie presiding" ("On the Turn" 34). The idea is intriguing, and one is certainly grateful for an interpretive key to a book as formidable as Peck's first effort. The circumstantial evidence strongly suggests both motive and opportunity for Peck to have written a book that pits Ezra Pound against Winters. Not only had Peck been something of a disciple of Winters' during the Old Man's last days at Stanford, but he had gone on to write his doctoral thesis on Pound under the direction of Donald Davie, Winters' successor at the university. When Davie arrived at Stanford, he had said that his project was to reconcile the projects of Pound and Winters. While he never quite managed to pull off that particular squaring of the circle, Davie kept at the problem, siding first with traditional formalism (in *Thomas Hardy and British Poetry*) and then with the Poundians (in *Under Briggflatts: A History of Poetry in Great Britain, 1960–1988*). Peck was always one to take his mentors seriously, and the debate between Pound and Winters was central to Davie's thinking for decades. In fact, Peck posed the debate between modernist and premodernist poetics in essentially the same terms as Davie when, in 1972, he published the essay "Pound and Hardy" in *Agenda*. It is hardly surprising that the debate would find its way into Peck's early poetry.

There is strong textual evidence to back up Wilmer's view of *Shagbark* as a weighing of Winters' case for an Augustan poetry. In the last of the book's four parts, for example, we find a number of poems reminiscent of the work of Winters' disciples: discursive, formal, and traditional, even to the point of being written in rhymed triplets. These are not among the strongest poems in the book, and, according to Laurence Lieberman, are probably "among the earliest writings" in the collection (272). The poems of the second and third sections also reflect the influence of Winters in that, like his mature poems, they are often addressed to specific individuals (friends, relatives, and mentors). For Winters, such dedications had been an element of Augustan sociability as well as a reaction to what he felt was the solipsism of modernist verse. Peck, though, uses the technique differently. He seems to be assessing different ways of being in the world, looking for possible selves—acts that in themselves lend credence to Wilmer's view of the book as a contest between Winters and Pound.

Two poems in particular, "Upper Trace" and "Involuntary Portrait," put forth the case for Winters and weigh it carefully in the balance. The former, dedicated to "Y.W.," tells the story of a young man and his mentor traveling into a rough, canyoned western landscape. While it would be going too far to read the poem as a literal representation of Peck and Winters journeying into the landscapes of Winters' youth, the dedication and the characterization of the tough old man in the poem support a reading as an elliptical assessment of Winters. As

the cold numbs the two men, they look at the glimmering floor of a
rocky valley:

                              I asked
    What is it throws the light back
    In steady points from the valley?

    He said, that is the sheer face
    Of granite sliced and smoothed by this,
    The tributary ice.
    A horse strange to this country
    Will smell the polished stone
    And test it with his hoof,
    Thinking it water.

The old man sees beyond the illusions that confuse animals. By implication this includes our sense-based animal selves who would, but for
the power of reason, also think the rock surface water. This character,
like the actual Winters, trusts in conscious reason rather than sense
experience. The Wintersian view is not criticized here, but if one were
to read the stanza closely, one might wonder about the apparently permanent stone of the valley being given shape by "tributary ice"—that
is, by water that appears as illusion, the prerational sense data trusted
only by animals. The poem asks just how far past illusion the old man's
reason really lets him see.

    In the next stanza, the actions of Peck's speaker provide material
for a slightly more explicit assessment of the Wintersian position:

    We made camp, my hands stung
    Back into feeling over fire,
    Remembering sundered heft
    Of things they made once.
    Ruddy, the fingertips of the pines,
    Brushing the silence, were so steep.
    His set face in the flickering
    Wash of embers
    Was yet the same

That I had seen,
But was far
As it had ever been.
Dumb blood, how long warmed,
Reached now from my hands
Into my own face in flood,
Barbed with sleep.

We might say that as his numbed limbs warm with the "dumb blood," the speaker is removed from the cold world of reason and reconnects with the animal world of the senses. He forges a bond with the world dismissed by the old man in the previous stanza. When we note that the pine trees rise in "fingertips," we can say that the whole realm of bodily nature returns to the speaker. We could also consider the "set face" of the old man in relation to the "sheer face" of the granite in the previous stanza. Here we see a contrast between the old man's view of himself as firm and permanent, set against his actual status as one being formed by large processes of natural change. Seen this way, the poem becomes an implicit critique of the Winters who believed in permanence and reason but was unwilling to embrace the inevitably prerational animal elements of the self.

"Involuntary Portrait" can also be read as a weighing, and in some respects a respectful rejection, of Winters. The poem presents us with an older figure, a mentor of sorts, who like Winters has "made spite and justice somehow both [his] friends." He stands on a headland against the ocean, in a pose reminiscent of that in one of Winters' major poems, "The Slow Pacific Swell." We are invited to read Peck's poem as a reply to Winters'. In "The Slow Pacific Swell," Winters opposes the conscious self to the kind of mindless natural forces that he had described in "At the San Francisco Airport" as "the rain of matter upon sense." He recollects a near-death experience (an actual event in Winters' life, sailing off Cape Flattery), and how

　　　　　　　　　　the sea
Hove its loose weight like sand to tangle me
Upon the washing deck, to crush the hull;
Subsiding, dragged flesh at bone. The skull

Felt the retreating wash of dreamy hair.
Half drenched in dissolution, I lay bare.
I scarcely pulled myself erect; I came
back slowly, slowly knew myself the same.
That was the ocean.

The destruction is literal but also figurative—a destruction of the conscious self, an oceanic dissolution from which he is fortunate to come
back and know himself to be the same. Now wary of the sea with its
brute, unreasoning force, he "would be near it on a sandy mound" where
"one may come/Walking securely, till the sea extends/Its limber mar-
gin, and precision ends." Terry Comito glosses the point with reference
to Allen Tate's two heresies, that of quality ("immersion in unmedi-
ated sensation," in Comito's words) and that of quantity (the desire to
"subsist wholly in intellectual constructs"). "The result of the first,"
writes Comito, "is disintegration," while the result of the second is "the
reduction of the world and the self to abstraction. One must live on the
brink," like the shore-walking speaker of "The Slow Pacific Swell" (148).

While the speaker of Peck's "Involuntary Portrait" expresses ad-
miration for the Winters figure, he finally lets his deep reservations
come to the fore. Thinking of the war that his mentor has been waging
against his times, the speaker says,

                    I see instead
    Your figure strangely set at a great remove

    Against a headland, posing there
    Before my camera. And as I watch,
    The focus will not hold you, and the air

    Works changes like a fantasy:
    Starts a scenario I cannot stop,
    Gives me the island exile by his sea.

    Fat sags along his poster jaw.
    His eyes twist vacantly, regardless still
    Of curlews overhead that wheel and call.

The cliffs march on the combers, deal
Their dull rebuff, and wait. Deal it and wait.
The curlews in their volley call and wheel.

Suddenly we shift from address to description. The "you" becomes a
"he" as the imaginary portrait continues:

And as he turns away,
The swift, high-angle shot of sentiment
Throws him steep upon the hill's flank —
His greatcoat slowly creasing the grass, and bent
In the slightest parabola of blank

Intention. He ignores the road.
The crest might not be there. Below and always,
The slope-heaved billows stupidly explode.

The shift from second to third person marks a separation from the Winters figure: the speaker is no longer in dialog with him but assesses
him from a distance. He sees the limits of the old man's perceptions,
notes the things against which he blinkers himself. The old man is unaware of, or uninterested in, the persistently circling birds—a fact that
gains significance when we remember that over the course of *Shagbark*
birds become symbols of augury.

The old man's refusal to make his peace with the sea, prerational
and billowing "stupidly," marks his limitations. The speaker, in contrast, is willing to follow the prerational and unbidden insight, building his meditation on a "scenario [he] cannot stop," a "fantasy" that
he nevertheless trusts will lead to insight. The very shape of the poem,
which depicts a mind following unwilled imaginative associations, is
to some degree anti-Wintersian. It implicitly rejects Winters' idea,
articulated in *Primitivism and Decadence*, that the "progression . . . of
reverie" and the pattern of "proceeding from image to image wholly
through the coherence of feeling" is an inferior form of poetic development (*In Defense of Reason* 57). This is not to say that Peck actually
proceeds by reverie or automatic writing: the poem seems far too coherent for that Bretonesque gesture. Rather, Peck depicts a process

of reverie-based meditative development in a poem whose rigorous, rhyming formality and semisyllabic measure indicate a highly deliberate, rational, and conscious act of composition.

If syllabics represented, as Pinsky claimed, "the official daringness of the Wintersians," then this poem pushes up against the outer limits of official daringness ("Robert Pinsky" 246). The prosodic form lies just within the boundaries of Wintersian acceptability, and the imagery and ideas are drawn from the Wintersian lexicon, but both the flirtation with reverie as a principle of progression and the critical distance from the Wintersian program are signs of incipient rebellion. Peck is very much Winters' student here, but a student who cannot live within the confines of his master's poetics. In the case of Winters versus Pound, Peck was a juror deeply ambivalent about the first party's case.

Pound or Round?

Just as surely as Peck owes Winters, Peck owes Pound. On this, all of his critics agree: Peck's work "has a kinship with that of Ezra Pound," says Wilmer ("On the Turn" 34); "Peck's project has been to honor and extend the Poundian tradition," says Jules Smith (22); Peck is "a devoted Poundian," says Frederick Pollack (205); "Peck's first father has been Ezra Pound," says Joan Hutton Landis ("John Peck" 751). I have joined the chorus myself, claiming somewhat hyperbolically that "John Peck isn't just a Poundian, he's a fully credentialed, card-carrying Poundian" ("John Peck: Modernist after Modernism" 164). But how right is this distinguished jury? In the case of *Shagbark*, one finds a great deal to support the idea that Peck is a true son of Ezra. But in the end, I have come around to Peck's own assessment of his work: "Pound I never was," Peck once wrote me, "opinions to the contrary notwithstanding. Round(er) and not Pound(ing), I believe. . . . An open-eyed look at what I've managed to do so far would not lend signal emphasis to Pound's example" (131). The very real Poundian elements of his work are subordinate, I think, to something else, something that would eventually lead Peck to give up tenure at a first-rate college and set him on the road to Zurich.

Let us begin with the very real Poundian influence. The file of *Shagbark*-based evidence begins with Peck's Imagist techniques. Some parts of the poems would have been suitable for inclusion in the early Imagist anthologies. In "Viaticum," for example, we find the following couplet:

Dust runs after the deer
Cloud prints the mountain

The "visual chord" technique described by T. E. Hulme (64) is very much in evidence, as is Pound's notion of the image as "a radiant node or cluster . . . from which and through which, and into which, ideas are constantly rushing" ("Vorticism" 57). As notions of wet versus dry, organic versus inorganic, elevated versus earthbound, motion versus stasis, and the like ricochet through the lines, one almost sees Pound nodding, stroking his scraggly beard and saying, "yes, *that's* what I meant by a poem of the *first intensity.*"

One might also make a convincing claim that Peck's orientalism and some of his more adventurous patterns of organization well up from Poundian sources. Poems such as "Colophon for Lan-T'ing Hsiu-Hsi" and its companion piece, "Colophon for Ch'ing-ming Shang-ho T'u," would not look out of place in Pound's *Cathay*, while the reverie-associative pattern of development in poems such as "Hunger-Trace" looks much like the poetics of Pound as described by Winters. But despite these traces of Pound, the more one looks at the poems of *Shagbark*, the more one finds some very real differences from Pound.

Peck's cryptic remark about being "round(er)" than Pound offers a clue about the nature of the differences between the two poets. For Peck, the round is the organic, and it exists in contrast to Poundian modernism, which he identifies with the hardness of stone. Consider the dedication in the copy of *Shagbark* that Peck presented to Davie (Davie, *Trying to Explain* 174): "To Donald Davie, / Master stone-carver, / This tree-rind." It references Davie's 1964 book, *Ezra Pound: Poet as Sculptor*, which identified Pound's art as the poetic equivalent of stone carving. Peck distances his book from the Poundian model and instead defines it as a circle of bark. The metaphor merits some consideration. Inert carved stone is worked by the will of the carver, who imposes his vision while respecting the limits imposed by the material. In contrast, the rinds or rings of a tree represent only the newest in an ongoing series of growing circles. Each ring is dependent on all those that have preceded it in the life of the tree and will be superseded over time as the tree continues to grow. The metaphor connects to the poems of *Shagbark* in three ways: in indicating a preference for growth over permanence; in hinting at the book's very un-Poundian sense of revelation as a slow process rather than a flash of insight; and in reflecting the book's interest in cumulative, collective historical experience.

Ideas of growth and change, and the accompanying rejection of any ideas of permanence, inform many of the poems of *Shagbark*. As we saw in "Upper Trace," for example, the apparently permanent granite is "sliced and smoothed" by "the tributary ice." As Davie puts it, "stone—emblem of the immobile and the enduring—is seen to be conditioned, if not indeed commanded, by what is on the contrary infinitely mobile and fluid, the element of water frozen and thawing and again frozen" (*Trying to Explain* 175). The ever-changing sea at the end of "Involuntary Portrait," the seasonal imagery of "Under Virgo," and the host of vegetative images that permeate the verses in *Shagbark* all point toward a world of process rather than a world of permanence. In fact, Peck sometimes presents the longing for permanence as an understandable but limited response to trauma. In "Spring Festival on the River," for example, we read about a panicked crowd as it flees across a bridge. We move from horrifying image of human suffering to horrifying image of human suffering, constantly reminded of historical cycles of violence and carnage. As the emotional pitch rises to the unbearable, the perspective suddenly shifts. We are among the crowd, and we look out at the hills beyond the city, asking:

> was it them I saw,
> Glancing and running? Red, then, they were,
> And silent: the bright and clear—
> Slabs of jasper, crystals of mica.

Running and glancing in a world of torturous change, the speaker longs for some sublime transcendence, and he seeks it in the great and distant stone of the hills. But this is not some Romantic moment of transcendence; it is not a version of Shelley's "Mont Blanc" or Coleridge's "Hymn before Sunrise in the Vale of Chamouni." Instead, we see such longings as the product of a traumatized mind that cannot bear exposure to the too-real world of flux, process, and change. Peck's is not the world of an Yvor Winters, who sought permanent values and wanted literature to be "absolutist" and convey a transhistorical "objective truth" (*In Defense of Reason* 11). Nor is it the world of an Ezra Pound, who wrote in his manic prose that *The Cantos* were meant to show the "moment of metamorphosis" when the quotidian world would "bust thru . . . into 'divine or permanent world.'" ("Letter to Homer Pound" 93). In his rejection of permanence, the young Peck was at odds with both of the litigants in the case of Winters versus Pound.

Related to this concern with processes is Peck's idea of revelation as a slow process rather than a sudden Poundian apprehension or a rational Wintersian conclusion. We recognize the progression inherent in the four-part structure of *Shagbark*. The first section, or first "ring" of "this tree book," as Landis puts it ("'Shipwreck, Autochthony and Nostos'"161), gives us the self isolated or alienated, striving in a world devoid of meaningful human contact. It is a world full of thresholds promising an entry into a world of permanence and revelation. In "Viaticum," for example, we undertake a journey that is both literal and spiritual (*viaticum* refers both to provisions for a journey and the Eucharist given in the last rites). We walk through a remote and isolated mountain landscape, up to the passes that loom as "Sills, thresholds" and that hold out the promise of a "firmness beyond."

In the second section, we enter a social world. No longer alone, we find ourselves surrounded by friends and mentors in the poems. This world expands in the book's third section, where the poems are populated by artists and others (Kierkegaard in "Soren," the anatomist Vesalius in "Cider and Vesalius," among them). We are linked to shared wisdom, as we read in "Colophon for Lan-T'ing Hsiu-Hsi," "the dead felt as we do,/Read them." The fourth and final section takes us not to some moment of firm and permanent wisdom, such as longed for in "Viaticum," but to the present. Landis understands the nature of the journey that Peck has undertaken as well as the nature of its conclusion: "in section IV, like Ulysses returning home to Ithaka, Peck breaks through into a present which has been there throughout the journey but is only at this point representable; he meets, as if for the first time, the Penelope whose 'sweater on the couch' now seems rich and an object allowable in his poems" ("John Peck" 751). *Shagbark* leads us away from isolation and the yearning for the timeless. We can arrive at the present moment and know it anew only because we have undertaken the long, slow journey from isolation through sociability and cultural heritage and have come back to where we started, knowing it for the first time.

The idea of collective historical experience that surfaces in a number of the poems of *Shagbark* is another manifestation of Peck's commitment to process and the organic over permanence. Perhaps the clearest instance comes in "The Factor Remembers His Lady," where we read:

> when I asked her what plan
> She would follow were she to lose her way, then
>
> She said her father once learned from his father
> An oath in runes for entry into the core
>
> Of their old wood; and learned the path leading there
> And learned the look of that hid place, forever.

Ancestral knowledge is cumulative, held for us in the "runes" of culture. Things learned are learned "forever," and our present abilities and consciousness must be regarded (to use Hegel's formulation) as "previously present, as an inheritance, and as the result of labor—the labor of all past generations of men" (Hegel 211). Such a view implies a deep interest in history that could be mistaken for a Poundian trait, but the nature of the interest is quite different from that of Pound and, indeed, from modernism in general. There is no sense of the present as an ironic or degraded repetition of the past (as in much of Pound, or in the Eliot of *The Waste Land*), nor is there a sense of the simultaneity of past and present from the perspective of eternity (as in the work of David Jones, or, say, the Apollinaire of "Zone"). Rather, the past is taken up in a present that grows out of and beyond it. The growth of knowledge, as one tree ring over another, is another instance of the non-Poundian "roundness" of Peck's *Shagbark*, the tree-rind he dedicated to Davie.

"The Litany of Fear Transmuted"

Since Peck is drawn to the organic and is skeptical of our ability to reason our way to timeless truths, it should come as no surprise that he is interested in the irrational as a key to both writing and knowledge. In "Cider and Vesalius," the most important and ambitious poem in *Shagbark*, Peck treats the work of the great sixteenth-century Belgian anatomist as an emblem of the processes of creativity and intellectual discovery. In doing so, he affirms both the rational, calculating, judging intellect and the primal, irrational realm of fear and fantasy. Winters could well have admired the poem's formal fluency and control but would have rejected it for legitimizing the irrational. Indeed, this sense of the legitimate nature of the irrational was one of the things that Peck himself brought to *Shagbark*, quite apart from the influences of Winters and Pound.

The poem tells about the assembly by the young Vesalius of an articulated skeleton, the basis of his important anatomical illustrations. He had had to undertake the work under the most gruesome of circumstances, covertly pulling limbs from the still-decaying body of a convict hanged by the roadside:

> The young
> Student went from Louvain
> Out to the roadside gibbet
> Late at night, and he pulled
> The femur off the hip—
> The bones were bare, still joined
> By ligaments—and then
> Each night thereafter, piece
> By piece, till finally

    Only the thorax hung
        From its chain. His desire
            Was great: he clambered up
    And yanked it off, and made
        His first articulated
            Skeleton.

Vesalius's "great desire" is important here: he must confront the irrational on his route to knowledge, and he must do so even to the point
of fearful hallucination ("Look again," says the speaker to Vesalius, "It
did not move, it stands/. . . dressed/in half its muscles"). "Recovering
those moments of terror . . . in which Vesalius' pioneering consciousness rode over a border, a subliminal as-yet-unbroken threshold, in the
racial mind of us all," writes Lieberman, "the poem reenacts the terrible
aura of discovery." Vesalius must encounter what Lieberman calls the
primal "fear of entering forbidden frontiers of man's brain" (271).
    Picking up on Peck's comparison of Vesalius and Hieronymous
Bosch as artists of the grotesque, Lieberman describes both men as
"oracles, prophets" exploring "unplumbed secrecies"(271). But this is
only half of the story. Peck's artists here are part *vates* or oracle, delv-
ing into the depths of the irrational, but they are just as much deliberate makers, creatures of reason and deliberation. They are powerful in
both unreason and reason. We do not want the fearful and irrational
straight, writes Peck: we turn to Vesalius because we "want the litany/
Of fear transmuted." Without the understanding born of the union of
the rational and the irrational, we live "without joy/or knowledge" in
mere animal existence, "bone against/Muscle, muscle against/Nerve
and vessel." Winters would say that we become merely animal when
we have surrendered our capacity for reason; for Peck such a fate is reserved for those who do not find a way to bring the rational and the
irrational into accord.
    The hanged and hanging skeleton itself becomes an emblem of the
rational and irrational:

    Its arm crooks in the quick
        Arrest of intuition,
            Its finger lightly bent

> Toward a zone haloing
> The smooth cope of the skull.

The body offers a gesture of prerational "intuition," a gesture that nevertheless points toward the skull as the seat of reason. We see here a synthesis that points toward Peck's attraction to Jung.

At the level of form and verbal surface, "Cider and Vesalius" has much in common with Winters: it is controlled, rather formal, and somewhat discursive. This is true of the majority of the poems of *Shagbark* (with a few notable exceptions, such as "Hunger-Trace," which, were it in French, would have been acceptable in one of the Surrealist salons). In his next books, though, Peck would increasingly allow his interest in the irrational and his sense of the intuitive as a legitimate part of our being dictate the formal bearings of his poetry.

Forms of Augury

"Augury" becomes one of Peck's key words in his second book, *The Broken Blockhouse Wall*, and for good reason. His concern with revelation as a slow process and his sense of the prerational as a legitimate part of the self lead him more and more to the conviction that the reading and writing of poetry are acts of augury, of divination and the interpretation of mysterious signs. Meaning was never really a matter of Wintersian statement for Peck, even in *Shagbark*. In *The Broken Blockhouse Wall*, though, Peck goes further in shunning the idea of the poem as an instrument for saying something definite and clear. The poem (for its writer as well as for its reader) becomes something to which one listens, hoping to understand what its mystery portends. Peck hints at this program in a number of poems, notably "Bounds." Here, he gives us a "gadfly questioner" moving among "the powerful sons/Of the powerful," whose questions "took them . . . through the gate/Into the half-formed, along the ravelling/Lifeline of his sentence." The questioner's role is not to lead his interlocutors to a definite truth, but rather to take them toward a half-emerged truth, still in the process of "ravelling." His work is a kind of "augury," Peck writes,

As when a swallow streaks

Up from the warehouse roofline, or erupts
Clearing the noon glare of the careful fields,
    Sensing already a changed air,

The shape of other weather in its climb
And dizzy spinout. Scrawled intelligence
    Of the turn.

The auger of classical antiquity would read the future in the flight of
birds, seeing in their paths and turns a "changed air," an obscure but
still readable knowledge in the "scrawled intelligence/Of the turn."
This is the kind of knowledge with which Peck has become concerned.

Many of the poems of *The Broken Blockhouse Wall* reflect this concern at the level of formal organization. "March Elegies," for example,
a 355-line poem in nine sections, eschews any easily ascertainable
order of coherence. The poem, whose sections take us through the
Pennsylvania landscapes of Peck's childhood, stories from his family
history, and the heroes of myth and legend, challenges its readers to
scrutinize it for the scrawled intelligence of its turns. No less a critic
than Alfred Corn has thrown up his hands at the task, saying that this
"striking poem" of "intricate verbal texture" can "be read a dozen, two
dozen times without its local clarities ever coalescing into any feeling
of coherence or verifiability" (*The Metamorphoses of Metaphor* 87–88).

It is not the case, though, that Peck surrenders to "the unwilling-
ness of experience to yield up anything intelligible," as Helen Vendler
has claimed ("Poets" 166). Rather, Peck lays down his landscapes, an-
ecdotes, and legendary heroes side by side in order for a variety of intelligible shapes to come forth. Total coherence may in the end remain
elusive, but intelligibility is not entirely sacrificed: significance in this
poem does not simply emerge at our command. The hermeneutic must
humble itself here. Peck knows this, writing in the fifth section that:

The temptation, the believable
Illusion, is
        that significance

Falls into place under one's need like land
  In its spread fullness.

Our inability to reduce the poem to total coherence is not, in Peck's view, tragic. He is no Ezra Pound lamenting, as in Canto 116, "I CAN-NOT MAKE IT COHERE." Instead, he is content to arrange the poem's parts side by side like the divination patterns of the *I Ching*, allowing us to find the various patterns of significance. Jere Odell once wrote that the joy of reading Peck lay in "the gradual and unending ascent to understanding. After reading and rereading, new strands of music, new levels of complexity float to the surface" (see Archambeau, "Outside the Penumbra of Postmodernism," 2). This is certainly true of "March Elegies," and it is also true of an increasing number of Peck's poems in the books that come after *The Broken Blockhouse Wall*.

Consider "Rhyme Prose Three" from Peck's next book, *Poems and Translations of Hî-Lö*. The initially apparent coherence is minimal, along the lines of a dream:

> The one finding his way to me will uncover in my cave the skull of his first similar, and the trickle of saving blood rusting its sutures, and the onset of storm, through eclipse and down-breaking flashings, in the twelfth hour approaching. But he will find too that the crown of my hill presages alternations with the breath of browsing deer I seem to remember from before time, auguring a last great change. He will find the exiled path of the stone.

Saving blood, a crown, a hill, and a "first similar," are all gathered into this dream vision. But the genre here is not free-form prophecy: in fact, the iconography turns out to be quite specific, having to do with Christ at Golgotha, and Adam as a prefiguration of Christ. This does not lead us to a convincing sense of the poem's total coherence or reduce it to a single meaning that can be claimed with authority. We do, though, begin to read the poem's "scrawled intelligence." We are the augurs of the poem's flight.

We cannot get past the title of Peck's next book, *Argura*, without encountering the poetics of augury. "Argura" is a neologism, as Peck tells us in the front matter: "My title corresponds to no single Latin word, but rather to elements that derive from roots shared among several terms" (*Argura* v). Rooting around in our Latin lexicons will yield *augere* (from which we derive "augury") as well as *argumentum* (inductive argument by evidence as opposed to *ratio*, or deductive reasoning) and *arguro* (to make clear but also to censure or reprove). The title tells us two things. First, through evoking the content of these three Latin words, the poems will make revelations (*arguro*) through combining the prerational intuitions of augury with the rational world of *argumentum*. Second, the title communicates not through statement but through connotation, through summoning up word-echoes from the cultural past. It offers no firm ground for a conclusive, coherent interpretation, only suggestions as to how it might be made intelligible. In this way it offers a clue for the reading of the poems that follow, which will also eschew statement and conclusiveness for polysemy and suggestiveness.

One of these poems, "Ars Poetica," explains Peck's project by comparing the composition of poetry to the geological formation of stone (another incremental natural process, like the tree-ring formation of *Shagbark*):

By silvery increment, by mineral touch of the remorseless,
The irregular stone takes shape, though it derives shape
From the ruled lattice, denuded hegemenous crystal.

The form of the stone is irregular, not reducible to a simple pattern, and the process of formation is cumulative, rather than a matter of architectural planning. To read other poems from *Argura* is to see what such an incremental, auguric art entails. "Little Frieze," "Rhapsody for the Gatekeepers," and "Frieze from the Gardens of Copenhagen," for example, offer moments when one feels as if the full shape of the whole will come into view, but in the end one finds irregularities that refuse to fit into the interpretive map that one has been constructing.

The poems of *Argura* were written when Peck was well into his studies at the Jung Institute, and in some important respects they are informed by Jung's own ideas about poetry. To understand Peck's relation to Jung, we need first to understand the latter's fundamental distinction between the two types of poetic art that he calls the introvert and the extravert. In his great essay "On the Relation of Analytic Psychology to Poetry," Jung describes the first of these as comprised of those literary works that

> spring wholly from the author's intention to produce a particular result. He submits his material to a definite treatment with a definite aim in view; he adds to it and subtracts from it, emphasizing one effect, toning down another . . . all the time considering the overall result and paying close attention to the laws of form and style. He exercises the keenest judgment and chooses his words with complete freedom. His material is entirely subordinated to his artistic purpose; he wants to express this and nothing else. He is wholly at one with the creative process. . . . the artist is so identified with his work that his intentions and his faculties are indistinguishable from the act of creation itself. (787)

Jung calls this "introvert art" because the author, rightly or wrongly, finds the source within himself: he identifies with the creative process and sees it as an expression of his will. This kind of artist "is characterized by the subject's assertion of his conscious intentions and aims against the demands of the object" (787). One could certainly see the mature Yvor Winters as such an artist, and damned proud of it. One might also say that, in Peck's terms, such an artist is a stone-carver rather than one whose books are gradually growing "tree-rinds."

The second kind of artist sees the creative act as somehow external to his or her conscious self, hence the term "extravert artist." Such an artist feels "subordination to the demands which the object makes upon him" (787). The works of such an artist, says Jung,

> force themselves upon the author; his hand is seized, his hand writes things that his mind contemplates with amazement. The work brings with it its own form; anything he wants to add is rejected, and what he himself would like to reject is thrust back at him. While his conscious mind stands amazed and empty before this phenomenon, he is overwhelmed with a flood of thoughts and images which he never intended to create and which his own will could never have brought into being. Yet in spite of himself he is forced to admit that it is his own self

speaking, his own inner nature revealing itself and uttering things which he would never have entrusted to his tongue. . . . Here the artist is not identical with the process of creation. (787)

The distinction between the two types is not absolute in Jung: sometimes, for example, one who perceives himself as an introvert poet "thinks he knows what he is saying but actually says more than he is aware of" (788). The two types represent extreme versions of the way poets can relate to their own creations. While Peck's work exhibits tight formal control and elaborate syntax of a kind that indicates a strong element of conscious composition, it seems clear that he embraces the extravert position.

We get a fuller sense of Peck's affinities with the extravert position when we consider what Jung has to say about the formal properties of extravert art: "It might be expected that this difference in origins would be perceptible in the work of art. For in the one case it is a conscious product shaped and designed to have the effect intended." In this case, Jung says, we would expect poems to

> nowhere overstep the limits of comprehension, [and] their effect would be bounded by the author's intention and would not extend beyond it. But with works of the other class we would have to be prepared for something suprapersonal that transcends our understanding to the same degree that the author's consciousness was in abeyance during the process of creation. We would expect a strangeness of form and content, thoughts that can only be apprehended intuitively, a language pregnant with meanings. (788)

When Corn despairs over how "March Elegies" can be read many times over without ever coming together into coherence, he is despairing at the extravert nature of Peck's art. Wilmer reacts more positively to the same qualities when he says that to read Peck is often "to feel on the verge of revelation," to be in a kind of hermeneutic tantra where "the full revelation never comes," but the poetry nevertheless "registers our sense of living in a world charged with meaning, some of which we can read, but most of which eludes us" ("Patterns of Flight"

23). The nature of a poem pregnant with meanings is, of course, that those meanings are never fully born to us but are instead on the verge of birth. This is where Peck often keeps us, in (to turn the metaphor back to an earlier point in the process of fertility) a kind of *jouissance*. His preference for a poetry of this kind takes him away from both Winters and Pound and draws him into the orbit of Jung.

Within You, Without You

Jung plays into another of Peck's core concerns, the interrelation of self and culture. The title of *Argura* itself speaks volumes about Peck's sense of the inevitable interpolation of the self in the cultural matrix. "Argura," is as we know, a made-up word. Let us also consider "kuboaa," a word invented by the great modern Norwegian novelist Knut Hamsun and put into the mouth of the starving hero of his masterwork, *Hunger*. For Hamsun's delirious hero, the word was a pure sound outside the realm of signifying language. "Kuboaa" was the verbal equivalent of one of Kasimir Malevich's paintings of a red square on a white background: everything familiar was to be left behind in the encounter with the unassimilated. "Kuboaa" was the word of the modern primitive, away from the freight of civilization. Peck's "argura," though, is a creature altogether different, a word that bears the weight of several etymologies. The point of a word such as "argura" is not to lift the reader up above the trails of cultural signification, but rather to send him down those trails in pursuit of historical and linguistic references. We cannot, in Peck, jettison the cultural past: we are always living with its echoes.

Jung's reverence for the idea of a lattice of cultural possibilities from which we draw—his often-misunderstood notion of the collective unconscious—must certainly have played a part in drawing Peck from Mount Holyoke to Zurich. The collective unconscious, for Jung, offers us a matrix of figures and emotions drawn from common experiences over the centuries, figures that represent "the psychic residua of innumerable experiences of the same type." Just as Peck sees the work of art as an incarnation of possibilities from an invisible lattice,

Jung sees art as a way for the collective unconscious to make itself manifest. As he again puts it in "On the Relation of Analytic Psychology to Poetry,"

> In contrast to the personal unconscious, which is a relatively thin layer immediately below the threshold of consciousness, the collective unconscious shows no tendency to become conscious under normal conditions, nor can it be brought back to recollection by any analytic technique, since it was never repressed or forgotten. The collective unconscious is not to be thought of as a self-subsistent entity; it is no more than a potentiality handed down to us from primordial times in the specific form of mnemonic images or inherited in the anatomical structure of the brain. . . . They appear only in the shaped material of art as the regulative principles that shape it. (791)

Since art that participates in the collective unconscious does so through the "unconscious activation of an archetypal image" (Jung 791), it is the province of the extravert artist. Peck's concern with extravert poetics actually puts us more closely in touch with the Jungian collective unconscious than, say, Robert Bly's more self-consciously archetypal work ever could. In contrast to Peck's project, Bly's attempt to work with the collective unconscious is, by virtue of its conscious intent, misguided from the start.

For a poet who spent a dozen years at the Jung Institute, Peck lets remarkably few archetypical figures gallop through his poetry. His engagement with the idea of the collective unconscious, though, is both very real and very profound. In *Selva Morale*'s "Tobelwacht," for example, Peck compares our human experience to the ancestral or species memory that guides migrating birds:

> Into hidden symmetries of the known
> the unknown floods and withdraws, side to side
> over stained, disregarded walls the blown
> foliage shadows of fresh solar tides . . .
>
> into the flared cups of crane's eyes Arcturus
> funnels orientation now, distilling

beady burning points, *rex quondam futurus*

no more brimming there with the age spilling

The birds have an instinctive, preconscious, communal knowledge that lets them know when and where to migrate. The same sort of knowledge applies to human experience, as the invocation of the Arthur of legend implies (Arthur is *"rex quondam futurus,"* the once and future king). We, like the cranes, draw from a storehouse of collective experience.

A number of critics have taken Peck to task for his apparent lack of concern with the autobiographical or lyric self. Christian Wiman, for example, has said that Peck is "open to Basil Bunting's charge against the Modernists . . . that their poetry derived too much from books and not enough from life" (298); while Barbara Herrnstein Smith once said that she found Peck's "a cold poetry" for similar reasons (see Landis, "'Shipwreck, Autochthony and Nostos'" 163). Peck is surely open to Bunting's charge, but if we make the effort to understand Peck on his own terms, rather than on the terms of our postconfessional biases, we see that the bookishness of the poems is entirely explicable. If the self (with the exception of the "thin layer" of the individual unconscious) is largely governed by a collective unconscious, and if the collective unconscious emerges most fully in works of art and literature, then in a sense culture is self writ large. To examine, as Peck relentlessly does, the arcana of the cultural past is in this view the only really effective way to understand the self. Archive becomes confession, and personal confession the merest ephemera.

This intimate linkage between self and culture, between what is within us and what is apparently (and only apparently) without us, is central to Peck and rather alien to Pound. Most critics likely to read Peck are also likely to know their Pound and to see the points of connection between Pound's historio-cultural concerns and those of Peck. Such connections are real, and Peck is happy to point them out, as he does in the preface to *Poems and Translations of Hî-Lö*. But such Poundian connections too often obscure Peck's affinities with Jung and therefore obscure the link between self and culture. When this link is made clear, Peck comes across as no less bookish, but as far less impersonal than many of his critics would lead us to believe.

"Over One Field through Generations"

"M," John Peck's poem in ten parts and 1,000 lines, sends off epic signals with its heroic similes and its beginning *in medias res*; it creates
eclectically allusive landscapes like those of Pound's idylls; and it takes
on matters as diverse as Leo Tolstoy, Antarctic scientific investigations, and Socratic ideals of nonviolence. But its primary theme is the
inseparability of self from culture and culture from nature. In this
respect it is very much a Jungian poem, envisioning as it does a powerful link between individual, collective, and species-oriented forms of
experience.

Despite its allusive density and oft-remarked complexity, the overall organization of "M" could not be simpler: we begin with an unnamed
hero's journey up a mountainside, we travel upwards, and eventually
we reach the peak to look down at the route we had taken. The tradition of pilgrimage, filtered through the Romantic transposition of the
spiritual onto the naturally sublime, lies behind the trope. The journey,
though, is studded with recollection, reverie, and erudite perorations.
Because we begin in isolation in the first section, then pass through
sections dealing with artists and cultural icons, and end at a kind of
quotidian moment, our journey in "M" is in many respects parallel to
the one we take over the four parts of *Shagbark*. In both its form and
its concern with collective experience, it is a restatement and a fulfillment of Peck's first book.

Again and again the poem asserts the collective nature of experience and the role of art as the repository of that experience. We see
this near the end of the poem when Peck recollects some of the odd
jobs he held in Zurich during his studies at the Jung Institute. Here, for
example, he works as a tutor teaching English to an immigrant, and
he finds that the books he has chosen for her reflect her experiences
and those of her people:

> The young woman
> From Czechoslovakia trying to master English, so to teach German,
> met with me over *Lord of the Flies* and *Animal Farm*.
> Eva had the peasant woman's build. Her father had farmed,
> then was drafted into factory work after the takeover

instead of being shot. She was their only child.
This Orwell story, it is not just story to me,
this animals say to me things we feel from inside
and outside. One of my other jobs sat me at the desk
of the Nordamerika Bibliothek on flake-drifted afternoons.
Yes, I would have preferred not to, but Bartleby starved.

"They are, so to speak, the psychic residua of innumerable experiences
of the same type," wrote Jung of the archetypes of the collective unconscious, which can emerge in works of art, even though they are "like
a deeply graven river-bed in the psyche" (791). Orwell's story clearly
ran in the same riverbed as did the life of Eva's father and, indeed, the
Czech people as a whole. And Peck, like many a moonlighting student
desk-jockey, felt in Melville's Bartleby a familiar psychic residuum bred
from dust, quiet, penury, and boredom.

The identification of the self with icons and forms drawn from the
cultural matrix occurs in stranger ways as well, as when Peck imagines entering a cathedral and meeting a ritual procession of men from
several religious traditions:

Then they came, processing from behind the flags,
a file of men, the central one shrouded in gray
with a faint ring of blood over his sheeted head
where a crown would have fitted, which in fact
he carried in front of him, his arms through slits in the fabric.
Before him walked a guard of three, the focal one
lifting high a Hindu dagger. I recognized
the pattern, ritually designated for the murder
of the precious *moi,* Sir President, Sir Chairman,
sinuous snakings up the hilt among brass glintings.
And then I recognized the sleeves of the shrouded man
as those of my own shirt. His knobbly knuckles were mine.

In this odd vignette, Peck sees himself as an incarnation of the Christ
figure, and Christ himself as part of a large sychretic vision of religions.

For Peck, high culture, in the form of literature and religious
ceremony, connects with and encompasses our individual experiences.

But his long poem offers other forms of participation in collective experience as well. At one point, for example, Peck turns to Tolstoy's *Anna Karenina* to show our need to partake of the ordinary lived collective experiences of generations—to become "no longer individuals, but the race," as Jung says in a passage somewhat unsettling to those of us who have been taught to value individuality and to tremble at the mention of collective thought:

> Tolsoy's Levin, as he came closer to both the fiber
> of what bonded him to the woman whom he chose
> and the charge of the land that chose him, swung a blade
> in rhythm with his serfs, the owner at last owning
> in release and penetration the waves of the blown field
> passing, falling to his stroke, respouting the seasons
> in green, gold, scorched, then white and sodden flashes,
> over one field through generations of hands
> flashing there also, wiping the brow, gone. (791)

Generations of labor in the same fields coalesce into a single experience, and the hands that wipe the brow at the end of the passage could be the hands of a single individual as well as the hands of multitudes who have lived and vanished. We connect with the lives of generations. Peck makes a more general statement of the same kind in another passage when he presents us with an image of a surging wind that blows at once "along hair of a forearm" and through a wheat field. This correspondent breeze affects the individual as well as the world at large and consists of "one stream" that would be the "companion of the stony mind." That is, it would lift the isolated mind out of its stony isolation, showing us how "that mind [is] one stratum in the store of mind." The sentiment is pure Jung.

The journey out of isolation into a conscious sense of how we are linked by formative collective experiences fascinates Peck throughout "M." As in *Shagbark*, he devotes a great many lines to the praise of artists and writers. Here, though, they are specifically figures caught in isolation, but reading and writing their way out of that state. He invokes Bakhtin, Cellini, Constance Markievitch, Osip Mandelstam,

Antonio Gramsci, and others, and calls upon what gods there be to grant them "Philosophy/as the lady due each solitary" (the prayer is, of course, another invocation, from Boethius's *Consolation of Philosophy*). He sees their cells as "wadded shut by power yet penetrable" by their own awareness of their connection to our always-shared culture and experience.

Along with his sense of how the self is the product of a culture, Peck has a sense of culture as an integral part of the processes of nature. In one odd and astonishing passage, he envisions his writers bending to write in their cells and absorbed through their writing into nature:

> Paper, scratchings, and their backs bend, husks from piths
> rotting into dispersal, blind vegetable into soil,
> mineral glint into metal, all flaking off the spin
> of their horizons into the Great Bear, Centaur, and then
> the Hunter. . . .
>   . . . up into ventral fins
> beating Anahata's rhythm, or into the cloud's body
> leaning above, trailing a lace rain over shoulders
> dozing among the near valleys, cold smoke on skin, brain,
> to harbor there, silting portals, atlases, the new
> poisons and potencies, unforeseen, all yeasting
> into the *epithuma*, crud-burn in the ritual
> sacrificial vessel, along the veins and hands, feeding
> flame we breathe out smokelessly, odor of the kind.

The passage makes Ovid's *Metamorphoses* look like a naturalist novel, but it does make sense in the context of the poem. The writers become a part of nature, first as soil, then as constellations, and then they return as rain to the human world in the valley, becoming at last fuel for the "flame we breathe out smokelessly." I take this flame to be speech or discourse, which is figuratively the "odor of the kind," that is, of the human species. One might remember here what Jung said about what we should expect from extravert art: "a strangeness of form and content, thoughts that can only be apprehended intuitively, a language pregnant with meanings" (788). The point of all this strangeness in the present context is the status of culture as a part of nature, as a species-trait, the characteristic odor of our kind.

"M" begins by proposing two different ways of experiencing our collective being, and it ends with a choice of sorts having been made between them. As he sets out on his journey up the mountain, our hero encounters an abbess, who speaks to him of:

> *the thaumaturge*
> *who drew the ten thousand strings of the intelligibles*
> *into his hands*
> > *at Jena, looking past Bonaparte and Christ*
> *into mirrors, dragging it all close, sinking in*

The riddle of the thaumaturge's identity is one of the easier ones in "M"—he is, of course, Hegel, and is named as such a few lines later. "Hegel," we read, "had arced his compass across the whole." This is the Hegel who theorized about the "concrete universal," the individual phenomenon that could only be understood by seeing it as the product of the totality of all precedent nature and culture. This is the Hegel who maintained that "the true is the whole." Hegel appears in "M" as the one who would climb to the peak and look down at all that had gone before and know it consciously.

In contrast to Hegel is the abbess, who, like Hegel, senses the interconnectedness of the self, the culture, and the natural world. Unlike Hegel, though, she does not strive to know these things from above in all their particulars. Rather, she immerses herself in the wholeness of the world without seeking conscious mastery of its particulars. As our mountaineer hero watches, she "vanishe[s] into all things." At the end of the poem, and at the top of the mountain, the hero looks back at the particulars of the world beneath him but finds that there is "less and less to see." "That part was over," he continues, "but the whole of it I felt/piercing through." After 1,000 lines that give us an often bewildering kaleidoscope of cultural moments and references, Peck chooses, like the abbess, to accept the interpenetration of things without encompassing it all in the arc of his intellect.

Collective experience, culture as a growth emerging from centuries of shared human experience, a sense (as Jungian as it is Hegelian) of the self and the present moment as explicable only as incarnations of a long history of culture: we can see why Peck was drawn to Jung as strongly as he was. "M," through its engagement with these concerns, is a fuller, richer version of the project proposed in *Shagbark*. It is a further ring of that growth, another, more encompassing tree-rind.

The Poet Belated

One could easily quote a dozen or so reviewers to the effect that Peck is a difficult poet; indeed, it sometimes seems as if his reviewers are contractually obliged to make this statement. Let me offer my favorite, from Wiman's review of *M and Other Poems*: "Read John Peck for any extended period of time," he writes, "and you can palpably feel the furrows on your face deepening" (298). This difficulty inevitably leads to his obscurity—or so say most of his critics. But is difficult poetry inevitably excluded from the canon? To answer the question, we first need to understand what we mean by "difficult," and then ask whether poets with this kind of difficulty have ever achieved fame and canonical status.

George Steiner rightly claims that in almost all instances, "what we mean when we say that a line of verse or stanza or entire poem is 'difficult' does not relate to conceptual difficulty." More often, Steiner says, what we signify by "a difficulty" boils down to "something that we need to look up" (19). When we say a poem is difficult, we don't generally mean that it is conceptually difficult. The problem of difficulty in poetry is, in Steiner's view, generally one of diction and reference. Difficult poetry of this kind works through words that imply a great deal, and "the implication is effected by virtue of allusion, of reference." This allusion, often literary, depends on an understanding of a literary continuity "of specific 'elementals,' and guarantors of felt meaning, namely Virgil, Horace, and Ovid, without whom the entire climate of recognitions on which our sense of poetic meaning depends would be hollow" (22). According to Steiner, this archive of traditional reference means one thing:

> Homework: mountainous, and becoming more so as our twentieth-
> century brands of literacy recede from the vocabulary, from the gram-
> mars, and from the grid of classical and biblical reference which have
> mapped the contours of Western poetry from Caxton and Chaucer to
> the archival gathering or museum-catalogue in *The Waste Land* and
> *The Cantos*. (26)

So, can a poet with this type of difficulty become canonical? Steiner
has already answered the question by invoking Eliot and Pound, two
of the most canonical American poets of the twentieth century.

Peck's difficulty is, for the most part, exactly the kind that Steiner
describes: his diction is often archaic or eccentric in order to be allusive, and his range of reference is wide and obscure, frequently giving
one the brow-furrowing realization that there is much homework to
be done. To this I would add syntactical difficulty, since Peck's sentences tend to be long and grammatically complicated, at odds with
both the speechlike limpidity of most contemporary poetry and the neo-
Steinian dissolving of syntax we see in much language poetry. But if
Peck's difficulty has much in common with the most canonical modernist poets, why is it nearly invisible to the public? The oft-repeated
reviewer's claim—that Peck's difficulty leads to his unpopularity—
implies a necessary link between difficulty and uncanonizability that
is demonstrably false.

The answer to the question of unpopularity lies in Peck's historical moment, as distinct from the historical moment of either Pound
or Eliot. Peck is difficult in exactly the way that Pound and Eliot are
difficult—as Stephen Burt puts it, "in the old high modernist way"
(154). Peck simply comes on the stage too late to be taken up by the
movement that made Eliot and Pound canonical figures: the New Criticism. Like Winters, who gave up modernism before the New Critics
came along to recruit modernists for the course syllabi, textbooks, and
anthologies where they remain firmly lodged to this day, Peck's timing
was unfortuitous.

Instead of landing in the hands of New Critics eager to track down
classical allusion and untangle convoluted syntax, Peck's first books
fell into the hands of people for whom the Lowell of *Life Studies* was
beloved, and the Lowell of *The Mills of the Kavanaughs* was just shy of

unbearable. When *Shagbark* came out in 1972, it followed in the wake of the narrative of poetic breakthrough from complexity to the ease of speech and personal confession. It had been six years since M. L. Rosenthal coined the phrase "confessional poetry" (*The New Poets* 83), and critics had come to expect poems in conversational speech on personal matters. These were expectations that Peck could not meet, and he has been criticized for not meeting them time and time again. He has been taken to task for writing "lines no one else would ever *say*" and veering "too far from imaginable speech" (Burt 154, 156); for writing poems "derived too much from books and not enough from life" (Wiman 298); for an unnecessary and unconversational "searching for unusual words" (Corn, *The Metamorphoses of Metaphor* 87); and for being "rarely confessional" and demanding too high a "level of erudition" (Smith 22). Laurence Lieberman proved prescient when he wrote, in 1973, that "many readers may dismiss Peck's first volume of poems, *Shagbark*, as weak-spined, after a glimpse at the obvious control, the unobtrusively handsome glamours of technical firmness." His work was too wrought for a generation weaned on speech-and-confession poetics, where strength was not measured in technique but in the courage to speak plainly in baring the soul. "No poet novice is likely to imitate Peck's style," Lieberman continues, and "perhaps not many will even notice him; he may loom a little outside their sights" (269–70). That he did, his kind of difficulty having gone out of fashion, washed away in the post-Lowell deluge of confessional talk.

Zero-for-Four

John Peck, says Annie Finch,

is a crossover phenomenon, his work respected and enjoyed by poets from wildly differing aesthetic schools. His voice is opaque enough for some Language poets, accessible enough for some "mainstream" poets, and conspicuously structured enough for most formalists. At a time when formalism and language poetry are commonly believed to occupy opposite ends of the poetic spectrum, John Peck's combination of experimental and formalist poetics is most distinctive, providing a much-needed model of how a poet can use form without sucking the individual life out of language. (219)

Finch is a perceptive critic, but she is wrong when she calls Peck a "crossover phenomenon." While Peck ought to have the kind of crossover audience that Finch describes, *M and Other Poems* was one of the slowest sellers from TriQuarterly Books in the year it came out.[1] Charting ninth out of eleven in the publisher's sales at the height of your career does not qualify one for "crossover phenomenon" status. One might also look to the number of language poets who have reviewed Peck's work (zero); the number of appearances in anthologies associated with that movement (none); and the number of reviews by New Formalists (nil) and the number of appearances in their anthologies (one, in Jauss and Dacey's *Strong Measures* back in 1986). If this is crossover success, the bar seems set a tad low. As for Peck's phenomenal success with the "mainstream" (however defined), one may point to his classmates Robert Pinsky and Robert Hass, with their combined total of five U.S. laureateships, as examples of what mainstream success really looks like.

The picture remains similar when we move from Finch's model of American poetry (a horizontal axis with language poetry at one extreme, New Formalism at the other, and a broad mainstream in between) to Kellogg's two-axis model of the field. Peck finds no strong constituency on either end of Kellogg's self-community axis, and none on either end of his tradition-innovation axis, either. His lack of appeal to the self-pole of poetic value can be explained through his refusal of confessional poetics. While he is, at a profound level, concerned with the self, his sense of self as formed by culture and collective experience drive him away from immediate personal experience. History, the collective unconscious, and art as the expression of that unconscious are, for Peck, the royal roads to the self. Such understanding, though,

1. My rankings come from two sources: one an affiliate of Northwestern University Press (which distributes TriQuarterly Books), who asked not to be named; the other a comparison of Amazon.com sales rankings. Neither of these constitutes the kind of evidence one would want to take to a courtroom, but they do give a little more rigor than Finch's method, which she describes as only an informal survey.

is hardly the common view of our times, and certainly not the understanding of those who value confession in the manner of a Sharon Olds or a Louise Glück. One might think that Peck's concern with shared group experience and the collective nature of identity would endear him to those who value Kellogg's poetics of community. But no, the important thing about community poetics, for Kellogg, is differentiation from other groups, the poet's participation in "the social claims of one or more" identity-based groups ("The Self in the Poetic Field" 101), and the implicit exclusion from other groups. Peck's Jungian sense of collective experience at the level of species involves a community on too large a scale to register as significant from the perspective of identity poetics. Species is simply not a category for identity politics.

Peck has not been claimed by any of the prominent proponents of innovation in poetry. It is perhaps apparent that Peck's Poundianism has sidelined him with advocates of language writing. While Peck is deeply immersed in tradition and writes poems that are often masterfully metrical, his Poundianism does not play any better with New Formalists than it does with language writers. Peck's is a poetry that has quite clearly assimilated modernism, and as such it can never sit comfortably with a movement whose rhetoric is fundamentally anti-modernist. It is exactly the sort of poetry that, Dana Gioia argues, we need to get past if poetry is to matter.

One wonders how well Peck would have been able to fight his way upstream against the strong currents of self, community, innovation, and tradition, had he stayed on at Mount Holyoke rather than pursuing his studies in Zurich. The university, as Ron Silliman says, has become the "primary institution of American poetry," and it is there that one gains credibility with presses and publishers, that one builds the networks that result in prominent reviews and prize nominations. It is also the place where poets cultivate students and (more important, from the perspective of posterity) graduate students. Such people represent an audience schooled in the taste by which the poet-teacher's work is most sympathetically judged. They often go on to build other audiences when they become professors or enter the world of editing and publishing.

Think of Yvor Winters' students, and one sees the importance of a university position. Students of Winters have been the base from which his best critics have been drawn. It was his student Donald Hall who got Winters the Bollingen Prize. It was his student Helen Pinkerton Trimpi who introduced his 1999 *Selected Poems*. One wonders if a proper selection of Winters' poetry would ever have been produced had Winters not been an academic: it seems likely that Donald Davie, who edited the first posthumous collection of his poetry, would have felt less obliged to do so had he not been Winters' successor at Stanford. Not only can an academic position influence one's stake in posterity, but it can also prove a boon for one's own poetic or parapoetic output. Beyond the obvious provision of time in which to write (summers, sabbaticals, leaves), the academy is a source of assistants (student and otherwise) who can further one's causes and extend one's visibility. Ken Fields co-edited Winters' anthology, *Quest for Reality*, while a graduate student at Stanford, for example, and Boston University provided Maggie Dietz (as co-editor) and a small cadre of support staff for two of Robert Pinsky's best-selling books, *Americans' Favorite Poems* and *Poems to Read: A New Favorite Poem Project Anthology*.

How much may Peck have lost in terms of prominence by leaving Mount Holyoke for his studies in Zurich? The poor fit between his work and the dominant forces shaping the American poetic field would have kept his reputation somewhat marginal in any case, but his cause has certainly not been advanced by his having left the path of the happy, sentimental old college professor.

"For Lack of What Is Found There"

It is difficult
to get the news from poems
yet men die miserably every day
for lack
of what is found there.

These lines from William Carlos Williams's "Asphodel, That Greeny Flower" have always seemed a bit hyperbolic to me. I cannot picture any nonreaders of poetry clutching their chests and collapsing from a lack of poetry's defibrillatory cures. But Williams did have a point: we can be much the worse for not having what certain poems offer us. Thus, I would like to end this chapter with a question: Does it matter that Peck's work is, by and large, unknown and unread outside of a small circle of admirers? This is another way of asking whether there is something important in the poems, something that we need but have not yet realized that we need. Peck's poems, I think, do have something to offer—if not to everyone, then to more people than have had a chance to read them.

What is significant about Peck has, in fact, a lot to do with his unpopularity. He is part of no movement, and the more one gets to know his work, the less one sees of any substantial resemblance to the work of other poets, including Pound. Wilmer has even gone so far as to say that Peck "open[s] up territory no one else has attempted" ("Patterns of Flight" 23). This makes for no happy reception, but, as Peck's great mentor Jung pointed out, it is the unusual work that has the greatest potential significance. The "social significance of art," says Jung, lies in how "it is constantly at work educating the spirit of the age, conjuring up the forms in which the age is most lacking. The unsatisfied yearning of the artist reaches back to the primordial image in the unconscious which is best fitted to compensate the inadequacy and one-sidedness of the present" (791). What Peck's work offers is not so much any particular image or archetype or structure of feeling drawn from the past, but an attitude toward the past itself.

This attitude, which contemporary American poetry does not have in abundance, could be best described as a reverence for the past that is unguided by the willful intellect. Even among poets attuned to history, Peck's project is rare because it is not guided by a particular, consciously chosen intellectual agenda. Peck's most important historical poems (such as "M") can seem disjunctive because they do not set out to investigate particular problems or topics with any boundaries in mind. In this, they differ from, say, Olson's geographic and historical "saturation jobs" and the work that follows in that tradition, such as Clayton Eshleman's investigations of the prehistoric caves of the Dordogne. Peck's poems differ, too, from identity-group-specific poems of historical investigation and their projects of cultural recovery. They even differ from John Matthias's historical poems, in that Matthias's work tends to be bounded by a specific geography or a specific text.

For Peck, though, there are no limits on the allusive connections that his poetry will make, no textual or geographic boundary to the poems' potential area of significance. This is a source of much of Peck's difficulty and his occasional unreadability, since it presupposes something akin to a confluence of all possible knowledge on the part of the reader. It also represents a poetic that could well unearth connections between past and present that would otherwise go unnoticed. It is a powerful laboratory for discovery.

A poetry of this kind would, I think, be an important gift to a country where much of the most prominent poetry seeks to affirm the present and its values. To imagine what such a country would look like, think of a place where a three-time U.S. Poet Laureate writes an "Ode to Television" in praise of the wisdom of Oprah Winfrey (oh, gentle American reader, you live in such a stricken land). Peck's brand of exploration will never sell like the work of such a laureate, but from a certain perspective it simply matters more.

Epilogue

The shortest answer one could offer, if asked where Yvor Winters and his last students are now, would be, "all over the map." The map here would be David Kellogg's chart from "The Self in the Poetic Field," and the poets whom we have been reading continue to be spread across broad portions of the poetic landscape staked out by Kellogg. Some continue along the same trajectories they have been following for years, while others have, to a greater or lesser degree, shifted course.

Winters' posthumous reputation remains overwhelmingly that of a poet of traditional formalism. With a few notable exceptions, the major works in Winters studies remain those written by critics who were his students in his mature phase, and these tend to reflect what we might call a Wintersian view of Winters. The most significant contribution to this view in recent years has been Helen Pinkerton Trimpi's introduction to the 1999 *Selected Poems of Yvor Winters*. Her long essay, destined to be read by a good part of his followers, is not overtly partisan in its favoring the mature Winters over the younger poet, but her preference for the Augustan Winters shows in a number of places, as in the following passage:

> Winters appears in retrospect not to have lost much through his early experimental poetry, though he personally regretted the years he lingered under the ignis fatuus of poetic "immediacy." Rather, one positive result clearly was a carryover of a lifelong

solicitude for exact sensory detail in any phrase or descriptive line
within a poem written in traditional meter and form. (xxx)

In Trimpi's view, Winters' early work was not a total loss: it added a
certain visual precision to his later work. This is not hardcore anti-
modernism, but it is a continuation of the mature Winters' dismissal
of the young Winters. If all you can say of his experimental period is
that he had not "lost much" from having done the work, your own
preferences are clear enough.

Interestingly, the book that Trimpi introduces opens up the possibility of a different evaluation of Winters. The poems selected for
that collection by R. L. Barth include a few of the early works—"Two
Songs of Advent," "One Ran Before," "Alone," and "Song of the Trees."
The engagement with Imagism, Native American poetics, and Japanese poetry is clear and shows us not only the brooding moralist of
the late years, but also the young poet whose work appeared in avant-
garde journals alongside that of James Joyce and Gertrude Stein. If
this side of Winters becomes part of his public image, it is possible
that he will be claimed by advocates of innovation as well as tradition.
Such a development could lift his stock higher on the great posterity
exchange board. It remains for some ambitious critic to take advan-
tage of the opportunity for a reappraisal.

If Winters remains, for the moment, a poet of tradition, then
Robert Pinsky remains very much a poet of community, with the community in question being a large, populist, national one. His Favorite
Poem Project is an excellent example of the kind of inclusive American
community that Pinsky imagines for himself. The poems in the project's two anthologies were chosen by a broad cross section of people.
The community envisioned in the anthologies, like that envisioned in
An Explanation of America, is general, rather than specific. The only
group deliberately excluded consists of poetry professionals, poets,
and critics: an exclusion that emphasizes Pinsky's populism and his
aversion to a poetic economy based on the principle of production for
producers.

Pinsky's collection *Jersey Rain* often traffics in topics and images
with a broad and rather populist public appeal. "A Phonebook Cover
Hermes of the Nineteen-forties," for example, uses as its muse an old

version of perhaps the only book that can be found in every American household. "To Television" praises the medium that appeals most strongly to the vast majority of the population, taking a balanced view of it as a "Homey miracle, tub/Of acquiescence, vein of defiance" rather than condemning it from a cultural elitist's perspective. The elegy "In Memory of Congresswoman Barbara Jordan," as public a poem as can be written, mourns the loss of a well-known and well-loved figure in national politics. While there are deeply personal poems in *Jersey Rain* (such as "An Alphabet of My Dead"), the overwhelming emphasis is on topics that will appeal to a broadly defined American community, as opposed to any specific group defined by race, gender, class, or religion.

In some ways, Pinsky was made for a democratic, populist national laureateship, and he has never fully left the role behind. He has certainly seen it as his task to speak to moments of national importance. In *Gulf Music*, for example, he sets out, in "The Anniversary," to write an elegy on the events of September 11, 2001. The occasion sends him back to civic imagery, including the national Great Seal he had written about in *An Explanation of America*. By and large the poem does its difficult work well, but there are moments when the civic imagery skirts kitschiness, as in the final invocation of the Statue of Liberty with an Elvis Presley sneer. I suppose the Elvis reference is meant to give a sense of American defiance in the face of the attacks of that tragic day, but for those of us born too late to remember Elvis in his heyday, it is hard to avoid a certain campiness when his name is invoked. Pinsky deals with 9/11 more successfully in "The Forgetting," another poem from *Gulf Music*, which joins William Carlos Williams's "The Crowd at the Ball Game" as one of the finest American poems about thoughtless crowds and their ominous power.

While Pinsky has been consistently interested in broad American concerns in his poetry, his prose book, *The Life of David*, inaugurates a new series of books called "Jewish Encounters." If it indicates a turn toward religious or ethnic identity in Pinsky's work, then it will prove to be the first step down a new avenue for a poet who has heretofore been interested in more general concepts.

James McMichael's recent development may at first appear to be the most surprising of any of the poets under consideration here. After his flirtation with American Surrealism in the late 1960s and early

1970s, McMichael seemed to have charted a steady course into a kind of personal, discursive poetry, almost flat in its eschewal of anything other than what Pinsky called the prose virtues in poetry. In the new poems of *The World at Large: New and Selected Poems*, though, we see something of a departure from this personal, essayistic course. "Pretty Blue Apron," for example, looks at times as though it could have been written by a mathematically inclined experimental poet such as Stephanie Strickland or Randolph Healy:

> In the separate histories
> wanting writes
>
> zero doesn't count. Nothing had
> happened yet. Zero.
>
> Then it had.

The poem soon assimilates this strange abstraction to one of McMichael's recurring themes, the relationship of child to mother:

> There was placental
> discharge and infusion. These didn't
>
> follow one from another as the night the day,
> there wasn't time. With nothing
>
> private for it, undeprived
> the fetus took in everything as
>
> one one one one one without one
> "and" between . . .

The "undeprived" infant is destined for the kind of loss that McMichael writes of in "Four Good Things." While the form is less essayistic, the poem remains consistent with his self-oriented poetics.

The collection *Capacity*, too, is remarkable for its ability to keep the emotions at a distance. *Capacity* consists of seven poems, or rather seven parts, since they add up to a single, book-length whole. It is a

strangely disparate and restrained book, but no more so than Mc-
Michael's earlier long poems. Like the first of his truly ambitious long
poems, "Itinerary," from 1974's *The Lover's Familiar*, *Capacity* takes on
matters of historical importance (in "Itinerary," it was the Lewis and
Clark expedition; in the present volume he addresses the Irish potato
famine at some length). Like *Four Good Things* (McMichael's book-
length poem of 1980), *Capacity* deals with many apparently disparate
topics. It begins with a book of photographs of the English country-
side, goes on to describe the wave forces working in the North Atlantic, comments on the nature of Newtonian space, depicts a scene of
family drama, details the process of human fertilization and gestation,
outlines chilling episodes from Irish history, and works its way back
to the book of photographs via the Second World War and the nature
of the will to live. *Capacity* also has much in common with *Each in a
Place Apart*, McMichael's 1994 effort, most notably in its deep distrust
of our most primal impulses, especially our sexual urges, which lead to
ill-advised actions in both books.

No matter how interesting and unusual McMichael's work is,
though, one hardly expects it to gain him popularity with a public
whose expectations for personal poetry are still governed by the norms
of confessionalism, with its individual particularity and emotional
heat. The issues in McMichael's poetry remain personal, but the levels
of abstraction and emotional reserve have, if anything, increased.

Like McMichael, Robert Hass is not prolific, but his literary activities since the publication of *Sun under Wood* affirm his previous place
as a poet appealing to many different constituencies. *The Best American
Poetry, 2001*, which he edited, represents a more catholic taste than
that of most of the series' poet-editors, and his translation of Czeslaw
Milosz's *A Treatise on Poetry* represents his continued commitment
to a discursive poetic that complements his commitment to a poetics
of the image. He has also added a Pinsky-like civic component to his
work in poetry. Although Hass was more of a Bay Area campus radical than Pinsky back at Stanford, his poetry has rarely been as civic-
minded and political as that of his classmate. If one were to judge by
the poetry alone, one might think of Hass as more the California he-
donist than the Left Coast politico, but in 2007's *Time and Materials*,
some of the most ambitious poems turn to public themes.

Not all of the civic poetry plays to Hass's strengths, though. The eight-page environmentalist poem "State of the Planet," for example, was commissioned by the Lamont-Doherty Earth Observatory of Columbia University in New York, and it reads like a poem written on assignment for the benefit of a worthy cause. One understands why Hass structures the poem as a letter to the Roman poet Lucretius, whose *De Rerum Natura* took a scientific perspective on the universe and urged us to take responsibility for our actions. Too often, though, the addresses to Lucretius feel like they're giving exposition that Lucretius would not need to hear. This, combined with the device of paraphrasing the contents of an imaginary science textbook that Hass places in the backpack of a passing schoolgirl, results in a very didactic poem indeed. This didacticism was appropriate to its first venue of publication, the science pages of the *New York Times*, but here it comes across as terribly *worthy*. On the other hand, Hass has written one of only two wholly successful poems on the fiasco in Iraq. The remarkable "Bush's War" stands alongside Eliot Weinberger's "What I Heard about Iraq" as a major poem about a conflict that has produced almost no successful poetry.

John Matthias has been more prolific than Hass, publishing three volumes of new poetry and a *New Selected Poems* since his collected poems in two volumes were released by Swallow Press in 1995. The most ambitious poems of the first of these new books, *Pages New Poems and Cuttings* (2000), are just as allusive and information-oriented as those of *A Gathering of Ways*, but they investigate texts rather than geographies. Where *A Gathering of Ways* found subject-rhymes based on topographical connections, sequences from *Pages New Poems and Cuttings* find such connections in specific archives—botanical illustrations or a cache of old yearbooks found in Matthias's deceased father's closet.

Matthias's *Working Progress, Working Title* (2002), moves even farther from a poetry of place. The volume's most important long poem, "Automystifstical Plaice," is, among other things, an investigation of the strangely placeless world of information technology. Combining the stranger-than-fiction story of how the actress Hedy Lamarr and the experimental composer George Antheil collaborated on wireless technology with tales of the Parisian avant-garde, the poem could be regarded as a deconstruction of the very idea of place. It is perhaps Matthias's most experimental work to date, and the crossing of high culture and pop culture may help dispel the false impression that his work is somehow "just modernism." While he continues to resist taking on an active role in the promotion of his poetry through the usual channels (readings, frequent travel), the possibility is open for a greater appreciation of his work by those committed to innovation in poetry.

The poems of Matthias's 2007 collection, *Kedging*, continue his voyage into experimentalism. In "Laundry Lists and Manifestoes," for example, he works up variations and combinations of famous lists from history and literature (the contents of Tom Sawyer's pockets, the manifest of animals on Noah's ark, the catalogs of ships in the Homeric epics, the great roll call of Don Giovanni's loves in Mozart's opera) and mixes them with references to the manifestoes of the great disruptors of literary and artistic order: Klebnikov, Marinetti, Antonin Artaud, and Tristan Tzara. "Laundry Lists and Manifestoes" is almost impossible to excerpt effectively: all the action takes place in the reworking of variations of the lists, in which we watch connections alternately established and disrupted. To quote a few lines out of context would be like showing a couple of square inches of a Jackson Pollock painting to indicate the interplay of order and chaos on the canvas as a whole. One hardly knows how to describe the form of the poem without recourse to the vocabulary of poststructuralism: *multiplicity*, one thinks, or *heterogeneity*, or, above all, *rhizome*. In the hands of a poet who did not have Matthias's perfect ear for the connections between apparently disparate phenomena, it could have turned out to be somewhat of a train wreck, but here it creates an astonishingly rich music. "Laundry Lists and Manifestoes" even has a kind of sublimity to it, offering a glimpse into the infinite number of ways connections between things can be lost and found.

Like Matthias, John Peck does little to promote his poetry, especially since leaving the poetic-academic nexus with all its privileges. His current project is a continuation of "M," his long ambitious poem of 1996. As such, it promises to affirm his current course of unorthodox experimentation and to be both fascinatingly idiosyncratic and entirely unpopular. The same fate, I think, awaits *Red Strawberry Leaf,* the collection released by the University of Chicago Press in 2005. Peck's method in this book, as always, is to take a theme and treat it with reference to the past, specifically the intellectual past of what used to be called the Western Tradition, from the pyramids at Gizeh and the Acropolis onward. On "A Stock-Taking," for example, Peck offers us something like a statement of his cultural historian's poetic. Here, he gives us several images for his method of writing, which always treats contemporary experience in relation to its past parallels, or as a result of the cultural forces that have led up to it. Peck is, it seems, fully aware of the strenuous effort that his poetry requires for both writer and reader. He is also aware of its unfashionableness, noting that it may cause people to walk away from the work. That he remains committed to such a challenging and unfashionable aesthetic is the sign of a fierce intellectual integrity. It is also the result of an intellectual background as idiosyncratic as it is impressive. One imagines that *Red Strawberry Leaf* will slowly attract a few more readers to Peck, but one hardly expects him to become the "crossover phenomenon" described by Annie Finch.

Donald Davie argued, in his introduction to *The Poetry of Yvor Winters*, that Winters was larger and more various than his own doctrines. Looking at the remarkable variousness of the achievement of his last generation of students—each one of whom is deeply indebted to the teacher—one realizes the breadth of Winters' legacy. The legitimate legacy of Winters, like his own poetic achievement, extends far beyond the work of his most orthodox students. I have aspired to show that it spans almost the entire length and breadth of the American poetic field.

Works Cited

Alacalay, Amiel. *From the Warring Factions*. Venice, Calif.: Beyond Baroque, 2002.

"Allen Ginsberg Will Share the Stage with Robert Lowell." *New York Times*, 22 February 1977, A36.

Altieri, Charles. *Postmodernisms Now: Essays on Contemporaneity in the Arts*. State College: Pennsylvania State University Press, 1998.

————. *Self and Sensibility in Contemporary American Poetry*. Cambridge: Cambridge University Press, 1984.

Anania, Michael. "John Matthias' *Bucyrus*." *Word Play Place: Essays on the Poetry of John Matthias*. Ed. Robert Archambeau. Athens: Ohio University Press, 1998. 20–25.

————. Personal Interview. 20 May 2004.

————. "Talking John Matthias." *Samizdat* 9 (Spring 2002): 3–5.

Archambeau, Robert. "John Peck: Modernist after Modernism." *Notre Dame Review* 11 (Winter 2001): 164–68.

————. "Outside the Penumbra of Postmodernism." *Samizdat* 4 (Fall/Winter 1999): 2–3.

————, ed. *Word Play Place: Essays on the Poetry of John Matthias*. Athens: Ohio University Press, 1998.

Arnason, David. *Fifty Stories and a Piece of Advice*. Winnipeg: Turnstone Press, 1982.

Barthes, Roland. *Writing Degree Zero and Elements of Semiology*. Boston: Beacon, 1970.

Beach, Christopher. *Poetic Culture: Contemporary American Poetry between Community and Institution*. Evanston, Ill.: Northwestern University Press, 1999.

Bedient, Calvin. "The Retreat from Poetic Modernism." *Modernism/Modernity* 1.3 (1994): 221–31.

Berman, Paul. *A Tale of Two Utopias: The Political Journey of the Generation of 1968.* New York: Norton, 1997.

Bernstein, Charles. *My Way: Speeches and Poems.* Chicago: University of Chicago Press, 1999.

Bloom, Allan. *The Closing of the American Mind.* New York: Simon and Schuster, 1987.

Bloom, Harold. *The Anxiety of Influence: A Theory of Poetry.* New York: Oxford University Press, 1997.

Bly, Robert. "The Work of Robert Creeley." *The Fifties* 2 (1959): 10–21.

Bogen, Don. "A Student of Desire." *The Nation* 249.20 (11 December 1989): 722–23.

Boswell, James. *Life of Johnson.* London: F. Thomas, 1792.

Bourdieu, Pierre. *The Field of Cultural Production.* Trans. Randal Johnson. New York: Columbia University Press, 1993.

Bromwich, David. "John Ashbery: The Self against Its Images." *Raritan* 5.4 (1986): 36–59.

———. "Robert Pinsky." *Contemporary Literary Criticism*, vol. 9. Detroit: Gale Research, 1978. 416–17.

Brooks, Cleanth. "The Formalist Critic." *Twentieth Century Literary Theory.* Ed. K. M. Newton. New York: Macmillan, 1997. 26–29.

———. "The Heresy of Paraphrase." *Critical Theory since Plato.* 2d ed. Ed. Hazard Adams. New York: Harcourt Brace Jovanovich, 1971. 961–67.

Bunting, Basil. *Briggflatts: An Autobiography.* London: Fulcrum, 1966.

Burt, Stephen. "Poetry in Review." *Yale Review* 85.3 (July 1997): 142–58.

Carruth, Hayden. "Impetus and Invention: Poetic Tradition and the Individual Talent." *Harper's* 258.1548 (May 1979): 88–90.

Casey, Edward S. *Getting Back into Place: Toward a Renewed Understanding of the Place-World.* Bloomington: Indiana University Press, 1993.

Caws, Mary Ann, ed. *Manifesto: A Century of -Isms.* Lincoln: University of Nebraska Press, 2000.

Comito, Terry. *In Defense of Winters: The Poetry and Prose of Yvor Winters.* Madison: University of Wisconsin Press, 1986.

Corn, Alfred. *The Metamorphoses of Metaphor: Essays in Poetry and Fiction.* New York: Viking, 1987.

Davie, Donald. "Introduction: The Poetry of Yvor Winters." *The Poetry of Yvor Winters.* Ed. Donald Davie. Chicago: Swallow Press, 1978.

———. *Thomas Hardy and British Poetry.* New York: Oxford University Press, 1973.

———. *Trying to Explain.* Manchester, Eng.: Carcanet Press, 1980.

————. *Under Briggflatts: A History of Poetry in Great Britain, 1960–1988.* Manchester, Eng.: Carcanet Press, 1989.

Delville, Michel. *The American Prose Poem: Poetic Form and the Boundaries of Genre.* Gainesville: University Press of Florida, 1998.

Derrida, Jacques. *Of Grammatology.* Baltimore: Johns Hopkins University Press, 1998.

Doody, Terrence. "From Image to Sentence: The Spiritual Development of Robert Hass." *American Poetry Review* 26 (March/April 1997): 47–56.

Ellman, Richard, and Robert O'Clair, eds. *The Norton Anthology of Modern Poetry.* 2d ed. New York: Norton, 1984.

Empson, William. *Seven Types of Ambiguity.* New York: New Directions, 1966.

Finch, Annie. "Hypnagogic Poetry." *Agni* 46 (1998): 219–25.

Florby, Gunilla. "Holding Out against Loss and Jacques Lacan: Some Reflections on Robert Hass' Sensuous Line." *Studia Neophilologica* 63 (1991): 189–95.

Friedman, Jonathan. "Cultural Logics of the Global System: A Sketch." *Theory, Culture, and Society* 5.2-3 (June 1988): 447–60.

Fussell, Paul. *The Rhetorical World of Augustan Humanism: Ethics and Imagery from Swift to Burke.* Oxford: Oxford University Press, 1965.

Gerstler, Amy. *Bitter Angel.* Pittsburgh: Carnegie Mellon University Press, 1997.

Gioia, Dana. *Can Poetry Matter?* Minneapolis: Graywolf, 2002.

Glissant, Édouard. *Poetics of Relation.* Trans. Betsy Wing. Ann Arbor: University of Michigan Press, 1997.

Golding, Alan. *From Outlaw to Classic: Canons in American Poetry.* Madison: University of Wisconsin Press, 1995.

Graff, Gerald. *Professing Literature: An Institutional History.* Chicago: University of Chicago Press, 1989.

Gunn, Thom. "On a Drying Hill." *Southern Review* 17.4 (Autumn 1981): 681–706.

Hall, Donald. "Rocks and Whirlpools." *Paris Review* 121 (Winter 1991): 211–47.

Hamburger, Michael. "Robert Pinsky: An Explanation of America." *The Nation* 230.3 (26 January 1980): 86–87.

Hamsun, Knut. *Hunger.* New York: Farrar, Straus and Giroux, 1998.

Hass, Robert. *Field Guide.* New Haven: Yale University Press, 1998. Originally published in 1973.

————. *Human Wishes.* New York: Ecco, 1990.

————. *Praise.* New York: Ecco, 1980.

————. "Reason's Children: Economic Ideology and the Themes of Fiction, 1720–1880." Ph.D. Diss. Stanford University, 1977.

————. *Sun under Wood.* New York: Ecco, 1998.

————. *Twentieth Century Pleasures: Prose on Poetry.* New York: Ecco, 1997.

————, ed. *The Best American Poetry, 2001.* New York: Scribner, 2001.

————, ed. *The Essential Haiku: Versions of Basho, Buson, and Issa.* New York: Ecco, 1995.

Hegel, G. W. F. *On Art, Religion, Philosophy.* Trans. J. Glenn Gray. New York: Harper, 1970.

Hollander, John. *Selected Poetry.* New York: Knopf, 1993.

Hooker, Jeremy. "John Matthias' England." *Word Play Place: Essays on the Poetry of John Matthias.* Ed. Robert Archambeau. Athens: Ohio University Press, 1998. 104–14.

Hoover, Paul, ed. *Postmodern American Poetry.* New York: Norton, 1994.

Howe, Irving. *Decline of the New.* New York: Horizon, 1970.

Hughes, Ted. *Crow.* London: Faber, 1970.

Huk, Romana. "Between Revolutions, or Turns: John Matthias and the American Avant-Garde/British Experimentalism." *Word Play Place: Essays on the Poetry of John Matthias.* Ed. Robert Archambeau. Athens: Ohio University Press, 1998. 115–32.

Hulme, T. E. *Selected Writings.* London: Routledge, 2003.

Jameson, Frederic. *The Prisonhouse of Language: A Critical Account of Structuralism and Russian Formalism.* Princeton: Princeton University Press, 1972.

Jarrell, Randall. "The Obscurity of the Poet." *American Poetic Theory.* Ed. Carl Perkins. New York: Rinehart, 1972. 307–16.

Jauss, David, and Philip Dacey, eds. *Strong Measures: Contemporary American Poetry in Traditional Forms.* New York: Longman, 1986.

Johnson, Samuel. *Lives of the Most Eminent English Poets: With Critical Observations of Their Work.* London, 1783.

————. *Preface to Shakespeare's Plays.* Menston: Scholar Press, 1969.

————. *Rasselas.* London: Routledge, 1967.

————. *Selected Writings.* London: Longman, 1848.

Joris, Pierre, and Jerome Rothenberg, eds. *Poems for the Millennium: The University of California Book of Modern and Postmodern Poetry.* 2 vols. Los Angeles: University of California Press, 1995.

Jung, Carl Gustav. "On the Relation of Analytic Psychology to Poetry." *Critical Theory since Plato.* 2d ed. Ed. Hazard Adams. New York: Harcourt Brace Jovanovich, 1971. 783–91.

Kalstone, David. "Praise by Robert Hass." *New York Times Book Review* (4 May 1980): 15, 43.

Keats, John. "Letter to George and Thomas Keats, Dec. 21, 1817." *Critical Theory since Plato.* 2d ed. Ed. Hazard Adams. New York: Harcourt Brace Jovanovich, 1971. 494.

Kellogg, David. "The *Pages* of John Matthias and the Future of Critical Recognition." *Samizdat* 9 (Spring 2002): 15–16.

———. "The Self in the Poetic Field." *Fence* 3.2 (Fall/Winter 2000–2001): 97–108.

Kenner, Hugh. *The Pound Era.* Los Angeles: University of California Press, 1973.

Kinnell, Galway. *The Book of Nightmares.* New York: Mariner, 1973.

Kinzie, Mary. *The Cure of Poetry in an Age of Prose: Moral Essays on the Poet's Calling.* Chicago: University of Chicago Press, 1993.

———. "A Generation of Silver." *American Poetry Review* 10.4 (March 1981): 13–17.

Kunitz, Stanley. "Foreword." *Field Guide.* Robert Hass. New Haven: Yale University Press, 1998. xi–xvii.

Landis, Joan Hutton. "John Peck." *Contemporary Poets.* 5th ed. Ed. Tracy Chevalier. Chicago: St. James Press, 1991. 750–51.

———. "Shipwreck, Autochthony and Nostos: An Approach to the Poetry of John Peck." *Salmagundi* 47–48 (1980): 159–200.

Lepkowski, Frank. "John Ashbery's Revision of the Post-Romantic Quest." *Twentieth Century Literature* 39.3 (Fall 1993): 251–66.

Levine, Philip. "Looking for an Opening." *Naked Poetry: Recent American Poetry in Open Forms.* Ed. Stephen Berg and Robert Mezey. Indianapolis: Bobbs-Merrill, 1969. 388–92.

Lévi-Strauss, Claude. *Structural Anthropology.* New York: Basic Books, 1963.

Library of Congress Information Bulletin (October 1997).

Lieberman, Laurence. "Survivor: A Last Oak Leaf, The Critic in the Poet." *Yale Review* 57.2 (Winter 1973): 267–72.

Longenbach, James. "Figuring Multitudes." *The Nation* 262.17 (April 29, 1996): 25–28.

———. *Modern Poetry after Modernism.* New York: Oxford University Press, 1997.

Lowell, Robert. "An Interview with Robert Lowell." *Paris Review Interviews.* Second Series. Ed. George Plimpton. New York: Viking, 1963. 337–68.

———. *Life Studies, and For the Union Dead.* New York: Farrar, Straus and Giroux, 1967.

Marcuse, Herbert. *Eros and Civilization: A Philosophical Inquiry into Freud.* Boston: Beacon, 1974.

Martz, Louis. "Recent Poetry: Mending Broken Connections." *Yale Review* 66 (1976): 114–29.

Marx, Karl. *The Eighteenth Brumaire of Louis Napoleon.* Moscow: International Publishers, 1963.

Matthias, John. *Beltane at Aphelion: Longer Poems.* Athens, Ohio: Swallow Press, 1995.

———. *Bucyrus.* Chicago: Swallow Press, 1970.

———. *Crossing.* Chicago: Swallow Press, 1979.

———. "Foreword." *Northern Summer: New and Selected Poems.* John Matthias. Athens, Ohio: Swallow Press, 1983. 7–9.

———. *A Gathering of Ways.* Athens, Ohio: Swallow Press, 1991.

———. Letter to Robert Archambeau, May 1, 2003.

———. *New Selected Poems.* Cambridge: Salt, 2004.

———. *Northern Summer: New and Selected Poems.* Athens, Ohio: Swallow Press, 1983.

———. *Pages New Poems and Cuttings.* Athens, Ohio: Swallow Press, 2000.

———. Personal Interview. 15 January 2004.

———. *Reading Old Friends: Essays, Reviews, and Poems on Poetics, 1975–1990.* Albany: State University of New York Press, 1992.

———. *Swimming at Midnight: Shorter Poems.* Athens, Ohio: Swallow Press, 1995.

———. *Turns.* Chicago: Swallow Press, 1975.

———. *Working Progress, Working Title.* Cambridge: Salt, 2002.

———, ed. *Five American Poets.* Manchester, Eng.: Carcanet Press, 1979.

———, ed. *Selected Works of David Jones.* Orono, Maine: National Poetry Foundation, 1993.

———, ed. *23 Modern British Poets.* Chicago: Swallow Press, 1971.

Matthias, John, and Göran Printz-Pahlson, eds. *Contemporary Swedish Poetry.* Chicago: Swallow Press, 1980.

McCorkle, James. "Nimbus of Sensations: Eros and Reverie in the Poetry of John Ashbery and Ann Lauterbach." *The Tribe of John: Ashbery and Contemporary Poetry.* Ed. Susan M. Schultz. Tuscaloosa: University of Alabama Press, 1995. 101–25.

McGann, Jerome. "Contemporary Poetry, Alternate Routes." *Politics and Poetic Value.* Ed. Robert Von Hallberg. Chicago: University of Chicago Press, 1987. 253–76.

McMichael, James. *Against the Falling Evil.* Chicago: Swallow Press, 1971.

———. *Each in a Place Apart.* Chicago: University of Chicago Press, 1994.

———. *Four Good Things.* New York: Houghton Mifflin, 1980.

———. *The Lover's Familiar.* New York: Godine, 1974.

———. "Rhetoric and the Skeptic's Void: A Study of the Influence of Nominalism on Some Aspects of Modern American Poetic Style." Ph.D. Diss. Stanford University, 1966.

———. *The Style of the Short Poem.* Belmont, Calif.: Wadsworth, 1967.

———. *The World at Large: New and Selected Poems.* Chicago: University of Chicago Press, 1996.

McMichael, James, and Dennis Saleh, eds. *Just What the Country Needs: Another Poetry Anthology.* Belmont, Calif.: Wadsworth, 1971.

Michelson, Peter. "You Keep the Cart Before the Horse, See, So They See it Moving but They Don't Know How." *Word Play Place: Essays on the Poetry of John Matthias.* Ed. Robert Archambeau. Athens: Ohio University Press, 1998. 84–103.

Middleton, Peter. "Academic Development of *The Waste Land.*" *Glyph Textual Studies* 1 (1986): 153–80.

———. "1973." *The Mechanics of the Mirage: Postwar American Poetry.* Ed. Michel Delville and Christine Pagnoulle. Liège, Belgium: University of Liège Press, 2000. 49–66.

Miklitsch, Robert. "*Praise*: The Poetry of Robert Hass." *The Hollins Critic* 17.1 (February 1980): 2–13.

Milosz, Czeslaw. *Collected Poems, 1931–1987.* New York: Ecco, 1990.

———. *The Separate Notebooks.* New York: Norton, 1984.

———. *A Treatise on Poetry.* Trans. Robert Hass. New York: Ecco, 2001.

"NewsHour with Jim Lehrer." PBS. April 2, 1997.

Nussbaum, Martha. "Patriotism and Cosmopolitanism." *For Love of Country: Debating the Limits of Patriotism.* Ed. Joshua Cohen. Boston: Beacon, 1996. 3–20.

Orr, David. "The Job Market in English and Foreign Languages." *PMLA* 85 (1970): 1185–98.

Parini, Jay. "Explaining America: The Poetry of Robert Pinsky." *Chicago Review* 33.1 (Summer 1981): 16–26.

Peck, John. *Argura.* Lebanon, N.H.: University Press of New England, 1998.

———. *The Broken Blockhouse Wall.* Manchester, Eng.: Carcanet Press, 1979.

———. *Collected Shorter Poems.* Evanston, Ill.: TriQuarterly Books, 2004.

———. Letter to Robert Archambeau, 17 October 1999.

———. *M and Other Poems.* Evanston, Ill.: Northwestern University Press, 1996.

———. "Petitio, Repetitio, Agensay, Agengrownde, Matthias." *Word Play Place: Essays on the Poetry of John Matthias.* Ed. Robert Archambeau. Athens: Ohio University Press, 1998. 201–36.

———. *Poems and Translations of Hî-Lö.* Manchester, Eng.: Carcanet Press, 1991.

———. "Pound and Hardy." *Agenda* 10.2-3 (Spring–Summer 1972): 3–10.

———. "Pound's Idylls, with Chapters on Catullus, Landor, and Browning." Ph.D. Diss. Stanford University, 1973.

———. *Red Strawberry Leaf.* Chicago: University of Chicago Press, 2005.

———. *Selva Morale.* Manchester, Eng.: Carcanet Press, 1995.

———. *Shagbark.* Indianapolis: Bobbs-Merrill, 1972.

Perloff, Marjorie. *The Dance of the Intellect: Studies in the Poetry of the Pound Tradition.* Evanston, Ill.: Northwestern University Press, 1996.

Pinsky, Robert. "A Conversation with Robert Pinsky." *TriQuarterly* (December 1994): 21–37.

———. *Democracy, Culture, and the Voice of Poetry.* Princeton: Princeton University Press, 2002.

———. "Eros against Esperanto." *For Love of Country: Debating the Limits of Patriotism.* Ed. Joshua Cohen. Boston: Beacon, 1996. 85–90.

———. *An Explanation of America.* Princeton: Princeton University Press, 1979.

———. "Far from Prose." *Poetry* (January 1974): 241–47.

———. *The Figured Wheel: New and Collected Poems, 1966–1996.* New York: Farrar, Straus and Giroux, 1997.

———. Interview by Jere Odell. *Notre Dame Review* 3 (Winter 1996–97): 79–94.

———. *Jersey Rain.* New York: Farrar, Straus and Giroux, 2001.

———. *Landor's Poetry.* Chicago: University of Chicago Press, 1968.

———. *The Life of David.* New York: Schocken, 2005.

———. "The People's Poet." November 2003. <www.amazon.com/exec/obidos/cache/ categories/literature/pinsky-interview>.

———. *Poetry and the World.* New York: Ecco, 1988.

———. "Robert Pinsky." *Contemporary Authors Autobiography Series.* Vol. 4. Ed. Adele Sarkissian. Detroit: Gale Research, 1986. 237–51.

———. *Sadness and Happiness.* Princeton: Princeton University Press, 1975.

———. *The Situation of Poetry.* Princeton: Princeton University Press, 1978.

———. *The Sounds of Poetry.* New York: Farrar, Straus and Giroux, 1999.

———. "Syncopated Things: An Interview with Robert Pinsky." *Pequod* 31 (1990): 161–66.

———. *The Want Bone.* New York: Ecco, 1990.

Pinsky, Robert, and Maggie Dietz, eds. *Americans' Favorite Poems.* New York: Norton, 1999.

———, eds. *Poems to Read: A New Favorite Poem Project Anthology.* New York: Norton, 2002.

Plato. *Timaeus and Critas.* Harmondsworth, Eng.: Penguin, 1972.

Pollock, Frederick. "Axis of Passion." *Salmagundi* 114/115 (Spring-Summer 1997): 205–27.

Pound, Ezra. *The Cantos.* New York: New Directions, 1996.

———. *Cathay.* New York: New Directions, 2002.

———. "A Few Don'ts by an Imagiste." *Poetry* (Chicago) 1 (1913): 198–206.

———. "Letter to Homer Pound." *Ezra Pound.* Ed. J. P. Sullivan. Harmondsworth, Eng.: Penguin, 1970. 93–94.

————. *Literary Essays of Ezra Pound*. New York: New Directions, 1968.

————. "A Retrospect." *Literary Essays of Ezra Pound*. New York: New Directions, 1968. 3–14.

————. *Selected Prose, 1909–1965*. New York: New Directions, 1975.

————. "Vorticism." *Ezra Pound*. Ed. J.P. Sullivan. Harmondsworth, Eng.: Penguin, 1970. 46–56.

Powell, Grosvenor. *Yvor Winters: An Annotated Bibliography, 1919–1982*. Metuchen, N.J.: Scarecrow, 1983.

Prevallet, Kristin. "Writing Is Never by Itself Alone: Six Mini-Essays on Relational Investigative Poetics." *Fence* 6.1 (Spring/Summer 2003): 19–31.

Ransom, John Crowe. *The New Criticism*. New York: Folcroft, 1971. Originally published in 1941.

————. "Poetry: A Note in Ontology." *Critical Theory since Plato*. 2d ed. Ed. Hazard Adams. New York: Harcourt Brace Jovanovich, 1971. 866–73.

Rasula, Jed. *The American Poetry Wax Museum: Reality Effects, 1940–1990*. Urbana, Ill.: National Council of Teachers of English, 1996.

Rosenthal, M.L. "Robert Lowell and the Poetry of Confession." In *The New Poets*. Oxford: Oxford University Press, 1967. 25–78.

Sadoff, Ira. "Robert Hass' *Praise*." *Chicago Review* 31.3 (Winter 1980): 133–36.

Schmidt, Michael. *Lives of the Poets*. New York: Vintage, 2000.

Shapiro, Alan. "And There Are Always Melons." *Chicago Review* 33.3 (Winter 1983): 84–90.

————. *The Last Happy Occasion*. Chicago: University of Chicago Press, 1996.

Sherry, Vincent. "The Poetry of John Matthias: 'My Treason and My Tongue.'" *Word Play Place: Essays on the Poetry of John Matthias*. Ed. Robert Archambeau. Athens: Ohio University Press, 1998. 26–34.

Silliman, Ron. *The New Sentence*. New York: Roof, 1987.

Smith, Jules. "No Easy Access." *Times Literary Supplement*, 10 December 1993: 22.

Sontag, Susan. *Against Interpretation*. London: Picador, 2001.

Spiegelman, Willard. *The Didactic Muse: Scenes of Instruction in Contemporary American Poetry*. Princeton: Princeton University Press, 1989.

Staudt, Kathleen Henderson. "'To Find the Song'—John Matthias and the Legacy of David Jones." *Word Play Place: Essays on the Poetry of John Matthias*. Ed. Robert Archambeau. Athens: Ohio University Press, 1998. 154–67.

Stein, Gertrude. "Composition as Explanation." *Gertrude Stein: Writings, 1903–1932*. New York: Library of America, 1998. 520–29.

Steiner, George. *On Difficulty*. Oxford: Oxford University Press, 1978.

Stitt, Peter. "Summer Birds and the Haunch of Winter." *Poetry* (Chicago) 135.4 (January 1980): 229–37.

Trilling, Diana. *Claremont Essays.* New York: Harcourt Brace, 1964.

Trimpi, Helen Pinkerton. "Introduction: Yvor Winters as Critic and Poet." *The Selected Poems of Yvor Winters.* Ed. R.L. Barth. Athens: Swallow Press/ Ohio University Press, 1999. xvii–xlv.

Tuma, Keith. "Way Out in the Center: John Matthias." *boundary 2* 28:2 (Summer 2001): 33–45.

Varela, Francisco J. "The Creative Circle: Sketches on the Natural History of Circularity." *The Invented Reality, How We Know What We Believe We Know: Contributions to Constructivism.* Ed. Paul Watzlawick. New York: Norton, 1984. 310–30.

Vendler, Helen. "Poets." *The New Yorker.* 18 September 1978: 165–73.

Vincent, John. "Reports of Looting and Insane Buggery behind Altars: John Ashbery's Queer Politics." *Twentieth Century Literature* 44.2 (Summer 1998): 155–76.

Von Hallberg, Robert. "Yvor Winters." *American Writers: A Collection of Literary Biographies.* Supplement Two, Part Two. Ed. A. Walton Litz. New York: Scribner's, 1981. 785–816.

Wagner, Linda. "Four Young Poets." *Ontario Review* 1 (Fall 1974): 89–97.

Waters, Michael. "Salad Days." *Southwest Review* 60.3 (Summer 1975): 307–11.

Williams, William Carlos. *Autobiography.* New York: New Directions, 1967.

———. "Prologue to KORA IN HELL." *Selected Essays of William Carlos Williams.* New York: New Directions, 1969. 1–11.

Wilmer, Clive. "On the Turn." *London Review of Books* 22.12 (22 June 2000): 34–35.

———. "Patterns of Flight." *Times Literary Supplement,* 25 August 1995: 23.

Wiman, Christian. "John Peck's *M and Other Poems.*" *Poetry* (Chicago): 171.4 (February 1998): 298–305.

Wimsatt, W.K., and Monroe C. Beardsley. *The Verbal Icon: Studies in the Meaning of Poetry.* Lexington: University of Kentucky Press, 1967. Originally published in 1954.

Winters, Yvor. *The Anatomy of Nonsense.* New York: New Directions, 1943.

———. *Before Disaster.* Tryon, N.C.: Tryon Pamphlets, 1934.

———. "The Brink of Darkness." *The Poetry of Yvor Winters.* Ed. Donald Davie. Chicago: Swallow Press, 1978. 213–44.

———. "By Way of Clarification." *Twentieth Century Literature* 10.3 (October 1964): 131–34.

———. "Concerning Jessie Dismorr." *Little Review* 6 (1919): 34–35.

———. *Forms of Discovery.* Denver, Colo.: Swallow Press, 1967.

———. *The Giant Weapon.* New York: New Directions, 1943.

———. *The Immobile Wind.* Evanston, Ill.: M. Wheeler, 1921.

———. *In Defense of Reason.* Denver: Swallow Press, 1947. A collection of works including *Primitivism and Decadence.*

————. *Poems.* Palo Alto, Calif.: Gyroscope, 1940.

————. *The Poetry of Yvor Winters.* Ed. Donald Davie. Chicago: Swallow Press, 1978.

————. *Primitivism and Decadence: A Study of American Experimental Poetry.* New York: Arrow, 1937.

————. *The Proof.* New York: Coward McCann, 1930.

————. *The Selected Poems of Yvor Winters.* Ed. R. L. Barth. Athens: Swallow Press/Ohio University Press, 1999.

————. *Uncollected Essays.* Ed. Frances Murphy. Chicago: Swallow Press, 1973.

————, ed., with Kenneth Fields. *Quest for Reality.* Chicago: Swallow Press, 1969.

Witcover, Jules. *The Year the Dream Died: Revisiting 1968 in America.* New York: Warner, 1998.

Index

studies at C. G. Jung Institute,
190–91, 214
as Wintersian, 191–92
and Yvor Winters: assessment
of Winters by Peck, 193–98;
temperaments compared, 190
Peck, John, works of
"Ars Poetica," 208
"Bounds," 208
"Cider and Vesalius," 201, 203–5
"Colophon for Lan-T'ing
Hsiu-Hsi," 201
"Factor Remembers His Lady,
The," 202
"Hunger-Trace," 205
"Involuntary Portrait," 193,
195–98
"M," 214–19, 225
"March Elegies," 206–7
"Pound and Hardy," 193
"Pound's Idylls," 190
"Rhyme Prose Three," 207
"Spring Festival on the River,"
200–201
"Stock-Taking, A," 234
"Tobelwacht," 212–13
"Upper Trace," 193–95, 200
"Viaticum," 201–2
Perloff, Marjorie, 34, 128
Pinsky, Robert, 35–82
and Allen Ginsberg, 38, 42
and American identity, 60–67,
72–82
arrival at Stanford, 35
and Augustanism, 5, 38, 39–40,
60–66
and Favorite Poem Project, 228
and Imagism, 52
and James McMichael, 90–91, 96
and Jewish tradition, 39, 42, 66
and Keats, 44–45

and modernity, 68–72
and Nietzsche, 74
popularity, 51–55, 80–82
prizes and awards, 7–8, 60
and realist/nominalist debate,
43–51
rejects Wintersian label, 37
and traditionalism, 71–74, 77
and Yvor Winters, first meeting,
38–39
Pinksy, Robert, works of
Americans' Favorite Poems, 224
"Ceremony for Any Beginning,"
40
"Culture," 78–80
"Discretions of Alcibiades," 64
"Eros against Esperanto," 78
"Essay on Psychiatrists," 10,
23–24, 48, 52, 64–65, 71, 189
Explanation of America, An, 11, 38,
39, 54, 72–80, 82
"Figured Wheel, The," 69–70
"Ginza Samba," 70–71
Life of David, The, 229
"Memoir," 71–72
"Phonebook Cover Hermes of the
Nineteen-forties, A," 228
"Poem about People," 61–64
Poems to Read, 224
Poetry and the World, 9
"Sadness and Happiness," 11,
39–43, 46–51
"Samurai Song," 71
Situation of Poetry, The, 10, 38, 39,
42, 44–45, 52–53
"Tennis," 52
"To Television," 229
Plato, 171
postmodernity, 107–10
Pound, Ezra, 14, 16, 181, 192–93,
198–99, 201, 207

ROBERT ARCHAMBEAU

is associate professor of English at Lake Forest College.
He is the author and editor of a number of books,
including *Home and Variations*.